Studies on Entrepreneurship, Structural Change and Industrial Dynamics

The 'Studies on Entrepreneurship, Structural Change and Industrial Dynamics' series showcases exceptional scholarly work being developed on the still unexplored complex relationship between entrepreneurship, structural change and industrial dynamics, by addressing structural and technological determinants of the evolutionary pathway of innovative and entrepreneurial activity.

The series invites proposals based on sound research methodologies and approaches to the above topics. Volumes in the series may include research monographs and edited/contributed works.

This is a SCOPUS-indexed series.

João Leitão • Vanessa Ratten • Vitor Braga
Editors

Brazilian Entrepreneurship

New Perspectives and Ideologies

Springer

Editors
João Leitão
Department of Management and Economics, NECE - Research Center in Business Sciences
University of Beira Interior
Covilhã, Portugal

Vanessa Ratten
Department of Management and Marketing, La Trobe Business School
La Trobe Univesity
Melbourne, VIC, Australia

Vitor Braga
School of Technology and Management
Polytechnic Institute of Porto
Felgueiras, Portugal

ISSN 2511-2023 ISSN 2511-2031 (electronic)
Studies on Entrepreneurship, Structural Change and Industrial Dynamics
ISBN 978-3-031-09391-3 ISBN 978-3-031-09392-0 (eBook)
https://doi.org/10.1007/978-3-031-09392-0

This Springer imprint is published by the registered company Springer Nature Switzerland AG
The registered company address is: Gewerbestrasse 11, 6330 Cham, Switzerland

Acknowledgements

We thank Prashanth Mahagaonkar for this helpful feedback and guidance with this book. We would also like to thank the following people:

I thank the University of Beira Interior and the NECE Research Center in Business Sciences for their support to this research endeavour. This editorial project is only possible due to my family, friends, and research partners, thanks to their support during my lifetime. The Portuguese Foundation for Science and Technology (Grants and NECE—UIDB/04630/2020) provided support for this study.

João Leitão

The ideas for this book have been developed and refined over a long time due to the editors and authors' interest in Brazilian entrepreneurship. Whilst I have never been to Brazil I do hope to travel there at some point in the future. I thank my mum, Kaye Ratten, for all the fun times. I remember my mum and brother Hamish ringing very early for me Australian time on the landline phone first time they went to the USA from San Francisco and enjoying their time there. This was before we had mobile phones and unlimited Internet access, so it cost quite a lot to ring from overseas. I also remember fondly going to Falling Water in Pennsylvania where a house had been built over a waterfall and being amazed at the level of innovation. I dedicate this book to her for being the inspiration behind creating this book. I also thank my dad David Ratten, brothers Hamish Ratten and Stuart Ratten, niece Sakura Ratten, and sister-in-law Tomomi Ratten.

Vanessa Ratten

I thank the School of Technology and Management, Porto Polytechnic, for the institutional support, in particular my colleagues in the Business Sciences Department for their enthusiasm and constant willingness to help. I also thank my family and close friends, for their honest support throughout life.

This work has been supported by national funds through FCT—Fundação para a Ciência e Tecnologia through project UIDB/04728/2020.

Vítor Braga

Contents

The Role of Brazilian Entrepreneurship in the Global Economy 1
Vanessa Ratten and João Leitão

Microentrepreneurship in Brazil: Mind the Gap 11
Anna-Katharina Lenz and Renata Brito

Surfing the Amazon: Exploring Surf Tourism and Lifestyle Entrepreneurship in Brazil 27
Laura Bradshaw

Academic Entrepreneurship in Brazilian Universities 45
Mariza Almeida

Entrepreneurial Framework Conditions in Brazil 63
Esha Thukral and Vanessa Ratten

Toward an Entrepreneurial University: Analysis of the Fluminense Federal University Initiatives and Trajectory 75
Thalyta de Sá Carvalho Velasco, Edilane dos Reis Carraro, and Marcelo Amaral

Celta: Knowledge Building Model for Business Incubators 95
Andreia de Bem Machado and Maria José Sousa

Entrepreneurship in Brazil: Geography and History 119
Vanessa Ratten

Wine Tourism Entrepreneurship in Brazil 133
Paul Strickland and Vanessa Ratten

Brazilian Entrepreneurship: Implications for ASEAN Countries 143
Mercedes Barrachina Fernández, María del Carmen García Centeno, and Carmen Calderón Patier

Learning Intention in Brazilian University Students: Self-Legitimation of Independence and the Search for Entrepreneurial Culture 153
Jocilene Gadioli de Oliveira, Serena Cubico, Romina Fucà, Piermatteo Ardolino, and João Leitão

Brazilian Entrepreneurship: Future Research Avenues 165
Vanessa Ratten and Leila Afshari

Contributors

Leila Afshari La Trobe University, Melbourne, VIC, Australia

Mariza Almeida Industrial Engineering School, Federal University of the State of Rio de Janeiro, Rio de Janeiro, RJ, Brazil

Marcelo Amaral Triple Helix Research Group (THERG-Brazil), Postgraduate Program in Administration, Institute of Human and Social Sciences, Fluminense Federal University, Volta Redonda, RJ, Brazil

Piermatteo Ardolino Department of Business Economy, School in Public Management, University of Verona, Verona, Italy

Andreia de Bem Machado Department of Engineering and Knowledge Management, Universidade Federal de Santa Catarina, Florianópolis, Brazil

Laura Bradshaw Institute for Sport Business, Loughborough University London, London, UK

Vitor Braga Porto Polytechnic, Felgueiras, Portugal

Renata Brito PUC, Rio de Janeiro, Brazil

María del Carmen García Centeno CEU University, Madrid, Spain

Thalyta de Sá Carvalho Velasco Triple Helix Research Group (THERG-Brazil), Postgraduate Program in Administration, Institute of Human and Social Sciences, Fluminense Federal University, Volta Redonda, RJ, Brazil

Serena Cubico Department of Business Economy, School in Public Management, University of Verona, Verona, Italy

Maria José Sousa Mercedes Barrachina Fernández Departamento de Métodos Cuantitativos, Facultad de Ciencias Económicas y Empresariales, Universidad Pontificia de Comillas, Madrid, Spain

Romina Fucà Department of Business Economy, School in Public Management, University of Verona, Verona, Italy

João Leitão Department of Management and Economics, NECE - Research Center in Business Sciences, University of Beira Interior, Covilhã, Portugal

Anna-Katharina Lenz Miami University, Oxford, OH, USA

Jocilene Gadioli de Oliveira SEDU - State Department of Education, Vila Velha, Brazil

Carmen Calderón Patier CEU University, Madrid, Spain

Vanessa Ratten Department of Management and Marketing, La Trobe Business School, La Trobe University, Melbourne, VIC, Australia

Edilane dos Reis Carraro Triple Helix Research Group (THERG-Brazil), Post-graduate Program in Administration, Institute of Human and Social Sciences, Fluminense Federal University, Volta Redonda, RJ, Brazil

Maria José Sousa Political Science and Public Policy Department, ISCTE – Instituto Universitário de Lisboa, Lisbon, Portugal

Paul Strickland La Trobe University, Melbourne, VIC, Australia

Esha Thukral La Trobe University, Melbourne, VIC, Australia

List of Figures

Chapter 2

Fig. 1 Average monthly income for employees, microentrepreneurs, and larger entrepreneurs across states in Brazil. (Source: Authors based on data from PNADC (2021, fourth trimester). ©2022 Mapbox ©OpenStreetMap) 13
Fig. 2 Differences in average monthly income (in R$) per region between employees (not entrepreneur), microentrepreneurs, and larger entrepreneurs. (Source: Authors based on data from PNADC (2021, fourth trimester)) 14
Fig. 3 Percentage of microentrepreneurs with CNPJ across states in Brazil. (Source: Authors based on data from PNADC (2021, fourth trimester). ©2022 Mapbox ©OpenStreetMap) 16
Fig. 4 Percentage of microentrepreneurs who pay INSS across states in Brazil. (Source: Authors based on data from PNADC (2021, fourth trimester). ©2022 Mapbox ©OpenStreetMap) 18
Fig. 5 Percentage of illiterate microentrepreneurs across regions in Brazil. (Source: Authors based on data from PNADC (2021, fourth trimester). ©2022 Mapbox ©OpenStreetMap) 19
Fig. 6 Percentage of microentrepreneurs who live in an urban (vs. rural) area. (Source: Authors based on data from PNADC (2021, fourth trimester). ©2022 Mapbox ©OpenStreetMap) 21
Fig. 7 Men and women microentrepreneurs who contribute to INSS payment in Brazil across regions (in %). (Source: Authors based on data from PNADC (2021, fourth trimester). ©2022 Mapbox ©OpenStreetMap) 23
Fig. 8 Research directions on microentrepreneurship in Brazil 23

Chapter 4

Fig. 1 Number of university patent applications to the INPI (2000–2019). (Source: INPI, Industrial Property Statistical Yearbook (2000–2019)) 57

Chapter 5

Fig. 1 A conceptual overview of entrepreneurial ecosystems. (Source: Self-created) 65

Chapter 6

Fig. 1 University–company interaction. (Source: Bonaccorsi and Piccaluga 1994) 80
Fig. 2 Prior knowledge of U–I–G interaction. (Source: Developed by the authors) 86
Fig. 3 Professors' perception of entrepreneurship at UFF. (Source: Developed by the authors) 86

Chapter 7

Fig. 1 Generations of incubation concepts 99
Fig. 2 Brazilian business incubators (2019) 101
Fig. 3 Celta Model 115

Chapter 10

Fig. 1 Brazil location in South America. Source: Authors' own 144

Chapter 11

Fig. 1 General Brazilian students' key features. *Note: The shown percentages in the graph are the more prevalent in the 2015 sample by Oliveira and the Centre for Entrepreneurial Youth (University of Verona, Italy) 156
Fig. 2 Brazilian students' job world key features. *Note: The showed percentages in the graph are the more prevalent in the 2015 sample by Oliveira and the Centre for Entrepreneurial Youth (University of Verona, Italy) 157
Fig. 3 Assumptions and outcomes for ELPA. *Note: The shown percentages in the graph are those in the 2015 sample by Oliveira and the Centre for Entrepreneurial Youth (University of Verona, Italy) 158
Fig. 4 ELPA scores per group of respondents. *Note: ELPA final scores per group of respondents with average values and standard deviations 162

List of Tables

Chapter 2

Table 1 Distribution of industry sectors (CNAE) among microentrepreneurs in Brazil from PNADC sample ... 20
Table 2 Income difference (in R$) between men and women entrepreneurs and non-entrepreneurs (employees) among regions in Brazil ... 22
Table 3 Average amount of microentrepreneurs' hours spend in business by gender ... 23

Chapter 4

Table 1 Brazilian higher education institutions (2001–2020) ... 51

Chapter 6

Table 1 Evolution of the university's mission from academic revolutions ... 78
Table 2 Innovation supporting legislation ... 81
Table 3 Platform search strategy ... 82
Table 4 Levels and indicators of Oliveira-Amaral Maturity Assessment Model ... 83
Table 5 UFF innovation policies ... 84
Table 6 Institutional time of professors at UFF ... 85
Table 7 Application of Oliveira-Amaral Model at UFF ... 88

Chapter 8

Table 1 States of Brazil ... 121
Table 2 States in Brazil ... 129

Chapter 9

Table 1 Wine regions and grape varieties of Brazil 135

Chapter 11

Table 1 Data outputs 161

The Role of Brazilian Entrepreneurship in the Global Economy

Vanessa Ratten and João Leitão

Abstract Brazil is a large country in South America with an interesting history. For this reason, it makes it an interesting context in which to study entrepreneurship. This chapter focuses on the role of Brazilian entrepreneurship in the global economy. Thereby taking into account political and historical factors that have contributed to economic and social developments in the country. The chapter begins by discussing the demographic characteristics of Brazil and how this has contributed to societal change. The role of entrepreneurship in Brazil is then stated with a view to developing a theory of Brazilian entrepreneurship. The chapter concludes by highlighting theoretical and managerial implications as well as future work suggestions.

Keywords Brazil · Culture · Economic development · Emerging markets · Entrepreneurship · History · Internationalization

1 Introduction

Entrepreneurship has become a popular global topic and debatable issue in society. There are many discussions around what is and what is not entrepreneurship. This is due to most people acknowledging that entrepreneurship is important, but it can differ in impact and effect. This means there has been a general growth in academic discourse about country-level entrepreneurship behavior (Ferreira et al., 2018).

Following Gianesini et al. (2018), at the individual level, it must be underlined the importance of entrepreneurial competences acquired by an entrepreneur, according to the contextual factors, include historical, geographical, and cultural factors.

V. Ratten (✉)
Department of Management and Marketing, La Trobe Business School, La Trobe University, Melbourne, VIC, Australia
e-mail: v.ratten@latrobe.edu.au

J. Leitão
Department of Management and Economics, NECE - Research Center in Business Sciences, University of Beira Interior, Covilhã, Portugal

J. Leitão et al. (eds.), *Brazilian Entrepreneurship*, Studies on Entrepreneurship, Structural Change and Industrial Dynamics,
https://doi.org/10.1007/978-3-031-09392-0_1

The results of entrepreneurship are far-reaching and felt by different parts of society. The chapters in this book advance growing interest in Brazil and entrepreneurship. They identify gaps in the current literature and progress on new ideas. By doing so they help to explain how and where entrepreneurship originates and in particular its impact on the Brazilian economy and society. In compiling this chapter, we seek to address questions such as what does entrepreneurship mean for Brazilian society? How has entrepreneurship research informed our understanding of Brazilian culture? Does politics influence Brazilian entrepreneurship and if so, how? Does a new theory of Brazilian entrepreneurship need to be developed?

Entrepreneurship has become somewhat of a common activity in Brazil (Borges et al., 2018). This means it is not thought about in a special way but rather an ordinary task that people engage in. This book will serve as a resource for those interested in Brazilian entrepreneurship. In this chapter, we discuss what we know about Brazilian entrepreneurship, where we are right now in terms of practice and scholarship and what the future might look like regarding this topic.

2 Country Context

Brazil is a large country in South America that has a unique history (Coelho et al., 2018). Its official language is Portuguese due to Portugal colonizing the country and still playing a role in its economic development. The economy of Brazil is mostly based on agricultural exports such as coffee, cotton, and fruit but also includes manufactured products such as clothes. The capital city is Brasilia, which was built specifically for this purpose and has unique modern architecturally designed buildings.

The most famous river in Brazil is the Amazon due to its length and influence on the geographic conditions of the country. Lesser known but still important rivers include the Parana, Tocantin, and Sao Francisco. The flag of Brazil is green, yellow, blue, and white. It was officially adopted in 1889 when Brazil became a republic. In the flag, there is a green background with a yellow diamond that has a blue circle. The flag was designed to depict the culture of Brazil in terms of its vivaciousness. The blue circle represents the sky in Brazil and the country's motto "Ordem e Progresso" (Order and Progress) is written on it. The wording on the flag is unusual as many countries do not include words on their flags. The stars in the flag represent the states in Brazil. The green and yellow colors for the flag were chosen due to the land and wealth found in the country. The previous flag of the country did not have the blue circle that was added to the new flag's design. The stars on the flag are representative of the states in the country. As new states were added the number of stars did not change. The stars in the flag also represent the constellations visible in Brazil.

Brazil occupies a large percentage of South America and shares borders with many other countries in the region (Cassiolato et al., 2003). It has a long coastline that faces the Atlantic Ocean. The country has a large forest ecosystem with no desert environment. The capital city is located inland and was positioned there in order to open up the inland area. This is due to most of the population living along the eastern seaboard making the area highly concentrated. Brazil has an interesting history and has faced numerous political struggles that have meant financial constraints regarding innovation activities (Crisóstomo et al., 2011). This is due to the social inequality between rich and poor existing in the country that means informal forms of entrepreneurship can be more prevalent (de Oliveira et al., 2018).

The land area that comprises Brazil is quite large compared to other countries in South America, which has influenced the development of innovation activities (Etzkowitz et al., 2005). There is now an emphasis on knowledge-intensive entrepreneurship in Brazil as a way of fostering innovation (Fischer et al., 2018). Unlike other territories in South America that split into separate countries following their independence, Brazil did not do this. This means it is the largest Portuguese-speaking country outside of Portugal. Most people in Brazil speak Portuguese although there are some dialects and regional variations.

The Amazon, which is located in Brazil and other South American countries is the world's largest rainforest. The Amazon is a network of many waterways that form an ecosystem environment. There are many medicinal herbs and trees in the Amazon with some still yet to be discovered. In the central west part of Brazil is the Pantanal, which is a swamp area. It is mostly wetlands but also includes lagoons. Within this area are South American alligators called caimans.

Portugal established a colony in Brazil in 1530. Sugarcane plantations were created with much of the sugar exported to other countries. In addition, due to the mineral wealth of the country, many mines were established. In 1789, an unsuccessful rebellion against colonial rule occurred. Members of the Portuguese royal family lived in Brazil but most returned to Portugal. The King of Portugal's son Dom Pedro stayed in Brazil and proclaimed it an independent country in 1822.

The rapid development of Brazil has replaced the focus of interest in entrepreneurship from developed countries to emerging markets (Franco et al., 2011). Brazil is considered one of the fastest-growing economies in the world so there has been much interest in how it compares to other emerging economies such as China and India (Gupta et al., 2014). Inkizhinov et al. (2021, p. 1404) define emerging markets as "countries in economic, political, social and demographic transition from the contexts of higher degrees of volatility to stable institutional commitments." Emerging markets like Brazil are considered unique places to study the process of entrepreneurship and in particular the role of reactionary forces that influence entrepreneurship activity in metropolitan areas (Jones, 2000). Entrepreneurship is a field that constantly changes based on emerging societal needs (Jones et al., 2019). The current literature on entrepreneurship in Brazil is constrained by a series of shortfalls most of which relate to a generalization in studies that consider all emerging markets as the same (Karam, 2004).

Brazil as an emerging global superpower is making a transition to a democratic and entrepreneurial oriented economy (Marques et al., 2020). The scholarship on entrepreneurship in Brazil is dominated by economic studies that analyze the consequences and processes of entrepreneurship (Nagano et al., 2014). More recently, the scope of scholarship has been widened to include social issues such as sustainability (e.g., Marcon et al., 2017), university–industry interactions (e.g., Rapini et al., 2009) export performance (e.g., Oura et al., 2016) and the rural economy (e.g., Mendonça & Alves, 2012). Much less has been dedicated to developing a Brazilian theory of entrepreneurship that focuses on the Brazilian identity and experiences. This new area of inquiry will enable more research to focus on the Brazilian philosophy and culture regarding entrepreneurship (Severo et al., 2019).

3 Brazilian Entrepreneurship Research

Entrepreneurship research is well established and is a prominent area of study (Moreira et al., 2019). Within general entrepreneurship research, there are many subfields including international, minority, sport among others (Ratten et al., 2021). The overall research on entrepreneurship has increased substantially over the past decade due to the recognition of its importance in society (Ratten & Usmanij, 2021). How we come to know entrepreneurship has been influenced by certain economic and political events. Recently the COVID-19 crisis has influenced the direction th at entrepreneurship research has taken (Ratten, 2020a, b, 2021).

There has been an emphasis in general entrepreneurship research on education (Ratten & Jones, 2021). This is due to entrepreneurial intentions often being influenced by previous education experiences. Education in Brazil is linked to patent incentives as well as public/private networks (Ryan, 2010). In Brazil, there are different kinds of education including vocational education that influences entrepreneurship (Stadler & Smith, 2017). Due to there being many family businesses in Brazil, entrepreneurship education can have a positive effect on overall performance outcomes (Soares et al., 2021). Brazil has been focusing on literacy rates in vocational education policies as a way to foster entrepreneurship (Stadler et al., 2021). This is due to entrepreneurial forms of innovation influencing the development of new industries such as 3D printing (Woodson et al., 2019).

4 Contributions

In the second chapter, Anna-Katharina Lenz and Renata Brito address on the topic Microentrepreneurship in Brazil, by revealing the research gaps in terms of the process of resilience building, the outcome of human capital inequalities, the impact of gender, resource constraints, and boundary conditions under which entrepreneurial activity emerges and can thrive under different conditions and regional contexts in Brazil.

In the third chapter, Laura Bradshaw concludes that Brazil has an opportunity for rapid growth in the surf tourism segment. This can be achieved by capitalizing on underprivileged coastal areas, which could benefit from tourism and development and increase the economic benefit of the area for local communities by bringing in much-needed business and development and opening the coastline up to more overseas travellers seeking an adventure.

In the fourth chapter, Mariza Almeida analyses academic entrepreneurship in Brazilian universities, considering three periods of distinct characteristics and using the Triple Helix model as the theoretical framework. In each of these periods, varied interactions were established and the internal discussion of universities about entrepreneurship and innovation was changing, with an impact on teaching, research, and transference activities.

In the fifth chapter, Esha Thukral and Vanessa Ratten analyze the Entrepreneurial framework conditions in Brazil, pointing out that Entrepreneurial activity is generated by interactions between various elements of the socio-economic environment. Nevertheless, in the specific context of Brazil, it is well recognized that an ineffective regulatory framework poses a structural barrier to entrepreneurial development.

In the sixth chapter, Thalyta Sá de Carvalho Velasco, Edilane dos Reis Carraro, and Marcelo Amaral present an interesting case applied to an Entrepreneurial University, that is, the Fluminense Federal University, concluding that the university–industry–government relations and the incorporation of a third mission (socio-economic development) in the academic organizations, are critical elements for integrating production and innovation systems.

In the seventh chapter, Andreia de Bem Machado and Maria José Sousa, present a knowledge-building model for business incubators: The Celta; which is a model for confirming knowledge construction in incubators, which implies and encourages the incubator's ability to prospect and pick strong ideas sequentially, and then turn them into successful and lucrative companies. This innovative model can also be used to determine the level of knowledge maturity in incubators and other Innovation Habitats.

In the eighth chapter, Vanessa Ratten provides a rich guide about Entrepreneurship in Brazil, crossing geographical and historical dimensions. This is particularly useful for guiding researchers on Brazilian entrepreneurship, especially, pointing out how they can research the Brazilian state contexts.

In the ninth chapter, Paul Strickland and Vanessa Ratten explore the Wine tourism entrepreneurship in Brazil, highlighting how the wine industry in Brazil has grown based on its innovative and entrepreneurial characteristics, as well as providing guidelines for improving wine tourism entrepreneurship in Brazil.

In the tenth chapter, Mercedes Barrachina Fernández, María del Carmen García Centeno, and Carmen Calderón Patier, address an interesting topic devoted to: Brazilian entrepreneurship: Implications for ASEAN countries; unveiling that, in Brazil, there is a growing entrepreneurship environment blowing and the government is supporting its development, especially in large cities, such as São Paulo, Rio de Janeiro, Belo Horizonte, and Porto Alegre. Nevertheless, there are several challenges Brazil has to overcome, in order to increase the opportunities of the companies that are born in its territory and their growing possibilities.

In the eleventh chapter, Jocilene Gadioli de Oliveira, Serena Cubico, Romina Fucà, Piermatteo Ardolino, and João Leitão address the topic on: Learning intention in Brazilian university students: self-legitimation of independence and the search for entrepreneurial culture; provide evidence that small prior experience in firms coupled with ties with the entrepreneurial world encourages the students to have trust on the university as a driving force to understand jobs and careers, as well as it enables them to search for theoretical inconsistencies and gaps in the materials offered by educational settings.

In the twelth chapter, Vanessa Ratten and Leila Afshari address the problematics on: Brazilian entrepreneurship: Future research avenues; stating that a distinct research track regarding Brazilian entrepreneurship is needed in the broader entrepreneurship literature in order to incorporate more cultural and historical meaning.

5 Conclusion

This chapter has made a multifaceted contribution to the literature on Brazil and entrepreneurship. First, the chapter provided an overview of Brazil as a country and organized the discussion into historical context and cultural linkage. Second, the chapter highlighted the importance of entrepreneurship to Brazil, which helped us to identify a theory of Brazilian entrepreneurship. The key themes included in Brazilian entrepreneurship studies included (a) strategic innovation, (b) cultural considerations, (c) institutional environment, (d) crises responses, and (e) entrepreneurial outcomes. These themes highlight how entrepreneurship in Brazil is different from other countries contexts. They imply that the changing economic conditions in Brazil are the result of entrepreneurial activities. Moreover, the drivers of entrepreneurship range from learning oriented activities to necessity-based needs. The chapter stressed the need to address the gaps in the literature and the opportunities for further research.

6 Theoretical Implications

This chapter suggests a theory of Brazilian entrepreneurship is needed. At the moment, most of the theories that exist on entrepreneurship are general ones such as the theory of knowledge spillovers and entrepreneurial ecosystems. This means there is room in the literature for new theories based on country contexts. There are regional theories that are based on common cultural characteristics but these are not used much in the literature. Therefore, in this chapter we suggest that Brazilian entrepreneurship theory provides a way to incorporate cultural and historical considerations into theoretical frameworks. This will help to build the literature on Brazilian entrepreneurship by linking it to a theoretical model.

This chapter is based on Brazilian entrepreneurship theory, which highlights the need for country considerations in entrepreneurship research. Currently, the existing entrepreneurship theory is too broad and needs to be revised based on context. Therefore, this chapter overcomes these issues and suggests a new theory that requires further development. This will be helpful to entrepreneurship researchers to narrow their scope of inquiry into country contexts. This chapter suggested that there are various aspects of Brazilian entrepreneurship, which can be further studied by scholars. This means theme-based gaps in the Brazilian entrepreneurship literature need to be identified. The broader entrepreneurship literature has not done this as the emphasis has been on generalization.

7 Implications for Entrepreneurship Strategy and Practice

This chapter has a number of key implications for practitioners and managers of entrepreneurial ventures. The discussion of Brazilian entrepreneurship provided a comprehensive overview of the topic that can help managers identify new trends. For example, the overview highlighted how emerging technologies related to sustainability are changing the entrepreneurial practices of Brazilian enterprises. Accordingly, managers can adapt to the new technologies by putting plans into place to deal with the change. This will help them proactively identify market needs before competitors.

Managers need to continually assess the changing marketplace and come up with better responses. This means changing from a reactive approach to a proactive stance. Management needs to embed an entrepreneurial mindset into their organizational culture by explicitly emphasizing entrepreneurship. This means changing accepted workplace practices by focusing more on entrepreneurial behavior. Doing so would further advance an organization's international competitiveness and differentiate them in the marketplace.

The value of entrepreneurship in the pursuit of profitability should be emphasized by managers. This can include entering into different kinds of partnerships in order to obtain knowledge. The regulatory and institutional environment influences entrepreneurship so managers need to have a proactive approach. This will help them unite different entities in an entrepreneurial ecosystem to come together for a joint purpose.

8 Future Work

This chapter has provided an overview of Brazilian entrepreneurship and discussed its importance. More work is needed on Brazil in general entrepreneurship studies. This includes taking into account research written in Portuguese that might not be easily accessed by English speakers. At the moment many relevant studies in Portuguese about Brazil are omitted due to most publications being in English.

Due to the existence of computer programs that easily translate languages it might be easier in the future to access this research.

More focus needs to be applied to the different cultures in Brazil. While there is a common language and culture in Brazil, there are many other languages spoken in the region. This means research should take into account cultural heritage when discussing Brazilian entrepreneurship. This will highlight the diversity of Brazil and continue to make it an interesting country to study.

References

Borges, C., Bezerra, É. D., Silva, G., Andreassi, T., & Ferreira, V. D. R. (2018). Entrepreneurship policy in Brazil: Its focus and gaps. *International Journal of Entrepreneurship and Small Business, 34*(2), 183–203.

Cassiolato, J. E., Lastres, H. M. M., & Maciel, M. L. (Eds.). (2003). *Systems of innovation and development: Evidence from Brazil*. Edward Elgar Publishing.

Coelho, F. J. M., Marques, C., Loureiro, A., & Ratten, V. (2018). Evaluation of the impact of an entrepreneurship training program in Recife, Brazil. *Journal of Entrepreneurship in Emerging Economies, 10*(3), 472–488.

Crisóstomo, V. L., López-Iturriaga, F. J., & Vallelado, E. (2011). Financial constraints for innovation in Brazil. *Latin American Business Review, 12*(3), 165–185.

de Oliveira, J. A. S., Basso, L. F. C., Kimura, H., & Sobreiro, V. A. (2018). Innovation and financial performance of companies doing business in Brazil. *International Journal of Innovation Studies, 2*(4), 153–164.

Etzkowitz, H., de Mello, J. M. C., & Almeida, M. (2005). Towards "meta-innovation" in Brazil: The evolution of the incubator and the emergence of a triple helix. *Research Policy, 34*(4), 411–424.

Ferreira, J. J., Fayolle, A., Ratten, V., & Raposo, M. (Eds.). (2018). *Entrepreneurial universities*. Edward Elgar Publishing.

Fischer, B. B., Queiroz, S., & Vonortas, N. S. (2018). On the location of knowledge-intensive entrepreneurship in developing countries: Lessons from São Paulo, Brazil. *Entrepreneurship & Regional Development, 30*(5–6), 612–638.

Franco, E., Ray, S., & Ray, P. K. (2011). Patterns of innovation practices of multinational-affiliates in emerging economies: Evidences from Brazil and India. *World Development, 39*(7), 1249–1260.

Gianesini, G., Cubico, S., Favretto, G., & Leitão, J. (2018). Entrepreneurial competences: Comparing and contrasting models and taxonomies. In *Entrepreneurship and the industry life cycle* (pp. 13–32). Springer.

Gupta, V. K., Guo, C., Canever, M., Yim, H. R., Sraw, G. K., & Liu, M. (2014). Institutional environment for entrepreneurship in rapidly emerging major economies: The case of Brazil, China, India, and Korea. *International Entrepreneurship and Management Journal, 10*(2), 367–384.

Inkizhinov, B., Gorenskaia, E., Nazarov, D., & Klarin, A. (2021). Entrepreneurship in emerging markets: Mapping the scholarship and suggesting future research directions. *International Journal of Emerging Markets, 16*(7), 1404–1429.

Jones, K. (2000). Psychodynamics, gender, and reactionary entrepreneurship in metropolitan Sao Paulo, Brazil. *Women in Management Review, 15*(4), 207–217.

Jones, P., Ratten, V., Klapper, R., & Fayolle, A. (2019). Entrepreneurial identity and context: Current trends and an agenda for future research. *The International Journal of Entrepreneurship and Innovation, 20*(1), 3–7.

Karam, J. T. (2004). A cultural politics of entrepreneurship in nation-making: Phoenicians, Turks, and the Arab commercial essence in Brazil. *Journal of Latin American Anthropology, 9*(2), 319–351.

Marcon, A., de Medeiros, J. F., & Ribeiro, J. L. D. (2017). Innovation and environmentally sustainable economy: Identifying the best practices developed by multinationals in Brazil. *Journal of Cleaner Production, 160*, 83–97.

Marques, C., Leal, C., Ferreira, J., & Ratten, V. (2020). The formal-informal dilemma for women microentrepreneurs: Evidence from Brazil. *Journal of Enterprising Communities: People and Places in the Global Economy, 14*(5), 665–685.

Mendonça, P. M. E., & Alves, M. A. (2012). Institutional entrepreneurship and professionalization of the rural development of the sisal region in Brazil. *Revista de Administração, 47*(3), 489–499.

Moreira, J., Marques, C. S., Braga, A., & Ratten, V. (2019). A systematic review of women's entrepreneurship and internationalization literature. *Thunderbird International Business Review, 61*(4), 635–648.

Nagano, M. S., Stefanovitz, J. P., & Vick, T. E. (2014). Innovation management processes, their internal organizational elements and contextual factors: An investigation in Brazil. *Journal of Engineering and Technology Management, 33*, 63–92.

Oura, M. M., Zilber, S. N., & Lopes, E. L. (2016). Innovation capacity, international experience and export performance of SMEs in Brazil. *International Business Review, 25*(4), 921–932.

Rapini, M. S., da Motta, E., Chave, C. V., Silva, L. A., de Souza, S. G., Righi, H. M., & Cruz, W. M. (2009). University—industry interactions in an immature system of innovation: Evidence from Minas Gerais, Brazil. *Science and Public Policy, 36*(5), 373–386.

Ratten, V. (2020a). Coronavirus (covid-19) and entrepreneurship: Changing life and work landscape. *Journal of Small Business & Entrepreneurship, 32*(5), 503–516.

Ratten, V. (2020b). Coronavirus and international business: An entrepreneurial ecosystem perspective. *Thunderbird International Business Review, 62*(5), 629–634.

Ratten, V. (2021). COVID-19 and entrepreneurship: Future research directions. *Strategic Change, 30*(2), 91–98.

Ratten, V., & Jones, P. (2021). Entrepreneurship and management education: Exploring trends and gaps. *The International Journal of Management Education, 19*(1), 100431.

Ratten, V., & Usmanij, P. (2021). Entrepreneurship education: Time for a change in research direction? *The International Journal of Management Education, 19*(1), 100367.

Ratten, V., da Silva Braga, V. L., & da Encarnação Marques, C. S. (2021). Sport entrepreneurship and value co-creation in times of crisis: The covid-19 pandemic. *Journal of Business Research, 133*, 265–274.

Ryan, M. P. (2010). Patent incentives, technology markets, and public–private bio-medical innovation networks in Brazil. *World Development, 38*(8), 1082–1093.

Severo, E. A., Becker, A., Guimarães, J. C. F. D., & Rotta, C. (2019). The teaching of innovation and environmental sustainability and its relationship with entrepreneurship in southern Brazil. *International Journal of Innovation and Learning, 25*(1), 78–105.

Soares, G. G., da Silva Braga, V. L., da Encarnação Marques, C. S., & Ratten, V. (2021). Corporate entrepreneurship education's impact on family business sustainability: A case study in Brazil. *The International Journal of Management Education, 19*(1), 100424.

Stadler, A., & Smith, A. M. (2017). Entrepreneurship in vocational education: A case study of the Brazilian context. *Industry and Higher Education, 31*(2), 81–89.

Stadler, A., Alberton, A., & Smith, A. M. (2021). Entrepreneurship education in Brazil: Brazilian and Scottish approaches to policy and provision in vocational education. *Journal of Small Business and Enterprise Development*, https://doi.org/10.1108/JSBED-12-2020-0440

Woodson, T., Alcantara, J. T., & do Nascimento, M. S. (2019). Is 3D printing an inclusive innovation?: An examination of 3D printing in Brazil. *Technovation, 80*, 54–62.

Microentrepreneurship in Brazil: Mind the Gap

Anna-Katharina Lenz and Renata Brito

Abstract In this chapter, we call attention to the research gaps that circumvent microentrepreneurship in Brazil and which motivate applied research at the Center of Microentrepreneurship (NUME) at PUC-Rio. Founded in 2019, the goals of NUME are to understand growth potential and growth enablers for microentrepreneurs to advance sustainable economic development and social change. Among the research topics we highlight: the process of resilience building, the outcome of human capital inequalities, the impact of gender, resource constraints, and boundary conditions under which entrepreneurial activity emerges and can thrive under different conditions and regional contexts in Brazil.

Keywords Microentrepreneurship · Institutional support · Brazil

1 Introduction

In initial terms, microentrepreneurs are here defined as people who work as self-employed or have up to five employees. We choose this definition based on theoretical and practical reasons. From a discipline perspective, microentrepreneurship has been traditionally identified as entrepreneurial activity of individuals or small firms with less than ten, but often only one or two people employed (Birks et al., 1992) and as such incorporated in empirical studies (Honig, 1998; Mead & Liedholm, 1998). While some studies are even considering

All maps were created using Tableau (2022.1).

A.-K. Lenz (✉)
Miami University, Oxford, OH, USA
e-mail: lenza@miamioh.edu

R. Brito
PUC, Rio de Janeiro, Brazil
e-mail: renata.brito@iag.puc-rio.br

J. Leitão et al. (eds.), *Brazilian Entrepreneurship*, Studies on Entrepreneurship, Structural Change and Industrial Dynamics,
https://doi.org/10.1007/978-3-031-09392-0_2

employees with up to 50 employees "microentrepreneurs" (Mensmann & Frese, 2019), articles that cover the concept within the Brazilian context typically focus on very small entrepreneurs or self-employed (e.g., Lenz et al., 2021; Rocha et al., 2018). This makes sense from a practical perspective in Brazil, as specific local legislation incentivizes the business formalization for initiatives such as self-employed individuals and microbusiness structure of up to one employee. Focusing on ventures with up to five employees, however, allows us to follow the growth pattern of this individual and brings us closer to our understanding of microbusiness operations that we have empirically observed over the years.

Despite microentrepreneurship being in the interest of entrepreneurship scholars and policy makers for more than three decades (i.e., de Soto, 1989; Honig, 1998; de Castro et al., 2014) research on microentrepreneurship still suffers from a number of shortcomings. Ranging from a "too broad categorization of the types of problems micro-entrepreneurs face" to a lack of addressing "the practical problems microentrepreneurs encounter as they pursue their short-term goals of achieving daily sales" to "limited insights into the relationship that exists between the approaches microentrepreneurs implement with short-term tactical problems and those they use to address longer-term strategic barriers" (DeBerry-Spence & Elliot, 2012). Microentrepreneurship is also a prosperous field for the investigation of the multilevel influence of macroeconomic, institutional, social, and local aspects on human capital development and venture growth. Microentrepreneurs are naturally more vulnerable to macro and micro changes in the environment, and the interaction of the variables at different levels increases the complexity of these impacts. For example, economic expansion may favor business growth, but as the job market expands, the microentrepreneur might lose existing help (i.e., due to family members finding employment in the formal labor market) and with it important human capital for the business. The many directions in which changes in the environment affect the entrepreneurial process of microentrepreneurs makes it an interesting and challenging field of research.

To provide insights into the research gaps and to bring an updated view of microentrepreneurship in Brazil that can assist the development of supportive public policies, we use microdata from the Continuous National Sample Survey of Households (Pesquisa Nacional por Amostra de Domicílios Contínua—PNADC) produced by the Brazilian Statistics Institute (IBGE). The sample is collected through a survey that produces quarterly indicators on the workforce, with a sample of Brazilian households being the unit of analysis. We use the survey data from the fourth quarter of 2021 for our descriptive analysis in this chapter. We coded the answer "self-employed" and "entrepreneurs with up to five employees" within the primary occupation question to create the "microentrepreneur" dummy for our analysis. By that definition, a total of 63,523 microentrepreneurs are in the PNADC sample and part of the analysis is presented below. Entrepreneurs with more than five employees are summarized in the data as "larger entrepreneurs," employees are summarized as "non entrepreneurs."

We continue by presenting the data and by showing the regional and gender inequalities that emerge from the PNADC sample of microentrepreneurs in Brazil.

Along with the data, we indicate the knowledge gaps and possible directions for future studies.

2 The Status Quo of Microentrepreneurship in Brazil and Research Directions

The data of PNADC shows that entrepreneurial activity is generally associated with a higher income across Brazil. However, this does not necessarily count for microentrepreneurs. In Brazil, the average income of larger entrepreneurs is 3.6 times higher than the average income of employees. Whereas the average income of microentrepreneurs in Brazil is 16% lower than that of employees in the labor market (not considering the part of the population outside the labor market, i.e., due to unemployment). Figure 1 displays the average monthly income for employees, microentrepreneurs, and larger entrepreneurs across all states in Brazil. The comparison shows large differences in the income of microentrepreneurs across regions and compared to the average income of employees within the same region.

The income disparity increases with the location and the distance to the South and Southeast, as the major economic centers. In the North of Brazil, employees earn on average 53% more than microentrepreneurs, followed by the Northeast, where employees earn on average 39% more than microentrepreneurs. The difference is much smaller in the Southeast, where microentrepreneurs earn on average 17% less,

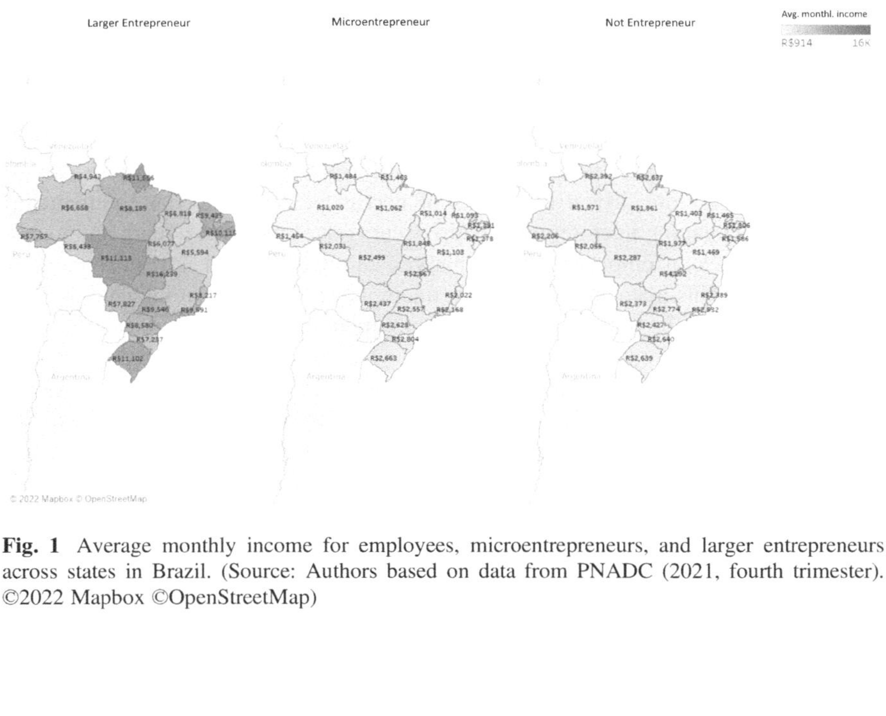

Fig. 1 Average monthly income for employees, microentrepreneurs, and larger entrepreneurs across states in Brazil. (Source: Authors based on data from PNADC (2021, fourth trimester). ©2022 Mapbox ©OpenStreetMap)

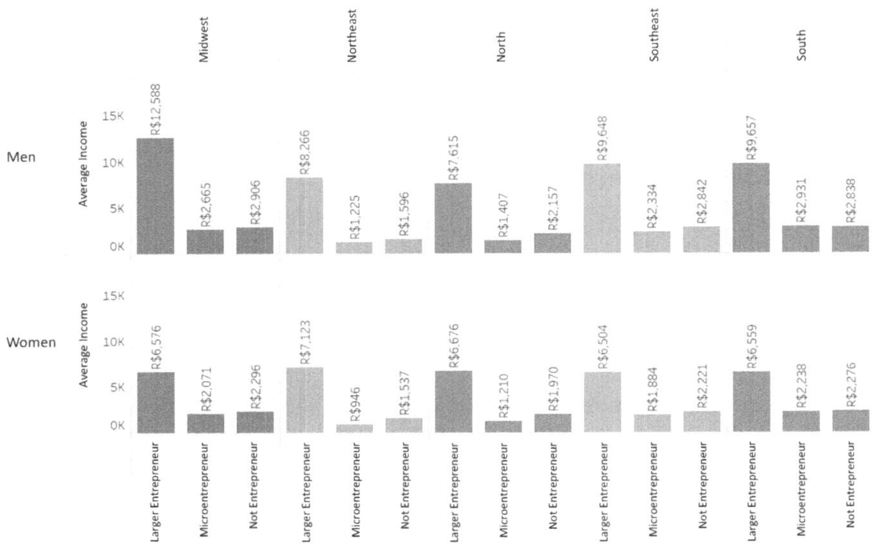

Fig. 2 Differences in average monthly income (in R$) per region between employees (not entrepreneur), microentrepreneurs, and larger entrepreneurs. (Source: Authors based on data from PNADC (2021, fourth trimester))

and even smaller in the Center-West with 7%. Distinct from all other regions, microentrepreneurs in the South earn 5% more than the average employee. The income of microentrepreneurs in the South is R$2703 also the highest across all regions in Brazil (Fig. 2). This indicates that the opportunity cost for becoming an entrepreneur is higher in the North and Northeast, compared to formal sector employment. This suggests that individuals in these regions enter microentrepreneurial activities due to a lack of formal employment options, which indicates that they are driven by means of necessity. Necessity entrepreneurship connotes that engaging in entrepreneurship occurs out of the need to earn an income and due to a lack of employment alternatives (Binder & Coad, 2013; Alvarez & Barney, 2014). This matches with data on unemployment rates that indicate that the South of Brazil has the lowest level of unemployment in the fourth trimester of 2021 (IBGE, 2022).

Previous research has pointed out that challenges for individuals not only persist due to a lower number of employment options, but also due to lack of skills and the absence of supportive institutional levers that push individuals toward necessity entrepreneurship (Alvarez & Barney, 2014; Karnani, 2007). We see both challenges more defined in the North and Northeast of Brazil, where microentrepreneurs, historically, have lower education levels and where the institutional environment is less developed (IBGE, 2021). However, institutional environment has changed, and there are attempts to enhance development and to foster decentralization. Research could explore the effects of the regional development (pushed, for example, through education and professional trainings) on the volume and type of microentrepreneurship over time, relative to larger entrepreneurs, and income levels in the formal employment market. The aim is to test the assumption that increasing institutional levels contribute to the transition of necessity entrepreneurs to more growth-oriented entrepreneurship.

Dencker et al. (2021) have argued that entrepreneurs with low levels of human capital, who are driven by physiological needs will engage in copying entrepreneurial business ideas related to basic services (e.g., food retail and farming activities) that they can observe in their immediate environment and that do not require any specialized skills. The imitation process is potentiated by the absence of supportive institutional levers to provide funding, advisory, and capacity building for microentrepreneurs (Dencker et al., 2021). Data from a survey study conducted with 4300 microentrepreneurs in Rio de Janeiro demonstrated the dominance of entrepreneurial activity in beauty salons, micro retail stores, and takeaway food (Lenz, 2018). Yet, it is less clear how these necessity entrepreneurs behave, if they start to generate an amount of income that puts them out of the need for immediate fulfillment of physiological needs. Would this lead to a change in the entrepreneurial process? We see a small percentage of necessity entrepreneurs growing into bigger ventures—what makes them different? At which stage of their entrepreneurial process does entrepreneurial opportunity exploitation set in?

The literature widely agrees that opportunity exploration activities are unlikely to happen by entrepreneurs with low human capital levels if they do not receive some support (Dutt et al., 2016; Bhatt et al., 2022). This collaborates with our empirical perceptions from necessity entrepreneurs in urban centers in Brazil, who typically neither have enough resources, nor capabilities to seize growth opportunities. To enable a shift into a more growth-oriented entrepreneurship, Dencker et al. (2021) propose that supportive institutional levers are needed to encourage necessity entrepreneurs to explore a broader range of market opportunities. In Brazil, several policy programs have specifically targeted microentrepreneurs over the last 15 years. The results are increased ease of business formalization (specifically through the MEI program, see Infobox 1), access to microcredit,[1] and access to institutional sponsors such as SEBRAE in more excluded areas such as Favelas.[2] These institutional changes allow for event studies that can observe core characteristics of microentrepreneurship in both, specific contexts (for example, favelas in Rio de Janeiro after institutional sponsors start their work) and as a regional country comparison over time (for example, using PNADC data). This can help to

[1] Several states promote reduced credit rates for microentrepreneurs in Brazil. See, for example, "Juro Zero"—a program that promotes access to investment capital in the state of Santa Catarina. https://www.jurozero.sc.gov.br/juro-zero.html.

[2] For concrete examples see, for example, "Favela Legal"—a program that promotes business registration and capacitation of entrepreneurs in Favelas in Sao Paulo, or "Sebrae nas Comunidades" in Rio de Janeiro.

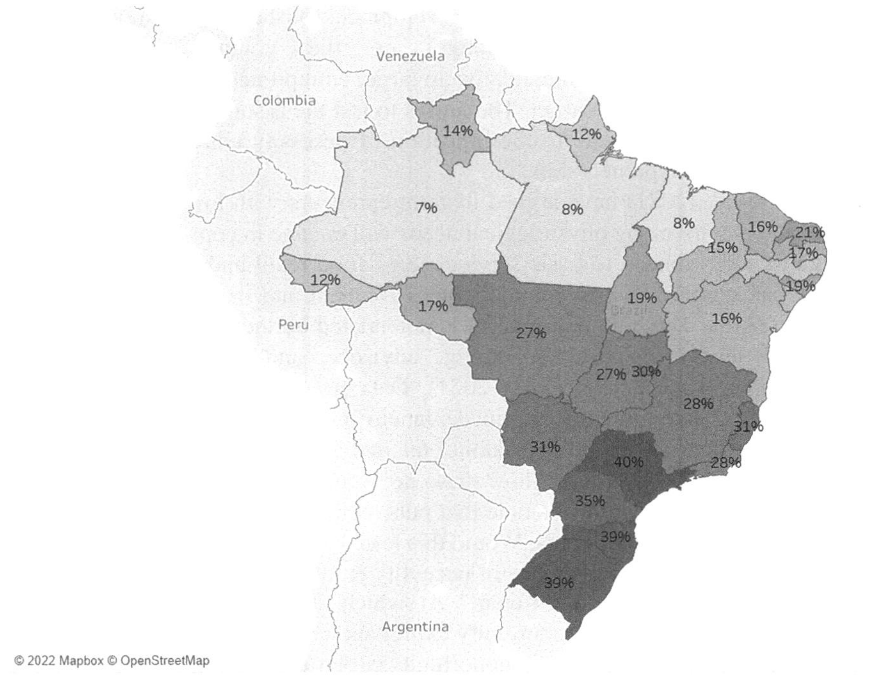

Fig. 3 Percentage of microentrepreneurs with CNPJ across states in Brazil. (Source: Authors based on data from PNADC (2021, fourth trimester). ©2022 Mapbox ©OpenStreetMap)

empirically test recent propositions around antecedents and outputs of necessity entrepreneurship (Dencker et al., 2021).

Effective institutional support and adequate development of public policies depend on the ability to observe the trajectory of microentrepreneurs. Business formalization plays a critical part in making these numbers visible. However, business formalization is still relatively low in Brazil, and even lower for the North and Northeast regions (Fig. 3). This corresponds with the lower institutional levers in the North and Northeast of Brazil. Formalization not only allows observing the numbers and follow-up on the development of microentrepreneurship, but also helps to target other support initiatives, such as access to financial resources. States like Santa Catarina in the South, with higher levels of formalization, stimulate business formalization by granting registered microentrepreneurs access to lower credit rates. Comparative life course perspectives could shed more insights into the dynamics that lead to formalization within different regions in Brazil. This could lead to a better understanding and use of more targeted incentives and policy interventions to increase formalization rates.

Even within the same city, interventions to increase formalization rates have shown different treatment effects. For example, Lenz and Valdivia (2021) and Zucco et al. (2020) are both linking information treatments with facilitated access to technical assistance to increase formalization in different neighborhoods in Rio de Janeiro. The results of both studies show heterogeneity in treatment effects that can be associated with differences in the local institutional environment and differences in the strength of the informal environment and crime levels, thus increasing, for example, the need for mobile technical assistance. We encourage the design and implementation of field experiments in different environments and regions to gain a deeper understanding of the take-up of these policy interventions.

Infobox 1: The MEI Program

- The Brazilian government instituted, in 2009, the Individual Microentrepreneur Program (Programa do Microempreendedor Individual, hereafter "the MEI program").
- The MEI program provides a low-cost, streamlined method for entrepreneurs to formalize (Rocha et al., 2018).
- MEI registration is completely online and free. However, it requires microentrepreneurs to pay a fixed monthly fee, which includes subsidized social security contributions—which is approximately half of what other employees or entrepreneurs have to pay—as well as state taxes and municipal taxes (Zucco et al., 2020).
- Bookkeeping is not required other than declaring once a year that the revenue is below the legally mandated limit of R$ 81,000 (US$ 18,000) as of 2021.
- MEI companies can employ up to one employee, which is tax subsidized.
- By becoming formal, entrepreneurs gain access to financing and the ability to do business with other formal firms. Furthermore, they receive a slew of social security benefits through the MEI program. In the event that entrepreneurs fulfill their monthly payments, and reach retirement age and have completed a minimum of 15 years of contribution, they are eligible for a monthly retirement benefit of one minimum wage for life.
- Those who become MEI and honor the monthly payments will also be able to receive disability pensions, sick leave, maternity leave benefits, as well as a limited life insurance benefit for children (Zucco et al., 2020).

Lower levels of formalization may not only impede business growth but also reduce the social security (INSS) coverage of entrepreneurs, which increases the risk associated with working as an entrepreneur due to a lack of eligibility for disability pension, paid sick leave, and paid maternity leave (Zucco et al., 2020). This may be particularly harmful to entrepreneurs in poorer regions as these contingencies may cause entrepreneurs to fall back into poverty (Hulme & Shepherd, 2003). However, as Fig. 4 points out, the percentage of microentrepreneurs who pay INSS is much lower in the relatively poorer North and Northeast than in all other states. It seems that in regions in which microentrepreneurs are in the most vulnerable situation

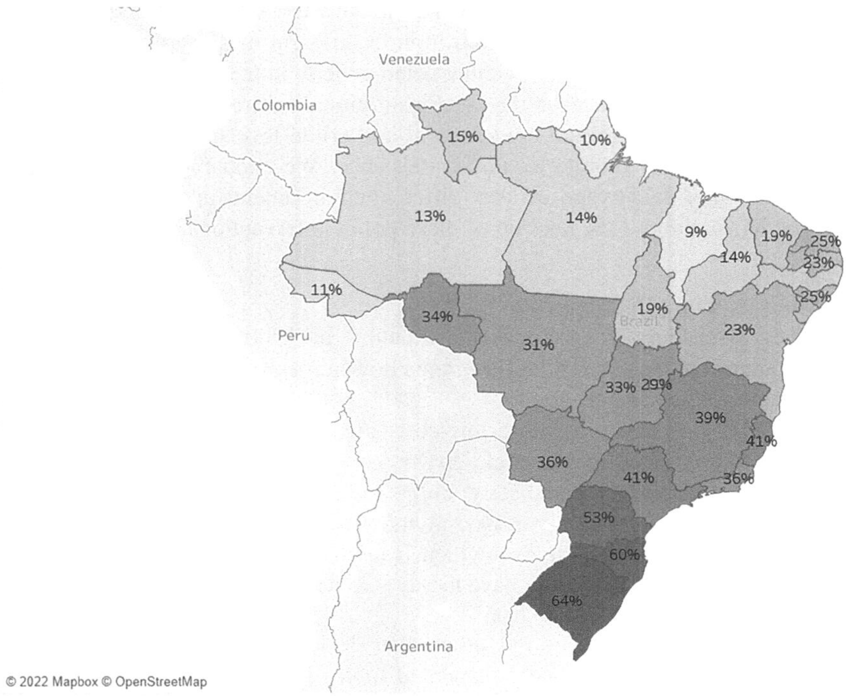

Fig. 4 Percentage of microentrepreneurs who pay INSS across states in Brazil. (Source: Authors based on data from PNADC (2021, fourth trimester). ©2022 Mapbox ©OpenStreetMap)

INSS coverage is lowest. We encourage research to explore why this is the case and how the entrepreneurial life journey is affected by decisions around formalization and associated social security coverage in Brazil.

Microentrepreneurship is generally characterized by lower levels of human capital compared to higher-growth entrepreneurship (Audretsch, 2012). However, in areas with lower institutional development, human capital acquisition is more constrained, limiting the development of managerial skills and the attraction of talent (Kluve et al., 2017; Cho & Honorati, 2013). In Brazil, this challenge has been linked to a lack of social entrepreneurial activity in disadvantaged areas (Barki et al., 2020) and the poorer chances for resilience building during crisis among microentrepreneurs (Brito et al., 2022, *forthcoming*). Figure 5 shows an estimate of the percentage of illiterate microentrepreneurs across regions in Brazil. Illiteracy, defined as the ability to read and write, is largely present among microentrepreneurs in the North and, particularly, the Northeastern region. On average, one in ten microentrepreneurs has severe human capital restrictions, and the likelihood to be illiterate is ten times higher among microentrepreneurs in the North and Northeast than in the South of Brazil. Despite findings that associate higher human capital levels with a stronger likelihood for venture survival, growth, and employment

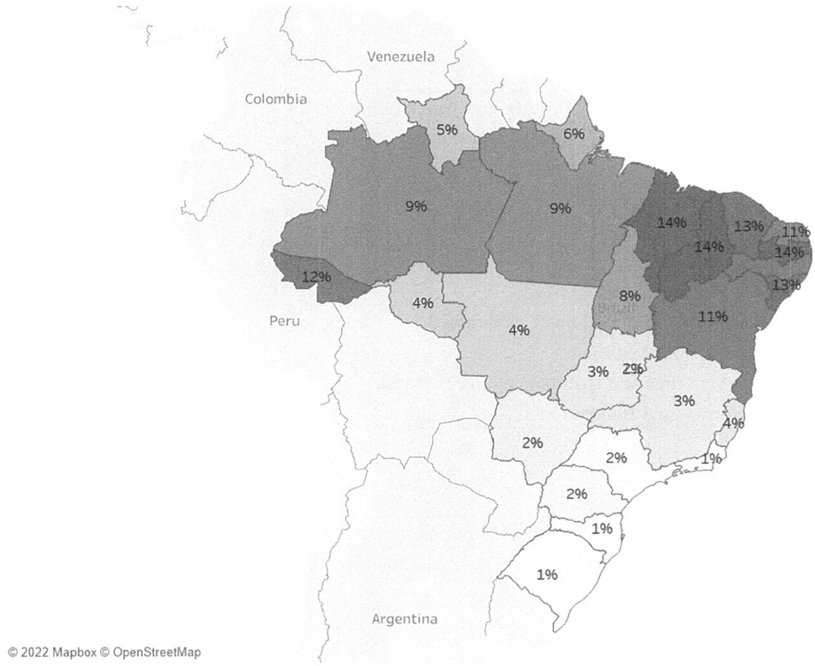

Fig. 5 Percentage of illiterate microentrepreneurs across regions in Brazil. (Source: Authors based on data from PNADC (2021, fourth trimester). ©2022 Mapbox ©OpenStreetMap)

generation, we know very little about the if and how the entrepreneurial process differs for entrepreneurs with very low human capital levels and particularly those that are illiterate. Given the high number of illiterate microentrepreneurs, we encourage studies to explore this question further in the Brazilian context.

In summary, the data on income, formalization rate, social security payment, and illiteracy paint the picture that entrepreneurs in the North and Northeast of Brazil are more likely to engage in microentrepreneurial activities due to necessity rather than opportunity.

These findings have consequences for the growth limits and growth enablers that entrepreneurs need. For example, microentrepreneurs with lower levels of human capital will need different support than educated entrepreneurs, or entrepreneurs that are already better structured through formal registration. Training may also be determined by the type of activity and industry sector in which microentrepreneurs are active. In this regard, Table 1 shows the distribution of industry sectors among Microentrepreneurs in Brazil from the PNADC sample.

Table 1 shows that very few microentrepreneurs operate in more technologically intense industry sectors, such as the information and communication sector. However, microentrepreneurs in these sectors may particularly benefit from support, as these sectors have higher growth rates (GEM, 2021). We expect these

Table 1 Distribution of industry sectors (CNAE) among microentrepreneurs in Brazil from PNADC sample

CNAE sector	Microentrepreneurs	
Agriculture, Livestock, Forestry, Fishing and Aquaculture	16,349	25.74%
Trade, Repair of Motor Vehicles and Motorcycles	12,987	20.44%
Construction	7904	12.44%
Processing Industries	5234	8.24%
Other Activities and Services	5153	8.11%
Accommodation and Food	4444	7.00%
Transportation, Warehousing and Mail	4037	6.36%
Professional, Scientific and Technical Activities	2619	4.12%
Human Health and Social Service	1162	1.83%
Administrative Activities and Complementary Services	1048	1.65%
Arts, Culture, Sports, and Recreation	685	1.08%
Education	666	1.05%
Real Estate Activities	421	0.66%
Information and Communication	380	0.60%
Financial, Insurance and related Service Activities	252	0.40%
Water, Sewage, Waste Management and Decontamination Activities	111	0.17%
Extractive Industries	44	0.07%
Poorly defined Activities	26	0.04%
Electricity and Gas	1	0.00%
Total Sample	63,523	

Source: Authors based on data from PNADC (2021, fourth trimester)

microentrepreneurs to have different demands for support organizations, as they are likely to enter the entrepreneurial activity with higher human capital levels. For example, microentrepreneurs might benefit from more personal growth trainings, market access and networking skills, and mentoring. We encourage policy makers and researchers alike to further explore industry-specific demands and microentrepreneurial outcomes.

Similarly important in the targeting of public policy efforts are the differences in demands of urban versus rural microentrepreneurs. Figure 6 shows the percentage of microentrepreneurs within the PNADC sample who live in an urban area. The data indicates that entrepreneurial activity in northern states tends to occur in rural and more isolated areas, than that in southern states, yet the majority of microentrepreneurial activities take place in urban areas across all states in Brazil. This stands in contrast to earlier studies from multicountry samples that have found the majority of microentrepreneurship taking place in rural areas (Mead & Liedholm, 1998).

In Brazil, like in the vast majority of countries worldwide, there is still a large income gap between women and men-led businesses (GEM Women Entrepreneurship Report, 2021). However, the gender income gap for microentrepreneurs is less defined compared to larger entrepreneurs, with male microentrepreneurs generating 26% more income than female microentrepreneurs, while men-led businesses in the

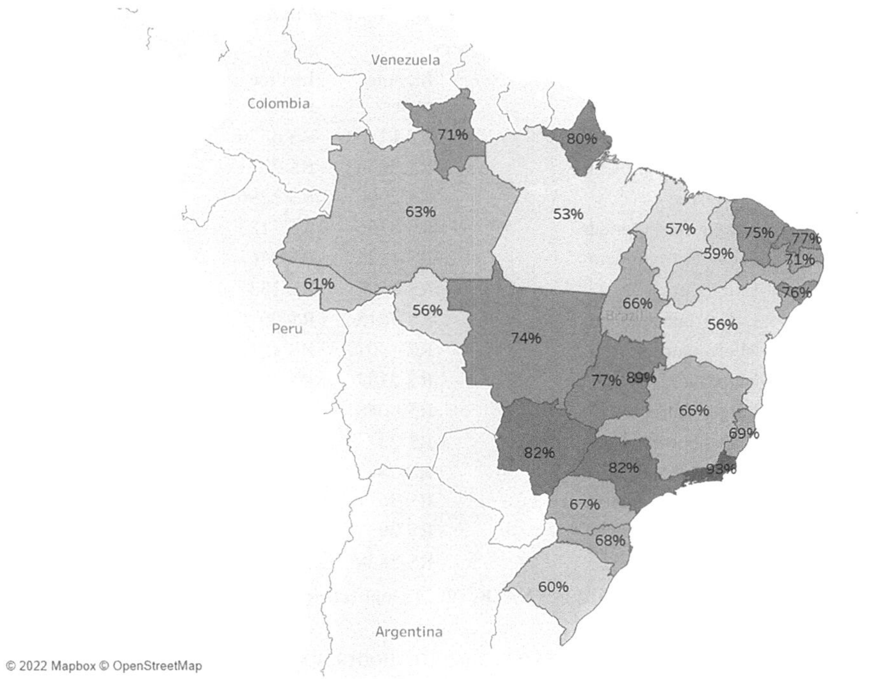

Fig. 6 Percentage of microentrepreneurs who live in an urban (vs. rural) area. (Source: Authors based on data from PNADC (2021, fourth trimester). ©2022 Mapbox ©OpenStreetMap)

category of larger entrepreneurs generate 43% more income than women-led businesses of the same category. Importantly, the gender income gap in Brazil seems to be driven by entrepreneurial activity, as men employees have on average 19% higher income. Furthermore, larger businesses seem to drive the gender income gap more than smaller businesses. Table 1 shows that the income gap varies by region and becomes larger with increasing incomes of larger entrepreneurs. Overall, regions with lower income appear to have lower differences in income between men and women. This may, for example, suggest that the economic surplus of richer regions in Brazil is more absorbed by men-led businesses than by women entrepreneurs, although the causal relationship cannot be established based on our observations. It may also suggest, a difference due to industry participation. As typical male-led industries, like finance, are more dominant in the Southeast and South, while the large gender pay gap among large entrepreneurs in the Center-West may be possibly explained with big agribusiness. We encourage future studies to further explore the reason for the income differences between men and women-led businesses and to contribute to the identification of suitable policy initiatives to fight gender inequality. Some parts of the gender income gap might be explained by a lower number of hours that women microentrepreneurs spend on average in their business (Table 2).

Table 2 Income difference (in R$) between men and women entrepreneurs and non-entrepreneurs (employees) among regions in Brazil

Region	Microentr. vs. larger entr. vs. employee	Income men	Income women	Income difference (%)
Midwest	Larger entrepreneur	R$ 12,588	R$ 6576	191%
Midwest	Micro entrepreneur	R$ 2665	R$ 2071	129%
Midwest	Employee	R$ 2906	R$ 2296	127%
Northeast	Larger entrepreneur	R$ 8266	R$ 7123	116%
Northeast	Micro entrepreneur	R$ 1225	R$ 946	129%
Northeast	Employee	R$ 1596	R$ 1537	104%
North	Larger entrepreneur	R$ 7615	R$ 6676	114%
North	Micro entrepreneur	R$ 1407	R$ 1210	116%
North	Employee	R$ 2157	R$ 1970	109%
Southeast	Larger entrepreneur	R$ 9648	R$ 6504	148%
Southeast	Micro entrepreneur	R$ 2334	R$ 1884	124%
Southeast	Employee	R$ 2842	R$ 2221	128%
South	Larger entrepreneur	R$ 9657	R$ 6559	147%
South	Micro entrepreneur	R$ 2931	R$ 2238	131%
South	Employee	R$ 2838	R$ 2276	125%

Source: Authors based on data from PNADC (2021, fourth trimester)

However, even when we adjust income for hours spent in the business a gender income gap remains.

Under a gender lens, missing access to social security is even more relevant, as women tend to stay out of the labor market for longer due to childbearing and motherhood. Figure 7 shows that, in general, women have a higher likelihood of paying social security (INSS) than men.

Missing social security directly affects the available income that women microentrepreneurs have in the month after giving birth. The lack of coverage might contribute to restricting the growth of women-led ventures. In addition, the lack of institutional assistance in childcare (e.g., kindergarten) may prevent women to pursue training and business opportunities, as they need to take care of children. Previous research has highlighted that women entrepreneurs have greater social obligations than men (Lenz et al., 2021). The higher number of hours that women spend on household and family care activities might be the reason for which female microentrepreneurs spend on average 6 h less working in their ventures than men (Table 3).

3 Conclusion

We are using PNADC data from the fourth trimester of 2021 to present an up-to-date view on microentrepreneurship in Brazil and to flash out possible research directions. Figure 8 shows the summary of our propositions along institutional, venture,

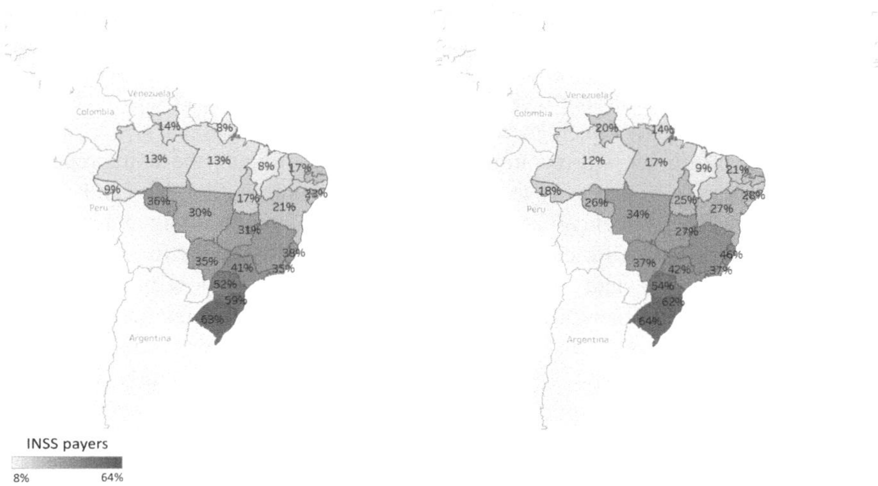

Fig. 7 Men and women microentrepreneurs who contribute to INSS payment in Brazil across regions (in %). (Source: Authors based on data from PNADC (2021, fourth trimester). ©2022 Mapbox ©OpenStreetMap)

Table 3 Average amount of microentrepreneurs' hours spend in business by gender

Gender	Avg. hours effectively worked	Avg. hours normally worked
Men	39.23	40.38
Women	33.11	34.11

Source: Authors based on data from PNADC (2021, fourth trimester)

Research directions on microentrepreneurship in Brazil

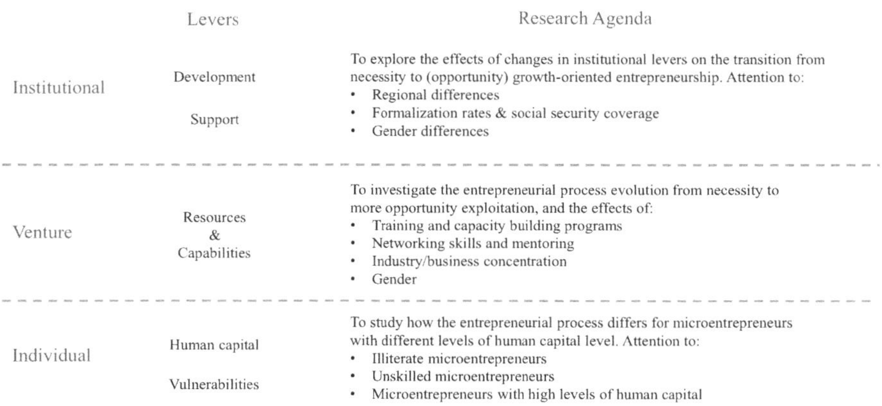

Fig. 8 Research directions on microentrepreneurship in Brazil

and entrepreneurial characteristics. While research has already provided evidence that institutional development and institutional support can help microentrepreneurs, more process research is needed to understand how changes in institutional levers affect the transition from necessity to growth-oriented entrepreneurship. Research in the Brazilian context could particularly focus on regional differences, formalization rates, and social security coverage, as well as gender differences.

On the venture level, we recommend to further investigate the entrepreneurial process evolution from necessity to more opportunity exploitation. Research in this area can benefit from evidence-based research on the different training and capacity-building programs, networking skills and mentoring, differences in industry and business concentration, and gender. On the individual level, low human capital levels and economic vulnerability characterize the majority of microentrepreneurs. However, human capital levels are different among microentrepreneurs and how these differences affect the entrepreneurial process is insufficiently explored. Research in this direction can contribute to the understanding of geographic and gender differences in microentrepreneurship and help to identify public policies to address regional and gender inequalities in Brazil.

References

Alvarez, S. A., & Barney, J. B. (2014). Entrepreneurial opportunities and poverty alleviation. *Entrepreneurship: Theory and Practice, 38*(1), 159–184. https://doi.org/10.1111/etap.12078

Audretsch, D. B. (2012, March). Determinants of high-growth entrepreneurship. In *Report prepared for the OECD/DBA International Workshop on "High-Growth Firms: Local Policies and Local Determinants*.

Barki, E., de Campos, J. G. F., Lenz, A.-K., Kimmitt, J., Stephan, U., & Naigeborin, V. (2020). Support for social entrepreneurs from disadvantaged areas navigating crisis: Insights from Brazil. *Journal of Business Venturing Insights, 14*, e00205. https://doi.org/10.1016/j.jbvi.2020.e00205

Bhatt, B., Qureshi, I., & Sutter, C. (2022). How do intermediaries build inclusive markets? The role of the social context. *Journal of Management Studies, 59*(4), 925–957. https://doi.org/10.1111/joms.12796

Binder, M., & Coad, A. (2013). Life satisfaction and self-employment: A matching approach. *Small Business Economics, 40*(4), 1009–1033. https://doi.org/10.1007/s11187-011-9413-9

Birks, S., Fluitman, F., Xavier, O., Salome, B., & Sinclair, C. (1992). *Skill acquisition and work in micro-enterprises: Recent evidence from West Africa*. Africa Technical Department, World Bank.

Brito, R., Lenz, A.-K., & Pacheco, M. (2022). Resilience building among small businesses in low-income neighborhoods. *Journal of Small Business Management* (Forthcoming). https://doi.org/10.1080/00472778.2022.2041197

Cho, Y., & Honorati, M. (2013). Entrepreneurship programs in developing countries: A meta regression analysis. *Labour Economics, 28*, 110–130. https://doi.org/10.1016/j.labeco.2014.03.011

De Castro, J. O., Khavul, S., & Bruton, G. D. (2014). Shades of grey: How do informal firms navigate between macro and meso institutional environments? *Strategic Entrepreneurship Journal, 8*(1), 75–94. https://doi.org/10.1002/sej.1172

De Soto, H. (1989). *The other path*. Harper and Row Publishers.

DeBerry-Spence, B., & Elliot, E. A. (2012). African microentrepreneurship: The reality of everyday challenges. *Journal of Business Research, 65*(12), 1665–1673.

Dencker, J. C., Bacq, S., Gruber, M., & Haas, M. (2021). Reconceptualizing necessity entrepreneurship: A contextualized framework of entrepreneurial processes under the condition of basic needs. *Academy of Management Review, 46*(1), 60–79.

Dutt, N., Hawn, O., Vidal, E., Chatterji, A., McGahan, A., & Mitchell, W. (2016). How open system intermediaries address institutional failures: The case of business incubators in emerging-market countries. *Academy of Management Journal, 59*(3), 818–840. https://doi.org/10.5465/amj.2012.0463

GEM. (2021). *Global entrepreneurship monitor global report*. Babson College.

GEM WE. (2021). *Global entrepreneurship monitor women's entrepreneurship report*. Babson College. Retrieved from https://www.gemconsortium.org/reports/womens-entrepreneurship

Honig, B. (1998). What determines success? Examining the human, financial, and social capital of Jamaican microentrepreneurs. *Journal of Business Venturing, 13*(5), 371–394. https://doi.org/10.1016/S0883-9026(97)00036-0

Hulme, D., & Shepherd, A. (2003). Conceptualizing chronic poverty. *World Development, 31*(3), 403–423. https://doi.org/10.1016/S0305-750X(02)00222-X

IBGE. (2021). *PNAD – Séries históricas*. Retrieved April 11, 2022, from https://www.ibge.gov.br/estatisticas/sociais/educacao/9127-pesquisa-nacional-por-amostra-de-domicilios.html?=&t=series-historicas

IBGE. (2022). *Desemprego*. Retrieved April 11, 2022, from https://www.ibge.gov.br/explica/desemprego.php

Karnani, A. (2007). The mirage of marketing to the bottom of the pyramid: How the private sector can help alleviate poverty. *California Management Review, 49*(4), 90–112.

Kluve, J., Puerto, S., Robalino, D., Romero, J. M., Rother, F., Stoeterau, J., Weidenkaff, F., & Witte, M. (2017). Interventions to improve the labour market outcomes of youth: A systematic review of training, entrepreneurship promotion, employment services and subsidized employment interventions. *Campbell Systematic Reviews, 13*(1), 1–288.

Lenz. (2018). *Perfil dos Microempreendedores – Rio das Pedras*. Retrieved April 11, 2022, from https://annakatharinalenz.com/policy_insights/pesquisa-empreendedores-rio-das-pedras/

Lenz, A.-K., & Valdivia, M. (2021). *Nudging microentrepreneurs into formalization under high drug-related violence: Evidence from a randomized field experiment* (Working Paper).

Lenz, A.-K., Sutter, C., Goldszmidt, R., & Zucco, C. (2021). Venture distress and problemistic search among entrepreneurs in Brazilian favelas. *Journal of Business Venturing, 36*(6), 106162. https://doi.org/10.1016/j.jbusvent.2021.106162

Mead, D. C., & Liedholm, C. (1998). The dynamics of micro and small enterprises in developing countries. *World Development, 26*(1), 61–74. https://doi.org/10.1016/S0305-750X(97)10010-9

Mensmann, M., & Frese, M. (2019). Who stays proactive after entrepreneurship training? Need for cognition, personal initiative maintenance, and well-being. *Journal of Organizational Behavior, 40*(1), 20–37. https://doi.org/10.1002/job.2333

Rocha, R., Ulyssea, G., & Rachter, L. (2018). Do lower taxes reduce informality? Evidence from Brazil. *Journal of Development Economics, 134*, 28–49.

Zucco, C., Lenz, A. K., Goldszmidt, R., & Valdivia, M. (2020). Face-to-face vs. virtual assistance to entrepreneurs: Evidence from a field experiment in Brazil. *Economics Letters, 188*, 108922. https://doi.org/10.1016/j.econlet.2019.108922

Surfing the Amazon: Exploring Surf Tourism and Lifestyle Entrepreneurship in Brazil

Laura Bradshaw

Abstract This chapter explores how entrepreneurs in the Brazilian market overcame and took advantage of differences with global competitors by rethinking their core competencies and creating sustainable business models around surfing lifestyles. Moreover, it is advocated that Brazil has a valuable opportunity to increase surf tourism around underprivileged areas where regions show the most potential for socio-economic development. Beaches in disadvantaged neighbourhoods could generate the potential for boosting surf tourism development and improving the flow of tourists to the area. Capitalising on underprivileged coastal areas that could benefit from tourism and development could also increase the economic benefit of the area for local communities by bringing in much-needed business and development and opening the coastline up to more overseas travellers seeking an adventure.

Keywords Surf tourism · Brazilian surfing · Lifestyle entrepreneurship · Adventure tourism · Surf etiquette · Localism

1 Introduction

Surfing is an ancient tradition, dating back thousands of years; despite ancient roots in Polynesia, Hawaii is considered the origin of modern surfing, where the ancients built stone temples and wooden surfboards and made religious offerings dedicated to surfing (Wieser, 2019). Surfing can be defined as "the act of riding an ocean wave while standing on a surfboard and broadly includes other aspects of wave riding such as riding prone on a 'bodyboard' or simply bodysurfing" (Martin & Assenov, 2012). The International Surfing Association (ISA) governs and defines Surfing as Shortboard, Longboard & Bodyboarding, StandUp Paddle (SUP) Racing and Surfing, Para-Surfing, Bodysurfing, Wakesurfing, and all other wave riding activities on any type of waves and on flat water using wave riding equipment (ISA, 2022).

L. Bradshaw (✉)
Institute for Sport Business, Loughborough University London, London, UK

J. Leitão et al. (eds.), *Brazilian Entrepreneurship*, Studies on Entrepreneurship, Structural Change and Industrial Dynamics,
https://doi.org/10.1007/978-3-031-09392-0_3

Surfing is a free activity practised recreationally by approximately 35 million people worldwide (O'Brien & Eddie, 2013). In search of the perfect waves, surfers regularly engage in surf tourism around the globe (Buckley, 2002; Ponting, 2009), which impacts thousands of coastal communities (Martin & Assenov, 2012; Ponting & O'Brien, 2015; Mach & Ponting, 2018).

In recent decades, the growth of surfing in sport and tourism has gained momentum in academic research. The World Surf League reported in 2017 that the sport of surfing was growing more than 30% annually and that the global surf industry generated more than $13 billion in that year alone (World Surf League, 2020). This increase has drawn the attention of researchers who have studied different aspects of surf tourism (Martin & Assenov, 2012). Traditional surfing and big wave surfing have increased in recent years, in both participation and researchers covering the topic. Surfing has also evolved for some into high-risk adventure sports such as Amazon river surfing and volcano surfing, wherein the latter, adventure enthusiasts, surf down the slopes of ash and sand on a Nicaraguan volcano (Horton, 2022). Surfing is one of the most popular sports in the world, with surfers willing to travel long distances in search of ideal surf conditions (da Rosa et al., 2020). Commercial surf tourism is recent in origin but now significantly contributes to the worldwide adventure tourism sector (Buckley, 2002). Tourism niches like adventure sports tourism have experienced significant growth in recent years, which has been developed to achieve more sustainable tourism, as is the case of surf tourism (Martin-Gonzalez & Swart, 2021). Two decades ago, Buckley (2002) described how surf tourism had become "a social phenomenon of sufficient economic, social and environmental significance to justify academic attention" (p. 406); this social phenomenon has since increased. Subsequently, this has led to an increase in academic focus that has established the topic as an area of interest far beyond tourism literature. Surf tourism spans tourism management, sociology, sport, event management, geology, environmental management, marine and coastal sciences, policy, and government and local authorities.

The increase in research on surf tourism highlights similar issues throughout coastal communities worldwide. However, in Brazil, where surf tourism is in its infancy, there is an opportunity to learn lessons from other regions that have experienced an increase in commercial surf tourism. Sustainable development issues have been highlighted in other coastal areas such as the Indo-Pacific islands. Problems have been documented in these regions concerning reef erosion, overcrowding, price hikes, crime, and negative impacts on local communities in popular surf resorts. All of which have put a spotlight on the dark side of this niche adventure tourism (Towner & Lemarié, 2020; Ponting & O'Brien, 2015). Heeding the warnings and learning from other resorts allows local coastal management and authorities of surf regions in Brazil to work on current issues such as sewage and pollution entering the sea, impacting local communities and visitors wanting to use the areas. Understanding the cost opportunity of surf spots may encourage local authorities to rethink current issues regarding sewage and conservation protection in these areas, to attract more lifestyle entrepreneurs and increase visitor numbers to the area.

For this chapter, lifestyle entrepreneurs are defined as "entrepreneurs who started up a tourism enterprise with the purpose of pursuing a desired lifestyle, with relatively less ambition towards achieving economic returns (Shaw & Williams, 1998; Williams et al., 1989). Many lifestyle tourists work in small business ventures referred to as micro-tourism segments that are "related to arts and crafts, ecotourism, adventure tourism, guesthouses, etc." (Fadda, 2020). Research reveals that in micro-tourism segments, many customers involved in particular recreational activities decided to create a business related to their hobby, i.e. by making their hobby their work (Peters et al., 2009; Shaw & Williams, 2004; Williams et al., 1989). It is hardly surprising that this segment of entrepreneurship has arisen in the tourism sector, where small businesses can have low threshold entry levels, with low financial resources and little to no relevant business experience required (Lashley & Rowson, 2010; Peters et al., 2009). This low entry threshold is perhaps part of the appeal of such micro-tourism segments that are open and accessible to all.

A micro-segment of the adventure sports tourism industry is surf tourism, which is defined as "an activity which takes place 40 m or more from the person's place of residence, where surfing or attending a surfing event is the primary purpose for travel. Surf tourists stay at their destinations for at least one night or can undertake their visit as a day trip" (Tourism New South Wales, 2009, p. 3). Research into the entrepreneurship of surf tourists revealed "an increase in surf tourism, as surfing has gained more international prominence and popularity. Many individuals travel to surf competitions as a form of leisure activity and enhance business connections" (Ratten, 2018a, b, p. 262). Findings revealed many surf tourists were interested in travelling for surfing as a leisure activity. In contrast, others saw the potential business opportunities of the sport, which indicates the entrepreneurial behaviour of surf tourists (Ratten, 2018a, b).

The most popular research spots for surf tourism are Australia, the USA, and Indonesia. Martin and Assenov (2012) identified that Australia and the USA benefit from universities located near the coastal resorts, attracting students and scholars who surf and have contributed to this area of research. Although surf tourism is a worldwide phenomenon, the research has mainly focused on a few countries, highlighting a potential knowledge gap. Surfing occurs in 162 countries (Wannasurf, 2022) and is officially represented in 109 countries across 5 continents (ISA, 2022). Yet academic research has thus far only covered a fraction of these countries (Martin & Assenov, 2012). With the success of Surfing as an Olympic sport in the Tokyo 2020 games, it can be anticipated that researchers will focus on surf tourism in a broader range of countries in the coming years. The inclusion of surfing into the Olympic programme in recent years is likely to generate a rise in participation in the sport, further coverage, and focus on the sport from a commercial perspective.

Surf tourism is a rapidly expanding market segment of the broader sports tourism industry (Martin & Assenov, 2012). Since Martin and Assenov carried out a comprehensive review of the surf tourism literature in 2012, there has been an increase in coastal coverage and research on surf tourism in the academic literature. However, research specifically focusing on Brazilian surf tourism remains sparse. While there has been more interest in the concept of surf tourism and academic focus on surf tourism appears to be on the rise, research on Brazil is not as established as other coastal surfing resources. This exploration attempts to fill the gap in the literature on lifestyle entrepreneurship and surf tourism in Brazil. By highlighting the role of lifestyle entrepreneurs and how developing tourism business activities have contributed to the broader surf tourism ecosystem. These discussion points can highlight to tourism bodies the opportunity cost of developing coastal surf towns and inspire future research on surf tourism in Brazil.

2 Surfing Brazil

Brazil is the largest country in South America, with arguably underrated surf (Denning, 2019). The preconceived idea that Brazil has only small waves is argued by those who enjoy the coastal waves each year (Wannasurf, 2022). Brazil was once famous for its Samba, food, and carnivals. Nevertheless, it is now adding surfing to its notoriety, attracting adventure tourists to breaks such as Praia Brava, Arpoador, Barra da Tijuca, Ipanema, Praia da Macumba, Pratigi, Joaquina Beach, and Maresias, to name a few (Surfer Girls, 2022).

From April to September, southern Brazil catches east to south swells, and from November to March, the North of Brazil (i.e. Fernando do Noronha) catches northern swells (Wannasurf, 2022).

For many, the attraction to Brazilian waves is the suitability of waves for all levels, the climate, water temperature, and the low-budget Brazilian lifestyle. The disadvantage to these conditions is that good surf, and tropical climate often results in crowded line-ups, generating problems such as limited carrying capacity and localism, aggression, and hostility. Deats et al. (2016) documented how surfers everywhere fight for waves; "this competition is inevitable as the demand for waves far exceeds the supply at most quality surf breaks near urban populations. The number of waves that a surfer will catch is a function of both the individual's characteristics and the local surf conditions (Deats, Martinez, & Shearer, 2016). It is helpful to view surfing as a common-pool resource problem, wherein surfers compete for waves in an ocean that is available to all" (p. 97) and uncrowded waves are a rarity (de Alessi, 2009). However, for experienced surfers, the lack of reef breaks can result in needing to travel to seek more powerful waves elsewhere (Wannasurf, 2022).

Brazilian surfing is now big business, "surfing generates R$7 (US$1.4) billion a year, according to estimates from the Brazilian Surfing Institute (Ibrasurfe). The amount includes expenses with clothing, boards, and accessories" (Latin American News, 2021). In recent years, Brazil has been riding high on the modern wave as four times Champion of the World (WSL, 2021). Previously Australia and the USA dominated global surfing, but since 2014, Brazil has taken over the reins, winning four world titles in the past decade, with athletes such as Gabriel Medina, Adriano de Souza, and Italo Ferreira all winning titles (WSL, 2021). Female surfers such as

Silvana Lima, Maya Gabeira, and Tatiana Weston-Webb (Surfer Girls, 2022) are all raising the profile of Brazilian surf in international competition.

Brazil has always been known for its dominance in football in the broader context of sport. Like its innovative style of football play, Brazil has also developed its unique style of surfing, with the reigning world surf champion, Gabriel Medina, representing Brazil on the World Surf Tour. A tour that has experienced Brazil's domination over global waves in the last decade and Maya Gabeira, a Brazilian big wave surfer, who recently took the Guinness World Record in 2020 as the biggest wave ever surfed by a female at 22.4 m high in Nazaré, Portugal (Ramsey, 2022). "Brazil has seen a boom in its surfing population due to the rise of the middle class, 2 years of Brazilian surfers winning premier surfing titles (US Open of Surfing 2015, 2016)" (Surfer Girls, 2022). The rise of female athletes such as the big wave surfing star Maya Gabeira, who after receiving endorsement from Lululemon may be the world's highest-paid surfer, male or female (Surfer Girls, 2022). Both male and female winning surfers make up a generation of surfing stars that are affectionately referred to as "The Brazilian Storm" and have blazed a trail, where world-class surf titles that were once dominated by Australians, Americans, and South Africans, are now being taken by the new generation of Brazilian surfers (Surfer Girls, 2022). For many surfers on the championship tour, their surfing life started through their entrepreneurial "surf parents" who were lifestyle entrepreneurs.

3 Lifestyle Entrepreneurs

The nexus of surf, tourism, and innovation is shifting (Bradshaw, 2021), and while research on lifestyle entrepreneurs is an acknowledged research domain, it still appears superficially understood (Wallis et al., 2020). Surf gear is now cheaper than a decade ago, and budget travel has made global adventure tourism an affordable passion for many (Buckley, 2002). Adventure tourism to far-flung private destinations used to be costly and reserved for the wealthy before budget air travel was introduced, yet in current times, surfing is more accessible than ever.

Surfers do not have to live next to the best surf breaks to catch a good wave. Adventure tourism companies now cater to mainstream foreign travellers seeking novel experiences engineered in unique locations, creating accessible solutions to finding the best waves. This commercial engineering of global surf tourism has grown in recent years, and surf tourists are no longer just the cash-rich, time-poor adventure tourists. Lifestyle entrepreneurs come in many guises but are defined as being predominantly motivated by the need to succeed at living a quality of life by sustaining an income that allows them to survive and maintain their lifestyle (Marchant & Mottiar, 2011). It is this incentive that sets them apart from other entrepreneurs. McKeever et al. (2015) stated that "context is now recognised as a critical factor in explaining the situatedness of the entrepreneurial process. According to this view, entrepreneurs are embedded in networks, places and communities which socially frame resources and opportunities" (p. 50). Likewise, this is true for lifestyle entrepreneurs who are also part of the embedded communities and networks.

Kaplan and Warren (2003) described lifestyle entrepreneurs as individuals who engineer the entrepreneurial activity around their preferred lifestyle and personal circumstances. Many of the professional surfers in today's competitive line-up had parents who were surf entrepreneurs. Surf entrepreneurs can loosely be defined as lifestyle entrepreneurs that run surf businesses. They can be referred to as Surfpreneurs, from those with surf businesses in hospitality to surf products and sustainable surf brands to travel and surf camps. In 2016 Peter Fabour and James Marshall founded Surfpreneurs Club, a surf entrepreneurs club that offers an online community connecting surf entrepreneurs. This community of entrepreneurs working in the surf industry reveals how enjoying the surfing lifestyle and running a related business has benefits; "life is good when surf trips can qualify as tax write-offs" (Marshall, 2017). Surf entrepreneurs are perhaps considered purist lifestyle entrepreneurs as they seek the lifestyle, and the business is simply to maintain that lifestyle, rather than being economically driven for commercial success (Marchant & Mottiar, 2011).

It is clear from existing research that many diverse types of lifestyle entrepreneurs have different goals, motives, and varying levels of business experience. Ratten (2018a, b) revealed how "some athlete entrepreneurs are interested in their lifestyles and pursue business ventures around certain themes that fit with their own ideologies. This helps provide a motive for innovations that is in line with personal goals" (p. 56). Some surf entrepreneurs set up surf shacks, while others run surf schools or move their businesses near the beach to allow their children to train or to enjoy the lifestyle.

Many of the current World Tour Brazilian surfers started their trade through entrepreneurial surf parents: firstly, Miguel Pupo (currently ranked 11th on the World Tour) learned to surf with a board made by his father, Wagner, who is a shaper by trade, who travelled, supported, and trained with Miguel for years, sleeping, eating, training, and sharing hotels together (Mellone, 2016) before moving onto coach Miguel's younger brother Samuel Pupo (currently ranked 18th on the World Tour); secondly, Filipe Toledo (currently ranked 4th on the World Tour) and father, coach, and hero Ricardo Toledo who are inseparable; Gabriel Medina (3 × World Champion), and coach/ stepfather Charlie Rodrigues who taught Gabriel to surf and went on to coach and manage his stepson to become World Champion and now coaches Gabriel's younger sister Sofia; Luana Reis, another rising Brazilian talent whose parents moved to Maresias, Brazil's surfing capital—so Luana could train daily (Associated Press, 2022). The influence that these "surfpreneurs" had on the future of surfing was impactful. Their actions and lifestyle choices enabled a generation of Brazilian surfers to develop and grow their talent to compete on the world stage. The impact that these lifestyle entrepreneurs had on the future of surfing was astonishing.

Despite the recent domination of world surfing, Brazil is not a country known for its big waves. Nevertheless, Brazilians have dominated traditional surfing and big wave surfing competition events over the past decade. Popular surf breaks in Brazil, such as Ipanema, Praia da Macumba, Pratigi, Praia da Joaquina, and Maresias, to name a few (Surfer Girls, 2022), serve the community of surfers and tourists fighting it out for a wave. However, despite surfing entering the Olympic line-up and rising commercial surf tourism, surfing has been difficult in recent years, with COVID-19 seeing surfing bans implemented in various global locations (Martin-Gonzalez & Swart, 2021). Still, surfing hotspots in Brazil such as Barra da Tijuca, Arpoador and Geribá, Rio de Janeiro; Praia Brava, Florianópolis, Santa Catarina; Fernando de Noronha, Pernambuco; Praia de Pipa, Rio Grande do Norte; Itacaré, Bahia and Pororoca, São Domingos do Capim receive a deluge of locals and adventure tourists enjoying the waves (Lees, 2018).

An economic study of surf tourism (Bosquetti et al., 2020) revealed: "as harmful coastal developments and pollution threaten surf spots, the evaluation of economic benefits derived from surfing, informally known as Surfonomics, has been utilised by internationally renowned enviro-surf NGOs such as the Surfrider Foundation and Save The Waves Coalition, to fully account for the economic benefits to communities from surf tourism and promote coastal conservation" (p. 12). Surfonomics has been used for over a decade now and offers those who govern coastal communities the opportunity to calculate the cost of regeneration and the economic benefits of promoting and sustaining a surf tourism destination. "Surf economics or Surfonomics applies natural resource economics to better understand the economic value of waves and surfing to local communities, as well as the consumer surplus that surf breaks provide to millions of surfers" (Nelsen, 2012). The ability to quantify the value of a wave has enabled surf resorts such as Guarda do Embaú to become a dedicated surf reserve. On 26 October 2019, Brazil's Guarda do Embaú was officially dedicated as the ninth World Surfing Reserve (Save the Waves, 2019). Formed by the Rio da Madre, "the Guarda do Embaú surf ecosystem is one of the most classic Brazilian surfing locations, as well as one of the most biodiverse areas in the Atlantic Coast Rainforest of Brazil" (Save the Waves, 2019). Furthermore, "Guarda do Embáu is home to a legendary wave that breaks at the Da Madre River mouth throughout the year. For generations, Guarda do Embaú was just a small, sleepy fishing village. In the 1970s, surfers discovered Guarda's epic waves, and it is now internationally recognised as one of the best surf spots in Brazil" (Bosquetti & da Souza, 2019). Now that the wave has World Surf Reserve status, the "Save The Waves staff and the Local Stewardship Council drafted the Stewardship Plan for the Reserve to define and implement important projects to improve the water quality of the Rio da Madre. This resulted in a new water quality monitoring program, municipal approval, and funding for construction of a wastewater treatment plant" (STWC, 2019). Social innovation schemes such as the World Surf Reserves Programme are created by collaborating with professional surfers, local stewardship councils, and local community members. Such entrepreneurial activities have "inspired the creation of and highlighted the need for a network of protected surfing areas throughout the coastline of Brazil" (STWC, 2019), and world-class waves now have an economic value that global surf tourism impacts. Therefore, local governing bodies can take action to protect their coastal communities and improve the attraction for future adventure tourists seeking their next wave.

4 The Brazilian Wave

As the largest country in South America, Brazil is home to some of the best surf spots in the world and some of the world's best surfers. "Brazil stretches from the Amazon Basin in the north to vineyards and massive Iguaçu Falls in the south. With over 4000 miles of coastline and a country that loves the beach life, Brazil is becoming a dominating factor in the surfing world" (Surfer Girls, 2022). There are many waves along its long Atlantic coastline, with different climates, environments, shapes, and sizes (Lees, 2018). Brazil has a great concentration of surf breaks (McGregor & Wills, 2017) and is a popular pastime, resulting in some spots getting crowded. The best waves can be found in the southern region, which receives more swell and offers a better variety of waves than the northern surf spots. Surfing hotspot such as Santa Catarina, Florianopolis, has over 40 surf beaches, the most popular being Barra da Lagoa, Praia Mole, and Praia Joaquina (Lees, 2018). While Rio de Janeiro has some excellent surf spots, crowding can be experienced around Rio de Janeiro, especially Arpoador, considered the birthplace of surfing in Brazil.

Similarly, in Rio Grande do Norte on the northeastern coast, Praia da Pipa is a popular surf town surrounded by quality waves (Lees, 2018). Brazil has a fast-growing surfing population (Bosquetti et al., 2017) offering year-round surfing, but for experienced surfers seeking more powerful swells, the best time to go is between April and October; the waves are less powerful for recreational surfers throughout the rest of the year. Brazil sits on a large continental shelf in the Atlantic, and there are many breaks along Brazil's coastline (Burgess, 2021). However, to gain experience on the more powerful waves, Brazilian surfers need to travel beyond their country to compete on the bigger waves, which means travel expenses, support, and technical assistance. When Gabriel Medina won the WSL tour in 2014, he was the first Latin American Surfer to do so and consequently, so began the Brazilian domination of the sport. However, developing competitive skills in surf locations such as Hawaii meant athletes needed support and financial assistance. Brazilians do not have the same calibre of waves to train on as Australians, Americans, and South Africans, so they must travel. However, expenses accumulate for travelling surfers, and Brazilian athletes did not initially have the same money or sponsorship to support their training as their fellow sponsored surfers in the line-ups; this meant they had to hustle, work harder than the rest and push their way into the media spotlight to gain the financial backing needed (Burgess, 2021). Adriano de Souza's breakthrough into the WSL opened the gateway for the next generation of athletes, such as Medina. Gabriel Medina then put Brazil on the surfing map and paved the way for others to follow with financial support and backing. To do this, Brazilian surfers had to rely on their underdog reputation and utilise the skills gained on the smaller waves, adapting to the powerful waves during competitions. Brazilian surfers are also currently dominating in Big wave surfing, such as Lucas Chumbo, Rodrigo Koxa, and Pedro Scooby. In 2017, Rodrigo broke the Guinness record for the biggest wave ever surfed in Nazaré at 80 ft (Bradshaw, 2021). Nonetheless, surfing is not limited to just the ocean and beaches of Brazil. In some parts of Brazil, experienced surfers risk life and limb to take on the challenge of the Amazon river wave, a tidal bore phenomenon referred to as Pororoca.

5 Pororoca: The Amazon River Wave

Away from the beaches of Brazil, another wave is surfed called the Pororoca, offering endless surfing along the Amazon rainforest. This wave is considered the world's longest surfable wave. Pororoca is the name of the tidal phenomenon in Brazil (Surfer Today, 2022). This tidal bore is located in the huge Amazon and can deliver up to 12-ft river waves in February and March during the dry season. However, Pororoca is a dangerous wave, only suitable for experienced surfers and should only be surfed with boat or jet ski support. The brown water is treacherous, full of trees, broken branches and debris, crocodiles, piranhas, and snakes. However, for experienced surfers, the powerful Pororoca wave offers the opportunity for long-lasting surf lines, cutbacks, aerial moves, and even barrels (Surfer Today, 2022). As with other tidal bores, it is possible to hear the Pororoca coming 30 min before it arrives, along with birds flying over as nature's warning. Picuruta Salazar, the iconic Brazilian surfer, holds the record of 12.5 km and 37 min of surfing a single Pororoca wave (Surfer Today, 2022). Like a small tsunami at 4 m (13 ft), the tide can travel at 800 km. It is a spiritual, mystical wave for many Brazilians living along the Amazon river banks. Unique waves like these create interest from adventure tourists and thrill-seekers searching for their next off-the-beat destination. While only for experienced surfers, the interest in seeking out the most dangerous waves increases as cash-rich, time-poor adventure tourists seek their next surf trip away from the crowded breaks (Buckley, 2002).

6 The Social Value of Waves

Waves are a natural occurrence and roll up on shores the world over. Yet, there is a potential economic and social value to these waves in terms of surf tourism. According to Save the Waves Coalition (STWC) (2022), surfonomics is a method that uses direct expenditure data from visiting surfer tourists to estimate the economic value that a world-class wave brings to the local community. This model was created in California but adapted to the Brazilian context (STWC, 2022). Following a surfonomics analysis of Guarda do Embaú, Brazil, Bosquetti and da Souza (2019) revealed that "world-class waves have an enormous social and economic value that may be underestimated by political leaders" (p. 6). Surf tourism value can be measured via socio-economic indicators. A weighting system for assessing the surf tourism potential of Brazil's beaches could be used based on socio-economic indicators. Aligned with scholarly recommendations (Martin & Assenov, 2014; Martin-Gonzalez & Swart, 2021), 24 indicators could be chosen based on the importance of demand on social, health, cultural, and economic development in the area concerning sustainability, value, use, quality, and integrity attributes. These suggested indicators are adopted from the range of possible indicators presented by Martin and Assenov (2014) based on the importance of demand. Economic indicators could also include accessibility, infrastructures, tourism accommodation, surfing companies, and information services (Martin-Gonzalez & Swart, 2021). This type of assessment tool would enable Brazil's coastal regions to calculate the potential for surf tourism development in the chosen area.

More popular areas of coastal regions can attract overcrowding and may require some form of etiquette, code of conduct, or informal system management to be in place to ensure good behaviour on the waves; this may be as minimal as the rules of surfing etiquette being publicly displayed on popular surf beaches. "Surf tourism is an increasingly popular niche in tourism that sparks economic development in many coastal regions around the world. Surfers make use of surf breaks which can be considered natural resources that experience issues of carrying capacity. Although no formal management system is in place (and desired), surfers utilise informal management systems such as localism and surf etiquette in an attempt to tune behaviours" (Knaap & Vanneste, 2021). Surfers regularly engage in surf tourism seeking the perfect wave; however, the rise in visitor numbers can impact thousands of coastal communities (Bradshaw, 2021; Martin & Assenov, 2012; Ponting & O'Brien, 2013). However, surf tourists are not always welcome in popular line-ups (Daskalos, 2007). Adverse changes in surfing are often attributed to the gentrification of their community and newcomers' importation of new values. A common theme in surf tourism and specifically with new surfers on a never-ending search for the perfect wave, cases of localism can occur. Olivier (2010) considered the concept of localism; "exclusionary and sometimes violent behaviours have historically been tacitly accepted in surfing under the banner of 'localism', or territorialism. In competition for an increasingly scarce resource (waves), vice is often celebrated and glorified within the subculture. Attempts at codifying acceptable behaviour have failed, not least because of an ingrained antipathy towards bureaucracy and formal organisation" (p. 1223). Localism for the purpose of this chapter is considered the antisocial behaviour of local surfers to newcomers on a wave. Olivier concluded that the most positive way forward without regulating wave access was the practice of virtue ethics. Foot (2006), stated, "virtues are in general beneficial characteristics, and indeed ones that a human being needs to have, for his own sake and that of his fellows" (p. 107). Olivier (2010) revealed virtuous actions are more likely to reverse the moral decline that localism is contributing to; "virtuous action could operate in an exponential process, through replication and reciprocation, and might result in changing the current moral climate in which harmful acts of localism are tacitly accepted" (p. 1233). It can thus be concluded that as with other sports, the solution to localism is demonstrating good behaviour through surfing etiquette such as following a surfing code of conduct and practising good sportsmanship. Foot (2006), stated, "virtues are in general beneficial characteristics, and indeed ones that a human being needs to have, for his own sake and that of his fellows" (p. 107). Olivier (2010) revealed virtuous actions are more likely to reverse the moral decline that localism is contributing to; "virtuous action could operate in an exponential process, through replication and reciprocation, and might result in changing the current moral climate in which harmful acts of localism are tacitly accepted" (p. 1233).

The social and recreational value of waves in Brazil has been documented by Leisner and de Paula (2021), who explored the social and recreational value of waves at Icaraí Beach, located in Caucaia municipality Ceará, Northeast Brazil. The evaluation of the wave resource followed the Zonal Travel Cost Method, a fundamental tool for obtaining economic estimates of ecosystem services that are not subject to market forces. The study revealed "social value of Icaraí's surf break was found to be strongly related to the surfers' familiarity with the beach and the perception of the wave resource as a profitable attraction for the local economy. It is estimated that the economic benefit of the surf break at Icaraí Beach is US$ 288,364 per annum, which is spent by 1185 surfers, averaging US$ 1.37 for each surf trip" (Leisner & de Paula, 2021). These quantifiable metrics can assist decision-making processes, as the values reveal economic benefits for the municipality of Caucaia. These results can contribute to the protection and maintenance of the beach by incorporating wave resources into an effective coastal management strategy (Leisner & de Paula). The values reveal economic benefits for the municipality of Caucaia. These results can contribute to the protection and maintenance of the beach by incorporating wave resources into an effective coastal management strategy (Leisner & de Paula).

From a tourism development perspective, the ideal trend in surf tourism is toward integrated ocean sports destinations that attract entire families and individual surfers (Buckley, 2002). Many entrepreneurial surfers have set up surf schools in Brazil, teaching visitors the skills of the ocean. However, surf tourism offers an opportunity for these local lifestyle entrepreneurs to increase the foot traffic of visitors to the area by understanding the value proposition of each surf spot. Once surf areas can be calculated in terms of socio-economic value, it is possible to understand how to enhance the opportunities for local businesses and entrepreneurs seeking to trade in the areas. Engaging local authorities in beach clean-ups and better sewage management might be easier if there was a quantifiable cost per wave. Suppose local authorities understood the socio-economic implications and increase in tourism would bring to the area. In that case, it may enhance the support offered to maintain coastal areas and improve the facilities for visitors.

Many lifestyle entrepreneurs have succeeded in Brazil, benefitting from the lifestyle, location, and surfing ecosystem to create a viable product, whether that is a surf school, surfboards, or an entire lifestyle brand. An interesting case study on a lifestyle brand Mormaii conducted by Bosquetti et al. (2017), revealed the successful lean business model of the Mormaii brand. A brand founded by a surfer doctor and entrepreneur who successfully anticipated the demand for wetsuits in Brazil. The company's rapid growth was due to the diversification of products. It was the first brand in the Brazilian surf industry to license its brand, allowing the brand's internationalisation to 80 countries. It subsequently became a global brand in response to Brazil's giant multinational surf companies. Fadda (2020) found lifestyle entrepreneurs to be "innovative, proactive in taking business decisions while tending to be neither risk-takers nor competitive...and that many entrepreneurs seized a business opportunity mainly for personal reasons related to enjoying a good lifestyle, being in an attractive natural and human environment, and seeking autonomy at work". Hence, lifestyle entrepreneurs are just that, innovators seeking to mix business with pleasure to enjoy their chosen lifestyle. Research has demonstrated that most lifestyle entrepreneurs are less economically driven but motivated by the balance between work, business and, most importantly, maintaining the lifestyle they enjoy (Fadda, 2020; Ratten, 2018a, b).

In the years to come, local governments may need to manage conflicts and issues of increasing surf tourism, and lessons can be learned from destinations such as Indo-Pacific islands. For example, the implementation of surf tourism retribution in Mentawai Islands, Indonesia, is an interesting case study to understand how surf tourism can coalesce with development agenda and policy (Pakan, 2022; Ponting et al., 2005). Likewise, the research on Fiji surf tourism (Ponting & O'Brien, 2013) where authorities deregulated surf tourism by cancelling the use of licenses for official breaks.

Nevertheless, the focus of this chapter was to contribute to the body of literature on tourism–development nexus by adding the case study of surf tourism in Brazil and considerations on the management of coastal areas. In developing nations, tourism can contribute to conservation by providing political and financial support, for public protected area agencies and the conservation of private and communally owned lands (Buckley, 2009). Managing surf tourism issues is complex and multi-layered (Bradshaw, 2021). However, there is value in carefully managing the coastal regions, for sustainable development of the local communities and regions, and the broader protection of climate change and environmental sustainability. Both help to build resilience to climate change (Buckley, 2009).

Bosquetti et al. (2017) stated, "the sport of surfing has been growing rapidly in popularity worldwide, and Brazil is among the countries with the largest surfing population, behind the United States and Australia. However, multinational surf companies are rushing into emerging markets like Brazil to find new opportunities for growth" (p. 110). Pakan (2022) described surf tourism research as rich in the narrative around tourism and how it is being used as a critical strategy or tool for socio-economic development in many parts of the world, including in developing countries (Almeida-García, 2018; Moscardo, 2005).

Government intervention and involvement in tourism are often interrelated (Truong, 2013) and linked to broader strategic development objectives of the local socio-economic development (Hussin & Buchmann, 2019). Pakan (2022) stated that "the rhetoric goes to say that, if being done well, the existence of tourism may help to enhance local economy, improve local resident's wellbeing, and alleviate poverty" (Musakwa & Odhiambo, 2020; Scheyvens, 2007) and such rhetoric is commonly found in surf tourism research, too.

Chok et al. (2007) described how "forecasts of high tourism growth in developing nations, where widespread poverty exists, has led to considerable interest in tourism as a tool for poverty alleviation. Powerful bureaucratic and business alliances have been forged to expand this programme. International development agencies are also turning to tourism as a way of alleviating poverty" (p. 144). Similarly, Scheyvens (2007) explored the current research surrounding "pro-poor tourism", suggesting that "tourism can effectively work as a tool to alleviate poverty" (p. 231). Pro-poor tourism is an interesting position, given that tourism is a dominant or increasing economic sector in most nations with prevalent poverty levels. Consequently, Scheyvens (2007) described how "the idea of utilising tourism to eliminate poverty has been embraced by donors, governments, non-governmental organisations, conservation organisations and tourism bodies, including the World Tourism Organisation" (p. 231). Surf tourism feeds into this strategic plan as it is often experienced in developing areas, where the infrastructure and coastal management are in their infancy. Countries with more developed infrastructure and governance appear to have systems in place to protect the environmental and socio-economic ecosystem and attract visitors in numbers that can be safely managed.

This chapter explored how entrepreneurs in the Brazilian market overcame and took advantage of differences with global competitors by rethinking their core competencies and created sustainable business models around lifestyles. Buckley et al. (2017) stated that "many tourism subsectors rely on particular sites and their natural resources, and commercial tourism enterprises compete to obtain or control access and use of those resources, such competition can occur through social, economic, administrative or political processes" (p. 185). Therefore, while the competition is fierce, especially against global competitors in the sports tourism sector, there is a niche for locally grown businesses, with local values and a nuanced lean approach to compete with the major players in the market, therefore perhaps homemade innovation that lifestyle entrepreneurs demonstrate is the key to sustainable tourism.

7 Conclusion

In conclusion, it is possible to agree with Bosquetti et al. (2017) that the socio-economic and environmental impact makes the surf industry an exciting area of research both in Brazil and globally. Brazil has a valuable opportunity to increase surf tourism around underprivileged areas where regions show the most potential for socio-economic development. Beaches in disadvantaged neighbourhoods could generate the potential for boosting surf tourism development and improving the flow of tourists to the area, much like the Nazaré wave did to increase tourism and economic growth in the Peniche area of Portugal (Bradshaw, 2021). Further research could inform government policy to determine the principal sites for surf tourism development in Brazil.

Surf tourists flock to tropical climates in unique destinations to achieve an experience that offers something different from their local surf breaks. As with other emerging global surf destinations, Brazil has an opportunity for rapid growth in this niche tourism segment. Capitalising on underprivileged coastal areas that could benefit from tourism and development could increase the economic benefit of the area for local communities by bringing in much-needed business and development and opening the coastline up to more overseas travellers seeking an adventure. Further research is required to better understand the Brazilian surf industry, explore the economic, social, and environmental impact and fully understand the stakeholders involved and the impact on local communities. However, surfers such as Gabriel Medina have stated their underdeveloped local breaks are special; speaking to the Associated Press in 2022, Gabriel Medina stated, "We don't have any tall buildings here. It is just houses, beaches and a lot of nature...I travel all over the world, but I still value the place where I live, where I came from. I feel complete here. This place gives me peace and ease to do everything I'm able to do". The $3 \times$ World Champions' hometown is Maresias in Sao Sabastian, with a 200-km stretch of shoreline in Sao Paulo state for surf communities to utilise. Nevertheless, it highlights the delicate balance of enabling a surf community to grow in an underdeveloped area. There is a need to tread carefully and navigate the delicate balance between coastal governance and the natural lifestyle that surfpreneurs and surfers are attracted to. Learning lessons from other international surf spots and prior planning could avoid the surf tourism pitfalls.

Surf tourism has the capacity to educate, empower, monetise, and develop areas through the power of a sport, which is on the rise. With its recent Olympic inclusion, the number of surf tourists will only continue to increase and there is an opportunity for further innovation in this industry, to use more sustainable materials and equipment, to raise awareness of conservation and tackle climate change and protect our environments for future generations.

References

Almeida-García, F. (2018). Analysis of tourism policy in a developing country: The case of Morocco. *Journal of Policy Research in Tourism, Leisure and Events, 10*(1), 48–68.

Associated Press. (2022, January 1). *In the shadow of the Rainforest, Brazilian Surf Capital Blossoms*. Associated Press. Retrieved from https://www.voanews.com/a/in-the-rainforest-s-shadow-brazilian-surf-capital-blossoms-/6374342.html

Bosquetti, M. A., & da Souza, M. A. (2019). *Surfonomics Guarda do Embaú, Brazil: The economic impact of surf tourism on the local economy*. UFSC.

Bosquetti, M. A., Fiates, G. G. S., & Ponting, J. (2017). Strategic management at Mormaii—The Brazilian Surf Industry Leader. *Brazilian Business Review, 14*, 110–129. https://doi.org/10.15728/edicaoesp.2017.6

Bosquetti, M. A., Pizarro, A., Tabago, M., Lang, E., & Hodges, T. (2020). *Surfonomics Lobitos, Peru: The economic impact of surf tourism on the local economy*. Save The Wave Coalition. Retrieved from https://www.savethewaves.org/wp-content/uploads/2021/02/Surfonomics-Lobitos-2020-eBook.pdf

Bradshaw, L. (2021). Surfing the innovation waves: Surf tourism in Portugal. In *Tourism innovation in Spain and Portugal* (pp. 149–166). Springer.

Buckley, R. (2002). Surf tourism and sustainable development in Indo-Pacific Islands. *Journal of Sustainable Tourism, 10*(5), 405–424.

Buckley, R. (2009). *Ecotourism: Principles and practices* (4th ed.). CABI.

Buckley, R., Guitart, D., & Shakeela, A. (2017). Contested surf tourism resources in the Maldives. *Annals of Tourism Research, 64*, 185–199. https://doi.org/10.1016/j.annals.2017.03.005

Burgess, A. (2021). Why Brazilians dominate the world of surfing? *Red Bull Surfing*. Retrieved from https://www.youtube.com/watch?v=JI9F0y4V-38

Chok, S., Macbeth, J., & Warren, C. (2007). Tourism as a tool for poverty alleviation: A critical analysis of "pro-poor tourism" and implications for sustainability. *Current Issues in Tourism, 10*(2), 144–165. https://doi.org/10.2167/cit303

da Rosa, S., dos Anjos, F. A., de Lima Pereira, M., & Arnhold Junior, M. (2020). Image perception of surf tourism destination in Brazil. *International Journal of Tourism Cities, 6*(4), 1111–1127. https://doi.org/10.1108/IJTC-11-2018-0090

Daskalos, C. T. (2007). Locals only! The impact of modernity on a local surfing context. *Sociological Perspectives, 50*(1), 155–173. https://doi.org/10.1525/sop.2007.50.1.155

de Alessi, M. (2009). The customs and culture of surfing, and an opportunity for a new territorialism? *Reef Journal, 1*(1), 85–91.

Deats, J., Martinez, M., Shearer, R., & Shearer, W. (2016). The tragedy of the waves. *Sport, Business and Management: An International Journal, 6*(1), 97–105. https://doi.org/10.1108/sbm-07-2013-0026

Denning, M. (2019, August 21). Brazil just might be the most underrated surf destination I've ever been to. *The Inertia*. Retrieved from https://www.theinertia.com/surf/brazil-just-might-be-the-most-underrated-surf-destination-ive-ever-been-to/*TheInertia*

Fadda, N. (2020). Entrepreneurial behaviours and managerial approach of lifestyle entrepreneurs in surf tourism: An exploratory study. *Journal of Sport & Tourism, 24*(1), 53–77. https://doi.org/10.1080/14775085.2020.1726801

Foot, P. (2006). Virtues and vices. In S. Darwall (Ed.), *Virtue ethics* (pp. 105–120). Blackwell Publishing.

Horton, B. A. (2022). Volcano surfing—Head to Nicaragua for a travel experience you'll never forget. *Euro News Travel*. Retrieved from https://www.euronews.com/travel/2022/03/29/volcano-surfing-head-to-nicaragua-for-a-travel-experience-you-ll-never-forget

Hussin, N. Z. I., & Buchmann, A. (2019). Understanding tourism development policies in Malaysia. *Journal of Policy Research in Tourism, Leisure and Events, 11*(2), 333–353.

International Surfing Association (ISA). (2022). *About the ISA*. Retrieved from https://isasurf.org/about-isa/

Kaplan, J. M., & Warren, A. C. (2003). *Patterns of entrepreneurship. Incorporated*. John Wiley & Sons.

Knaap, C., & Vanneste, D. (2021). Issues of conflict management in a context of increasing surf tourism. https://doi.org/10.17265/2328-2169/2021.02.001.

Lashley, C., & Rowson, B. (2010). Lifestyle businesses: Insights into Blackpool's hotel sector. *International Journal of Hospitality Management, 29*(3), 511–519.

Latin American News. (2021, July 27). In Brazil, the billion-dollar surfing business is heading for its peak. *The Rio Times*. Retrieved from https://www.riotimesonline.com/brazil-news/brazil/with-italos-gold-the-billion-dollar-surfing-business-heads-for-its-peak/

Lees, W. (2018). The best places to surf in Brazil. *The Culture Trip*. Retrieved from https://theculturetrip.com/south-america/brazil/articles/the-best-places-to-surf-in-brazil/

Leisner, M., & de Paula, D. P. (2021). Social and recreational value of waves: Application of the zonal travel cost method with surfers from Icaraí beach (Caucaia, Ceará, Brazil). *Ateliê Geográfico, 15*(1), 26–49. https://doi.org/10.5216/ag.v15i1.66540

Mach, L., & Ponting, J. (2018). Governmentality and surf tourism destination governance. *Journal of Sustainable Tourism, 26*(11), 1845–1862. https://doi.org/10.1080/09669582.2018.1513008

Marchant, B., & Mottiar, Z. (2011). Understanding lifestyle entrepreneurs and digging beneath the issue of profits: Profiling surf tourism lifestyle entrepreneurs in Ireland. *Tourism Planning & Development, 8*(2), 171–183. https://doi.org/10.1080/21568316.2011.573917

Marshall, J. (2017, July 6). What travelling with surfing entrepreneurs taught me about business and friendships. *The Inertia*. Retrieved from https://www.theinertia.com/surf/what-traveling-with-surfing-entrepreneurs-taught-me-about-business-and-friendships/

Martin, S. A., & Assenov, I. (2012). The genesis of a new body of sport tourism literature: A systematic review of surf tourism research (1997–2011). *Journal of Sport & Tourism, 17*(4), 257–287. https://doi.org/10.1080/14775085.2013.766528

Martin, S. A., & Assenov, I. (2014). Developing a surf resource sustainability index as a global model for surf beach conservation and tourism research. *Asia Pacific Journal of Tourism Research, 19*(7), 760–792. https://doi.org/10.1080/10941665.2013.806942

Martin-Gonzalez, R., & Swart, K. (2021). The Covid-19 crisis and the 'new' normality of surf tourism in Cape Town, South Africa. *African Journal of Hospitality, Tourism and Leisure, 10*(1), 194–213. https://doi.org/10.46222/ajhtl.19770720-95

McGregor, T. & Wills, S. (2017). *Surfing a wave of economic growth* (CAMA Working Paper No. 31/2017). https://doi.org/10.2139/ssrn.2955476

McKeever, E., Jack, S., & Anderson, A. (2015). Embedded entrepreneurship in the creative reconstruction of place. *Journal of Business Venturing, 30*, 50–65.

Mellone, A. (2016, September 21). Awesome father-son surfing duos on the world tour today. *The Inertia*. Retrieved from https://www.theinertia.com/surf/4-awesome-father-son-surfing-duos-on-the-world-tour-today/

Moscardo, G. (2005). Peripheral tourism development: Challenges, issues and success factors. *Tourism Recreation Research, 30*(1), 27–43.

Musakwa, M. T., & Odhiambo, N. M. (2020). Tourism and financial development in South Africa: A trivariate approach. *Journal of Policy Research in Tourism, Leisure and Events*, 1–17. https://doi.org/10.1080/19407963.2020.1856860

Nelsen, C. (2012). *Collecting and using economic information to guide the management of coastal recreational resources in California* [Doctoral thesis]. UCLA.

O'Brien, D., & Eddie, I. (2013). Benchmarking global best practice: Innovation and leadership in surf city tourism and industry development. In *The Global Surf Cities Conference*, Kirra Community Center, Australia.

Olivier, S. (2010). "Your wave, bro!": Virtue ethics and surfing. *Sport in Society, 13*(7–8), 1223–1233. https://doi.org/10.1080/17430431003780229

Pakan, S. P. (2022). Waves for development? Local perceptions on surf tourism retribution in the Mentawai Islands. *Journal of Policy Research in Tourism, Leisure and Events*. https://doi.org/10.1080/19407963.2022.2047989

Peters, M., Frehse, J., & Buhalis, D. (2009). The importance of lifestyle entrepreneurship: A conceptual study of the tourism industry. *PASOS–Journal of Tourism and Cultural Change, 7*(2), 393–405.

Ponting, J. (2009). Projecting paradise: The surf media and the hermeneutic circle in surfing tourism. *Tourism Analysis, 14*(2), 175–185.

Ponting, J., McDonald, M. G., & Wearing, S. L. (2005). Deconstructing wonderland: Surfing tourism in the Mentawai Islands, Indonesia. *Loisir et Société. Society and Leisure, 28*(1), 141–162.

Ponting, J., & O'Brien, D. (2013). Liberalising nirvana: An analysis of the consequences of common-pool resource deregulation for the sustainability of Fiji's surf tourism industry. *Journal of Sustainable Tourism, 22*(3), 384–402. https://doi.org/10.1080/09669582.2013.819879

Ponting, J., & O'Brien, D. (2015). Regulating "Nirvana": Sustainable surf tourism in a climate of increasing regulation. *Sport Management Review, 18*(1), 99–110. https://doi.org/10.1016/j.smr.2014.07.004

Ramsey, G. (2022). *How Maya Gabeira overcame a life-threatening accident to surf two record-breaking waves*. Retrieved from https://edition.cnn.com/2021/04/27/sport/maya-gabeira-big-wave-surfer-spt-intl-cmd/index.html

Ratten, V. (2018a). Entrepreneurial intentions of surf tourists. *Tourism Review, 73*(2), 262–276. https://doi.org/10.1108/TR-05-2017-0095

Ratten, V. (2018b). *Sport entrepreneurship*. Springer International Publishing.

Save The Waves Coalition. (2019). Brazil's Guarda do Embaú officially dedicated as the 9th world surfing reserve. *Save the waves*. Retrieved from https://www.savethewaves.org/brazils-guarda-do-embau-officially-dedicated-as-the-9th-world-surfing-reserve/

Save The Waves Coalition. (2022). *Guarda do Embaú*. Retrieved from https://www.savethewaves.org/guarda-do-embau/

Scheyvens, R. (2007). Exploring the tourism-poverty nexus. *Current Issues in Tourism, 10*(2–3), 231–254. https://doi.org/10.2167/cit318.0

Shaw, G., & Williams, A. (1998). Entrepreneurship, small business, culture and tourism development. In D. Ioannides & K. Debbage (Eds.), *The economic geography of the tourist industry: A supply-side analysis* (pp. 235–255). Routledge.

Shaw, G., & Williams, A. M. (2004). From lifestyle consumption to lifestyle production: Changing patterns of tourism entrepreneurship. In R. Thomas (Ed.), *Small firms in tourism. international perspectives*. Elsevier Ltd.. p. Ch. 7.

Surfer Girls. (2022). *Brazilian female surfers*. Retrieved from https://surfergirls.com/top-female-surfers-1/brazilian-female-surfers/

Surfer Today. (2022). *Pororoca: Surfing the endless Brazilian tidal bore*. Retrieved from https://www.surfertoday.com/travel/surfing-the-endless-wave-of-pororoca

Tourism New South Wales. (2009). *Tourism NSW's action plan to consolidate the state's position as Australia's premier surf destination: Catching the wave*. New South Wales Government and Author. Retrieved from https://www.yumpu.com/en/document/view/5614545/surf-tourism-action-plan-tourism-nsw-nsw-government

Towner, N., & Lemarié, J. (2020). Localism at New Zealand surfing destinations: Durkheim and the social structure of communities. *Journal of Sport & Tourism, 24*, 110–193. https://doi.org/10.1080/14775085.2020.1777186

Truong, V. D. (2013). Tourism policy development in Vietnam: A pro-poor perspective. *Journal of Policy Research in Tourism, Leisure and Events, 5*(1), 28–45. https://doi.org/10.1080/19407963.2012.760224

Wallis, L., Walmsley, A., Beaumont, E., & Sutton, C. (2020). 'Just want to surf, make boards and party': How do we identify lifestyle entrepreneurs within the lifestyle sports industry? *International Entrepreneurship and Management Journal, 16*(3), 917–934.

Wannasurf. (2022). *Brazilian South America*. Retrieved from https://www.wannasurf.com/spot/South_America/Brazil/

Wieser, N. K. (2019). *Causes and development impacts of the tourism boom exemplified by Nazaré* [Master's thesis]. University of Graz. Retrieved from https://unipub.uni-graz.at/obvugrhs/content/titleinfo/3512101/full.pdf

Williams, A. M., Shaw, G., & Greenwood, J. (1989). From tourist to tourism entrepreneur, from consumption to production: Evidence from Cornwall, England. *Environment and Planning A, 21*(12), 1639–1653.

WSL. (2020). World Surf League. *Sponsorship*. Retrieved from www.worldsurfleague.com/pages/sponsorship

WSL. (2021, September 9). *O Filme Brasil Do Surfe: The unprecedented rise of modern surfing*. WSL. Retrieved from https://www.youtube.com/watch?v=NBnyOStaRz4

Academic Entrepreneurship in Brazilian Universities

Mariza Almeida

Abstract The objective of this chapter is to analyze academic entrepreneurship in Brazilian universities, considering three periods of distinct characteristics and using the Triple Helix model as the theoretical framework. The first period began in 1986 when the first incubators were created. Those endeavors, mostly introduced in public universities, were organized in a bottom-up manner, on the initiative of professors returning from studies abroad, where came into contact with these organizational structures and visualized their transformative potential in the university and the ensuing impact of the university on economic and social development, innovation, and job creation. The second period began in 2003, with the implementation of the Industrial, Technology and Foreign Trade Policy (PITCE), in effect from 2003 to 2006. It was followed, with the approval of the Innovation Law, in 2004, and regulated in 2005, the internal environment of the university diversifies, with the organization of Technology Transfer Offices and a policy to encourage patenting, technology transfer, and university–company interaction. The third period begins in 2015, when there is a decrease in public R&D resources and a growth of private initiatives, such as co-working, organization of accelerators, and interaction of incubators with the initiatives of private companies to select enterprises to be supported for the development of solutions requested by those companies. In each of these periods, varied interaction was established, the internal discussion of universities about entrepreneurship and innovation was changing, with an impact on teaching, research, and outreach activities. Considering the current context of S&T&I in Brazil, the new prospects for the development of an entrepreneurial culture are outlined.

Keywords Entrepreneurial university · Academic entrepreneurship · Incubators · Triple helix

---

M. Almeida (✉)
Industrial Engineering School, Federal University of the State of Rio de Janeiro, Rio de Janeiro, RJ, Brazil
e-mail: mariza.almeida@unirio.br

J. Leitão et al. (eds.), *Brazilian Entrepreneurship*, Studies on Entrepreneurship, Structural Change and Industrial Dynamics,
https://doi.org/10.1007/978-3-031-09392-0_4

1 Introduction

The establishing of universities in Brazil is a historically recent phenomenon, as previous initiatives, both in the colonial and monarchical periods, were not successful, due to the control exercised by Portugal over activities that could generate signs of cultural and political independence in what was then a colony. Higher education courses started to be organized in 1808, following the arrival of the royal family in Brazil, with the aim of training professional staff to work in the state administration. So courses were developed that later became the colleges of Medicine in the states of Bahia and Rio de Janeiro (both in 1808), the school of Engineering in Rio de Janeiro (1810) and the Law faculties in São Paulo and Pernambuco, in 1827 and 1828, respectively (Fávero, 2006). Institutions of a more scientific nature, such as the National Observatory, the National Museum, the Ouro Preto school of Mining, the Bacteriological Institute (the famed Butantã Institute) in São Paulo, and the Manguinhos Institute (the well-known Oswaldo Cruz Foundation) in Rio de Janeiro, were set up as of 1870, to address specific needs or emergencies, and at that time encountered difficulties in extending their mandate on a more durable basis (Burgos, 1999).

The first university was only founded in 1920, bringing together three schools of higher education, and given the name University of Rio de Janeiro, later to be called the Federal University of Rio de Janeiro, in what was then the capital of the country, the city of Rio de Janeiro. The University of São Paulo was only founded in 1934, based on a broader project for an educational institution, rather than just bringing together existing schools. This rather late and slow development of higher education institutions generated specific characteristics, with emphasis on the reproduction of existing knowledge and incipient research.

Only after World War II did the federal government define a Science & Technology policy, beginning with the building of an institutional infrastructure and the development of human resources in the S&T field. During that period, the motivations driving this public policy were national security and technological autonomy. The setting up in 1951 of the National Council for Scientific and Technological Development (CNPq), for example, was mainly due to the desire to use the country's mineral resources for the production of atomic energy (Burgos, 1999). The Coordination for the Development of Higher Education Personnel (CAPES) was also set up in the same year, for the purpose of supporting the training and formal qualification of specialized human resources for the public and private sectors (Martins, 2003).

The military intervention of 1964 profoundly affected the universities and, from 1970 onward, a number of professors and researchers were fired, imprisoned, or exiled. In 1968, higher education underwent a profound change and also rapid expansion, mainly due to the establishing of higher education courses at private institutions. The first postgraduate courses at public universities and certain Catholic universities were also introduced as of 1968, marking the insertion of ongoing research activities at institutions of higher education (Schwartzman, 2010). Investments in education, at the postgraduate level, and in R&D activities at universities and research centers by the federal government during the last few years of the 1960s and early 1970s, endowed the country with reasonable scientific and technological infrastructure. The importance of those investments is highlighted by other authors, such as Freeman (2002).

The 1980s were marked by profound changes in the country that were also reflected in universities. The democratization of the state and the decentralization of power brought significant changes in the political and cultural life of the country: direct elections for governors and the mayors of state capitals, campaigning for full direct elections, the end of the military regime, and the emergence of new social agents, with the advent of civil society representation.

University segments, excluded by the military government from the formulating of policies in support of a democratic project, participated in putting together the political platforms developed during the state elections in 1982, which led to the appointment of a number of academics to the administration of certain institutions. The new governors were generally more receptive to proposals originating from the universities and particularly in relation to Science and Technology.

The first incubators were set up, in 1986, in the states of São Paulo (Souza & Garcia, 1999) and Santa Catarina (Cavagnari, 1987), within the context of this change in the direction of Brazilian scientific and technological policy, which was reflected in the search for alternative organizational formats, aimed at achieving greater university participation in the country's socioeconomic development, mainly through enhanced coordination between the academic, industry, and government spheres.

The incubators sought initially to support technology-based companies, originating from the existing university research groups, but they started to be employed for other aims, including social purposes and local development (Etzkowitz et al., 2005). The most recent data indicate a total of 363 business incubators, 43 technology parks, 3694 incubated companies, and 6143 graduate companies, 14,457 jobs in incubated companies and 55,942 in graduated companies (Anprotec, 2019; MCTIC, 2019a, b), as well as 270 Technology Transfer Offices (TTO) (MCTIC, 2019a, b). In various countries, incubators have been used in support of public S, T, and I policies. For example, in 2017, in China there were 4069 (Xiangfei et al., 2022), while in the USA there were 1400 (InBIA, 2016) and in India there are 520 incubators and accelerators (NASSCOM, 2020).

The main feature of academic entrepreneurship in Brazil is the establishment of incubators and technology parks. Technology transfers to companies are still at a low level, mainly due to the lack of innovation by Brazilian companies. Unlike other countries, such as the members of the OECD, the main hubs for innovation, particularly in high-tech areas, are the universities, rather than business, when one looks at the patent applications (Póvoa, 2008).

This critical factor can also be confirmed using triple helix indicators, showing that the country's economic policy has not (yet) been transformed into a national innovation system. At the state level, the synergies change according to geographical positioning and economic sector. In some states in the south and southeast, such as São Paulo, Minas Gerais, Rio de Janeiro, Rio Grande do Sul, and Paraná, the synergy levels were found to be above average. It was also observed that the country's capital, Brasília, has no impact on Brazil's innovation system (Almeida et al., 2022a, 2022b).

A survey of the Brazilian industry in 2018, covering a total of 116,962 businesses employing 10 or more people, shows an innovation rate of 33.6%. Problems in the economic situation, such as recession and diminished capital investment, have led to a decrease in the number of companies that have innovated during the period. Analysis of the results indicates a reduction in the main types of innovation observed: (1) internal processes (14.8%), typically the replacement of machinery and equipment; (2) innovation in both products and processes (13.7%); and (3) innovation in products (5.1%). The distribution of innovative activities by economic sector indicates that in the service sector, 32% of the companies developed some kind of innovative activity, while in manufacturing the rate was 33.9% and in electricity and gas it was 28.4% (IBGE/PINTEC, 2020).

The choice of Brazil for the study of academic entrepreneurship is significant in various aspects, whether because of the country's continental dimensions, its participation in the BRICS group or because it is listed by the World Bank as a middle income trap. In the context of the transition of S&T policies from a "top-down" approach to a post-linear model, the internal changes at the universities draw attention, with the creation of incubators using "inputs" from various university segments, companies, and government at the federal, state, and local levels. It can be seen that the first technology-based incubators arose as a result of "bottom up" initiatives by university professors, during a period when civil society was reorganizing itself, and since then they have become an instrument of national public policy (Etzkowitz et al., 2005).

The objective of this chapter is to analyze academic entrepreneurship at Brazilian universities, considering three periods with distinct characteristics, using the Triple Helix model as the theoretical framework. In each of those periods, varied interaction was established, the internal discussion at universities about entrepreneurship and innovation was changing and having an impact on teaching, research and outreach activities. Considering the current context of S&T&I in Brazil, the new prospects for the development of an entrepreneurial culture are outlined.

2 Triple Helix and the Entrepreneurial University

The triple helix model enables the description, analysis, and explanation of the process of technological innovation and the dynamics of institutional arrangements and public policy models, one of the concerns being the institutional integration of the S&T system among universities, companies, and government agencies. The innovation networks and complex relationships forged between university–industry–government are a key feature of this theoretical model for invigorating the innovation process and thereby generating economic and social development. Relationship networks create sub-dynamics of intentions, strategies, and projects that add surplus value by constantly organizing and harmonizing with the existing infrastructure in order to achieve their goals. The emergence of this new entity—the triple helix—thus represents a new synthesis between university, industry, and government. The complex dynamics comprise a number of sub-dynamics, involving market forces, political power, institutional control, social movements, technological regimes, and their trajectories. These sub-dynamics are constantly being rebuilt, as a result of the flow, reorganization and increasing of knowledge in society. The sources of innovation in the triple helix are not defined a priori, as they are a function of the group of participants, analysts, and policymakers who are present during the interaction (Etzkowitz & Leydesdorff, 2000). This approach can be used for studies at the national, state, or local level. The triple helix assumes different levels of complexity according to the technological trajectories observed in each country or region (Leydesdorff & Etzkowitz, 1996).

Under the triple helix model, the university is expected to be the core institution in the production of knowledge, while retaining its original mission devoted to education, since teaching offers a comparative advantage, especially when it is linked to research and economic and social development. The university blends continuity with change, organizational and research memory with new personnel, and new ideas across generations of students (Etzkowitz et al., 2000).

The universities initially devoted themselves to teaching activities and by adding the mission dedicated to research they underwent the first academic revolution (Etzkowitz, 1993). By incorporating activities linked to economic and social development, they engaged in a process of change that is called the "second academic revolution," according to Etzkowitz (1998, 2003, 2004), Etzkowitz and Leydesdorff (2000), and Etzkowitz et al. (2000). The increase in these kinds of activities within the university has led to the development of an entrepreneurial culture that affects both teaching and research activities (Etzkowitz et al., 2000). These new activities, also known as the "third mission," take on different formats, such as technology transfer to companies, the setting up of spin-offs and start-ups and the establishing of technology transfer offices, incubators, and technology parks (Etzkowitz & Leydesdorff, 1998). The diversity of activities covered under the third mission is divided into non-profit, with social characteristics, and entrepreneurial focus, aimed at innovation (Montesinos et al., 2008). In extending their traditional business model (teaching and research) and embracing the third mission, the universities have begun to work with diverse stakeholders, in order to sustain and expand the institutions, in response to intense domestic and international competition (Miller et al., 2021).

The entrepreneurial university is defined as an institution that engages in a process of change and innovation, identifying and creating opportunities, taking risks and working as a team, in order to drive organizational change that creates new possibilities for the future. To that end, it builds internal support structures so that professors, researchers, and students can initiate new intellectual ventures, whether they be of a social or commercial nature (Etzkowitz, 1983; Clark, 1998).

Several empirical studies, based on case studies, carried out in a number of developed and developing countries, have described the process of transformation of the universities, whether through teaching entrepreneurship (Katz, 2003; Klofsten

& Jones-Evans, 2000), the commercialization of research results (Perkmann et al., 2013), strategy, and structural changes (Jacob et al., 2003; Herrera et al., 2018), the impact on economic development (Audretsch, 2014), the setting up of spin-off companies at the universities (Shane, 2004) or in the development of the entrepreneurial university itself (Guerrero & Urbano, 2012; Etzkowitz, 2004).

A factor related to entrepreneurial universities that are still under development refers to the definition of indicators for their assessment. In the traditional university rankings, the indicators relate to the missions of teaching and research. To fill that theoretical gap, the International Triple Helix Institute developed a research project called the Global Entrepreneurial Metrics Initiative (GEUM), having held four workshops attended by researchers from various countries to discuss the subject. A research project for that purpose was developed in Brazil, culminating in the proposal of a set of indicators to evaluate the third mission in the context of the country, which involved the following: (1) entrepreneurship teaching for undergraduate and graduate students; (2) outreach projects (non-profit); (3) business activities and technology transfer (TTO, incubators, start-ups, technology parks, clusters, etc.); (4) knowledge capitalization (patents and other intellectual property measures); (5) university organizational changes, including introduction of innovation policy, intellectual property policy, and initiatives to reward researchers and students, among others. The analysis of these indicators enables the identification of gaps, existing problems, and successful features, as well as other factors that facilitate the transition toward an entrepreneurial university format (Almeida et al., 2022a, 2022b).

3 Brazilian Higher Education Systems

Higher education in Brazil is provided by universities, university centers, schools, higher education institutes, and technological education centers. In the last two decades, from 2001 to 2020, there was expansion of the Brazilian Higher Education System. This expansion occurred mainly in the private sector, which accounts for 88% of the total number of higher education institutions (HEI). Of the total number of higher education institutions, only 8% are universities. Thus, the majority is composed of university centers and colleges. Table 1 shows the changes in the number of HEIs during that period.

The postgraduation programs are divided into *lato* sensu (which refers to refresher courses, further education or specialization courses) or *stricto* sensu (which refers to programs that require previous courses or a diploma, most often referring to Master's and Doctoral programs).

The differentiation between higher education institutions in Brazil can be analyzed in accordance with the functions proposed by Laredo (2007): (1) mass tertiary education function, the HEIs where a bachelor's degree is a central feature; (2) professional specialized higher education. In this category of HEIs, *the core diploma is the professional master's degree and the core activity is problem-solving research*;

Table 1 Brazilian higher education institutions (2001–2020)

	2001	2002	2003	2004	2005	2006	2007	2008	2009	2010
HEI (total)	1391	1637	1859	2013	2165	2270	2281	2252	2310	2378
Public	183	195	128	141	141	156	153	139	145	177
Private	1208	1442	1568	1703	1848	1936	1945	1930	1980	2011
Universities (total)	156	162	163	169	176	178	183	183	186	190
Public	71	76	79	83	90	92	96	97	100	101
Private	85	84	84	86	86	86	87	86	86	89

	2011	2012	2013	2014	2015	2016	2017	2018	2019	2020
HEI (total)	2365	2416	2391	2372	2364	2407	2450	2537	2608	2460
Public	182	196	190	187	188	188	190	192	194	192
Private	1993	2027	2006	1990	1981	2022	2061	2146	2216	2065
Universities (total)	190	193	195	195	195	197	199	199	198	203
Public	102	108	111	111	107	108	106	107	108	112
Private	88	85	84	84	88	89	93	92	90	91

Source: INEP

and (3) academic training and research, included HEIs "*with the Ph.D. as the core diploma and academic papers as the core output.*"

The information on the number of universities shows that the majority (55%) is composed of public institutions. It should be emphasized that the research is carried out mainly at public universities. Paradoxically, activities aimed at entrepreneurship, such as the setting up of incubators and technology parks, and technology transfer, are carried out in public universities and in a few nonprofit private universities, such as Catholic universities. Therefore, most HEIs are devoted only to teaching activities (Almeida et al., 2022a, 2022b). For the purpose of this chapter, the analysis focuses on public universities, which perform academic training and research activities, as well as acting as entrepreneurial universities, with activities that include the third mission, in addition to the traditional missions of teaching and research.

The Brazilian Higher Education Evaluation System (SINAES) is a system for the assessment of HEIs, aimed at evaluating and disseminating quality in HEI undergraduate courses. Participation in the evaluation process is mandatory for all universities, whether public federal, for-profit or non-profit. The assessment carried out by the SINAES is based on three pillars: institutional evaluation, course evaluation, and the evaluation of student performance. The SINAES covers only the teaching and research missions and does not include entrepreneurial activities. Participation in the Third Mission is included as a social responsibility and is conceived of mainly in terms of social inclusion, economic and social development, protection of the environment, cultural history, artistic production, and cultural heritage (INEP, 2009).

Assessment of the *stricto* sensu graduate courses (master's and doctorates) is carried out by CAPES (Coordination for the Development of Higher Education Personnel), an agency linked to the Ministry of Education (MEC), which in 2019 revised the evaluation indicators, adopting a multidimensional model that includes five elements: teaching and learning, social impact and importance, scientific production, internationalization, and innovation and knowledge transfer.

That last element should strengthen the entrepreneurial culture and innovation at universities, as it includes aspects such as knowledge transfers in the sociocultural, economic, and environmental spheres that are effectively transferred to society by the professors, students, and technical specialists linked to the postgraduate programs (CAPES, 2019).

4 Academic Entrepreneurship in Brazil

In the analysis of academic entrepreneurship in Brazil, there are three distinct periods, marked by changes in the S&T&I context, which affected the institutional environment, involving internal discussions and strategic partners, generating changes in teaching, research, outreach, and the third mission. Those periods are analyzed below.

4.1 First Period

The first period began in 1986 when the first incubators were set up. These initiatives, mostly established in public universities, were organized in a bottom-up manner, at the initiative of professors returning from studies abroad, where they came into contact with these organizational structures and visualized their transformative potential in the university and the ensuing impact of the university on economic and social development, innovation and job creation. The transferring of this model to Brazil took on its own features, due to local problems and opportunities.[1]

The technology incubator is the outcome of the university's dual evolution,[2] as well as a consequence of the extension of its mission and its focus on economic development. The technology transfer offices, set up in the 1970s, represent a way for academia to transfer knowledge to government and the production sector. Under the incubation process, the opposite occurs, with the private sphere of incubated companies and cooperatives becoming established within the university (Etzkowitz, 2002).

The incubator is an example of the triple helix model of university–industry–government relations, considered to be hybrid organizations that internalize the relationship between the three spheres, creating and stimulating space for interaction. The premise of the incubators is that the founding of firms can be improved by being organized as an educational process (Etzkowitz, 2002).

The first incubators to be set up were intended for the incubation of technology-based companies. They were the result of an alliance between universities and local governments (municipality and state) that enabled the establishing of incubators, since the elected state governments (1986) were seeking alternatives for decentralized economic development in the regional context, in terms of general public policy and specifically in the fields of science and technology. The incubators were presented as a new instrument for technology transfer, by governments that were new to the task, not only in terms of proposals, but also in terms of administration, an open to the participation of other spheres, and in this specific case—the university.

The existing social and intellectual bases at the Brazilian universities, facing the difficulties of proceeding with the innovation policy introduced by the military government, due to economic crisis and the reorganizing of civil society, paved the way for the technology incubators. As a result, the university's educational

[1]Previous initiatives, such as the establishing of TTOs in the 1970s and the Technology Parks Program in 1984, were very weak, as they received little support in establishing themselves, did not achieve the proposed goals and encompassed few institutions, thus failing to attain critical mass or have an impact on the overall university environment.

[2]In addition to the transformation of the university, incorporating the economic development function on top of the two existing ones (teaching and research), the dual evolution of the university represents a parallel organizational change. That is to say, the change of focus from the individual to the group in all of the three missions (Etzkowitz, 2003).

mission was adapted to the new economic and social mission, through the training of individuals and organizations.

The internal context of the universities, on the occasion of the founding of the first technology incubators, shows that there was no consensus regarding this initiative, as well as a lack of guidelines or directions from the Ministry of Education or national government bodies for the founding of those incubators. Thus, the first incubators were set up by groups of professors with the support of intermediary bodies at the universities. Liaison with institutions in other spheres, and other support obtained, helped to legitimize the incubators internally.

Internal resistance, scarcity of resources, and changes in S&T policy in the 1980s and early 1990s are factors that contributed to these incubators being created within support networks at the federal and Catholic universities. From the first two incubators, set up in 1986 as a result of bilateral relations between university and government, the movement began to take off. Fundamental to that expansion were the initiatives of a nongovernmental organization, Anprotec (National Association of Entities Promoting Innovative Enterprise), founded by university professors, which targets technological development.

Although initially focused on technology parks, which also included hi-tech clusters and technology centers, Anprotec little by little started to pay particular attention to incubators. Among Anprotec's first partnerships, for the purpose of obtaining financial resources, were with the CNPq's Program in Support of Competitiveness and Technological Diffusion and the Program for the Preparation of Human Resources in Strategic Areas of the Ministry of Science and Technology, which provides for the granting of scholarships to entrepreneurs of incubated companies.

The cooperative incubators represent a variant created in Brazil within the university sphere. They arose from a desire for economic development through inclusion within the formal labor market of excluded social sectors. The emphasis on the education process, allied to the founding of enterprises—which underlies the incubator model organized, initially, to house the technology incubators—was thus seized upon for incubators of cooperatives (Etzkowitz, 2002). In this case, transplanting the language of the academic field to popular cooperatives required building new training and qualification strategies for those under incubation, as well as methodologies for education and learning, elements of citizenship, and cultural and anthropological factors that feature in these new groups but the university is not used to dealing with (Bocayuva, 2002).

It was only in August 1998 that the federal government introduced the National Incubator Program, as a priority under the Program for Technology Training in Industry, within the sphere of the Ministry of Science and Technology, when there were already around 60 incubators in operation within Brazil.

Between 1986 and 2003, 237 incubators were set up in the country, as follows: 107 technology-based, 51 traditional, 40 mixed, 29 cooperative, and 5 private (Almeida, 2004).

Embora com o foco inicial voltado para os parques tecnológicos, inclui também tecnópoles e pólos tecnológicos, a Anprotec, pouco a pouco, passa a dar uma atenção particular para as incubadoras. Entre as primeiras parcerias da Anprotec, para fins de obtenção de recursos financeiros, estão o Programa de Competitividade e Difusão Tecnológica (PDCT) do CNPq e o RHAE do Ministério da Ciência e Tecnologia que prevê a concessão de bolsas, para os empreendedores das empresas incubadas.

As incubadoras de cooperativas representam uma variante criada, no país, no seio da universidade. Surgem visando o desenvolvimento econômico através da inclusão no mercado de trabalho formal de setores sociais excluídos. A ênfase no processo de educação aliada à formação de empreendimentos - que está por trás do modelo de incubadoras, organizado, inicialmente, para abrigar as incubadoras tecnológicas - é, então, transposto para as incubadoras de cooperativas (ITCP/COPPE/UFRJ, 1998; Etzkowitz, 2002). Nesse caso, o transplante da linguagem do terreno acadêmico, para as cooperativas populares, exige a construção de novas estratégias de formação e capacitação dos incubados, de metodologias de educação e aprendizagem, de elementos de cidadania e de aspectos culturais e antropológicos que estão presentes nesses novos grupos com que a universidade não está acostumada a trabalhar (Bocayuva, 2002).

Somente em agosto de 1998, o Governo Federal cria o Programa Nacional de Incubadoras, como uma ação prioritária do Programa de Capacitação Tecnológica da Indústria, no âmbito do Ministério da Ciência e Tecnologia, quando já existem no país cerca de 60 incubadoras em funcionamento.

Entre 1986 e 2003 foram criadas no país 237 incubadoras, assim divididas: 107 tecnológicas, 51 tradicionais, 40 mistas, 29 de cooperativas e 05 privadas (Almeida, 2004).

4.2 Second Period

The second period began in 2003, with the implementation of the Industrial, Technology and Foreign Trade Policy (PITCE), in effect from 2003 to 2006. It was introduced by the Ministry of Science, Technology and Innovation (MCTI), which sought to strengthen and expand the Brazilian industrial base and improve the innovative capacity at companies. Proposals and priority economic sectors for public investment were discussed, in order to achieve the following aims: emphasis on domestic marketing, stimulating innovation to replace imports in certain economic sectors (pharmaceuticals and medical supplies); encourage innovation to increase software exports; build research capacity to generate future applications in economic sectors where the country does not have expertise, such as semiconductors and nanotechnology, and to also avoid the need for imports; modernization and enhanced competitiveness, enabling companies to replace capital goods; and strengthening of strategic fields such as biotechnology, biomass, and renewable energy.

To implement the PITCE, it was necessary to enact a set of laws proposed by the federal government and approved by Congress. Among the most important legal instruments one should mention the: Innovation Law (2004), Law in support of

R&D and incentives for the IT sector and automation (2004), Law of Tax Incentives for Innovation, known as the "Lei do Bem" (2005) and the Biosafety Law (2005), among others.

The Innovation Law had been under discussion since 2000, but it was only finally approved in 2004 and regulated in 2005. The purpose of this law was to stimulate universities and public research institutes in the process of innovation. It provided for the mandatory establishing of TTOs in universities and public federal teaching and research institutes; allowed the laboratories at those institutions to be used by private companies, as long as the institution set rules to that effect; allowed professors to request leave in order to set up spin-offs and that at the end of the 2-year period they could decide whether they wanted to continue their academic career; and set down regulations governing the intellectual property of research results. It was only with the passing of this law that regulation of the incubators and technology parks at public federal universities came into being, along with the total or partial concession of public property for the installation of incubators, parks, and incubated companies. Until that point, these organizations developed from the bottom-up, as described in the previous section, had no legal definition of their operations within the public sphere, providing public resources for companies to innovate.

Beyond the public federal HEIs, the law also authorized the government to grant direct nonreimbursable R&D support to private companies and provide incentives to establish a venture capital sector, which did not exist at the time, as well as various mechanisms for university–industry interaction.

This law was replaced by Law no 13,243/2016, called the Legal Framework for Science and Technology, which retained the same objective of encouraging innovation and scientific and technological research within the production environment, with a view to enhancing technological capacity and developing the country's national and regional production systems. It was noted that, following enactment of the Federal Innovation Law, the states started discussing and approving their own laws in support of innovation, increasing the resources available for that purpose and giving priority to local programs and other specific endeavors.

The passing of the Innovation Law brought about significant changes in the academic environment that can be analyzed on the basis of three characteristics: number of TTOs established, number of patent applications requested, and revenue earned from commercial contracts.

The annual report on the Intellectual Property Policy for Scientific, Technology and Innovation-based Institutions in Brazil (FORMICT), drawn up by the Ministry of Science, Technology and Innovation (MCTI), has the purpose of assessing the implementation of the legal measures provided for under the Innovation Law. It initially provided only for the collection and analysis of data from public federal institutions, which had the obligation to provide such data, but private institutions joined in and started to provide information, even though it was not mandatory for them. The FORMICT results (MCTIC, 2019a) indicate that 169 public ICTs (80.9%) reported that they had already implemented the NIT. Only 12 public ICTs (5.7%) reported that the NIT had not been implemented and 28 public institutions (13.4%) reported that they were in the implementation phase. As for the private ICTs,

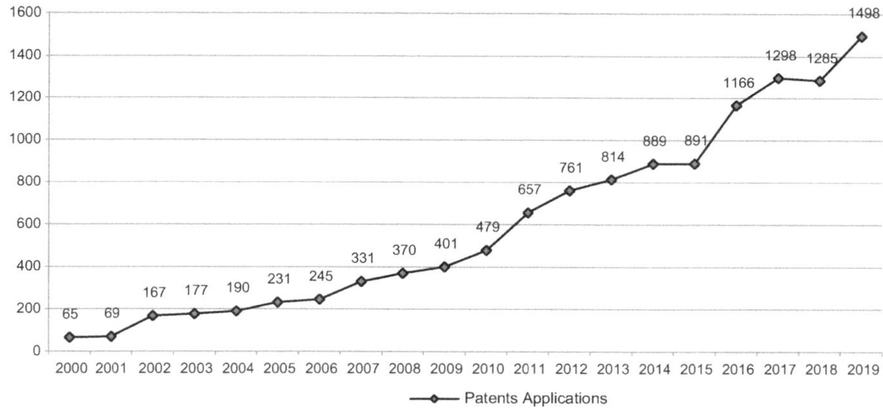

Source: INPI, Industrial Property Statistical Yearbook (2000-2019)

Fig. 1 Number of university patent applications to the INPI (2000–2019). (Source: INPI, Industrial Property Statistical Yearbook (2000–2019))

51 institutions (53.1%) reported that they had implemented the NIT, and 23 (24%) that they had not implemented the NIT, while 22 institutions (22.9%) reported that the NIT was in the process of being implemented.

There has been a significant increase in patent applications by universities since the innovation policy was first introduced, with the subsequent approval of the Innovation Law, as shown in Fig. 1, which presents the number of applications between 2000 and 2019.

An increase in technology contracts was also observed. In 2018, the number of institutions with technology transfer contracts increased to 66, of which 47 were public and 19 private. Of the 66 institutions that reported having technology contracts, 33 are Higher Education Institutions, followed by 19 Research Institutes, 8 Professional and Technological Education Institutes, and 6 Other Institutions. The total number of technology contracts amounted to 2374, covering R$1,217,700 for the year. Although the scale is small compared to institutions abroad, it represents a change in the behavior of Brazilian universities.

The enactment, in 2016, of the Legal Framework for ST&I obliged the public federal universities and other public ICTs to discuss and approve an internal Innovation Policy, providing the performance details in activities related to innovation, the protection of intellectual property and technology transfer. Among the institutions responding to the FORMICT, 71.7% of the public institutions and 59.4% of the private institutions reported that they had implemented an innovation policy (MCTIC, 2019a, b). The data are not broken down for each university.

With regard to the incubators, which are so important during the initial period, this package of laws and invested resources enabled the expansion and enhanced quality of the performance capacity. There was also an extension of activities, with the establishing of Technology Parks at some universities, supported by state and municipal governments, thus repeating the alliance in the development of incubators, since the perception of these governments regarding the positive impact on economic development was consolidating. The triple helix was no longer just an analytical concept for studying the process of innovation, but had become a strategy and instrument of S&T&I policy. However, the major change during the period was felt by the companies under incubation at the incubators and parks, which now had financial resources to carry out innovative projects, due to a set of programs introduced by the federal government and certain state governments, once the Innovation Law authorized that kind of financing.

4.3 Third Period

The third period begins in 2015, marked by diminished public funding by the federal government for investment in S&T&I, which strongly affected the activities of universities and reduced the possibility that they would expand the teaching activities in support of the third mission.

The impeachment of President Dilma Rousseff, in 2016, brought into the federal government conservative groups that do not prioritize science, research activities, and education. The role of science and research is no longer considered a path to and stimulator of economic and social development. Successive budget cuts, criticism of the work of researchers, and persecution of those who disagree with the political positions all worsened after the election of Jair Bolsonaro, in 2018. There was a significant exodus of young researchers to other countries, due to the lack of job opportunities in Brazil. Initiatives by certain government agencies, such as FAPESP (Foundation for Support to Research in the State of São Paulo) and FAPERJ (Foundation for Support to Research in the state of Rio de Janeiro), attempted to at least partially turn this situation around, by issuing public tenders for the awarding of scholarships for special projects. Young researchers have always been participants in the HEI feedback process and in academic entrepreneurship.

Following the international trend of organizing spaces for start-up activities and fostering entrepreneurship in the initial stages, a series of initiatives, such as co-working and accelerators, were organized in an environment outside the HEIs, which created opportunities for the strengthening and growth of enterprises whose first internships were initiated in the incubators at the universities.

The establishment of university–industry interaction during this period was important. Some examples can be mentioned, such as the partnership between the cosmetics company Natura and CESAR (Center for Advanced Systems and Studies in Recife), in the northeastern state of Pernambuco, through Natura Startup 2016;[3] the acceleration of start-ups in partnership with Telefônica Open Future and the Technology Park of the Federal University of Rio de Janeiro, through a project

[3]https://www.investe.sp.gov.br/noticia/programas-corporativos-aceleram-a-transformacao/

called CrowdRio;[4] the Ocean New Business Program, between Samsung and the University of São Paulo, for the selecting of projects;[5] or the agreement between the University of Passo Fundo, in the municipality of Passo Fundo, Rio Grande do Sul state, and Ambev, the country's largest beverage company, signed in 2021.[6]

This period revealed some interesting initiatives, both in terms of university–industry interaction and in government activities, which in this case was the government of the state of Rio de Janeiro. One of the challenges faced by those responsible for the academic entrepreneurship initiatives was the discontinuity or sectorizing of the sources of funding for these activities. Government agencies issued separate public tenders, on an irregular basis, sometimes for incubators, sometimes for TTOs, without noting that academic entrepreneurship embraces broader activities. In 2021, FAPERJ issued a distinctive public tender, for the financing of systemic activities in support of innovation at ICTs, especially those aimed at technological development, mechanisms in support of entrepreneurship, various sources for the transmission of knowledge and relations between institutions and the production sector. The amount of resources they could have access to varied according to the number of master's and doctoral courses, an unequivocal confirmation that the development of research will influence the opportunities for innovation. There was also the flexibility for each ICT to list the priority activities to be developed, according to their level of maturity and immediate need.

It was observed that the number of incubators remained stable, with only the number of technology parks increasing.

5 Conclusions

In this chapter, I have introduced key features of the path of academic entrepreneurship in Brazil, during three distinct periods, highlighting their characteristics, interactions, and results.

Based on the above analysis and discussion, it is possible to conclude that the academic entrepreneurship began in Brazil back in 1986, with the organizing of the first incubators and expanded with the founding of a civil society organization, Anprotec, was one of the factors that influenced the S&T&I policy scenario in Brazil. Its importance is emphasized by the fact that it is a source for the creation of new technology-based companies in a country with a low rate of innovation, when one analyzes the business context.

It can be seen that, in each period, there was an institutional evolution in the institutions involved. During the first period, the changes were concentrated within the internal space of the universities, since the creation of incubators generated the

[4] https://www.parque.ufrj.br/historico/consolidacao-de-parcerias-e-novas-empresas/

[5] https://oceanbrasil.com/educacaoempreendedora/

[6] https://www.upf.br/noticia/upf-e-ambev-firmam-parceria-com-foco-em-inovacao

need to restructure the institutional space and discuss and approve the rules, against the backdrop of an internal debate about the role of the university in economic and social development and discussion about the limits of the influence of the economic sphere and of companies on the production of knowledge. It also enabled the creation of a social innovation, in the incubator movement itself, with the establishment of cooperative incubators and the incorporation within the university environment of social segments that had previously had no access to knowledge. In the second period, the definition of innovation policies at the government level and the enacting of new laws broadened the horizon of academic entrepreneurship, opening up new possibilities. During the third period, the understanding of the business sector that universities could contribute to innovation in certain areas led cooperation programs to support the emergence of start-ups and creation of products necessary for the companies.

In each of these periods, varied interaction was established and the internal discussion of universities about entrepreneurship and innovation was changing, with an impact on teaching, research, and outreach activities.

References

Almeida, M. (2004). *The evolution of the incubator movement in Brazil. Ph.D. thesis COPPE*. Federal University of Rio de Janeiro.

Almeida, M., Plonski, A., Axelberg, J., Baeta, A., Terra, B., Simões, B., & Etzkowitz, H. (2022a). Entrepreneurial vision and Brazil's system of Higher Education Assessment. *Quality Assurance in Education, 30*(3), 370–386.

Almeida, M., Porto-Gomez, I., & Leydesdorff, L. (2022b, March 24). *Are Brazilian innovation systems innovative*? Regional and Sectorial Decompositions of Triple-Helix Synergies. Available at SSRN: https://ssrn.com/abstract=4065507 or https://doi.org/10.2139/ssrn.4065507

ANPROTEC – Brazilian Association of Science Parks and Incubators/Associação Nacional de Entidades Promotoras de Empreendimentos Inovadores. (2019). *Mapeamento dos Mecanismos de Geração de Empreendimentos Inovadores*. ANPROTEC. Retrieved July 28, 2021, from https://anprotec.org.br/site/wp-content/uploads/2019/09/Mapeamento_Empreendimentos_Inovadores.pdf

Audretsch, D. (2014). From the entrepreneurial university to the university for the entrepreneurial society. *The Journal of Technology Transfer, 39*, 313–321.

Bocayuva, P. C. C. (2002). Social subjects, human rights and their political relevance. In *Dignity and human rights: The implementation of economic, social, and cultural rights* (pp. 149–161). Brill Nijhoff.

Burgos, M. B. (1999). Ciência na periferia: a luz síncrotron brasileira. EDUFJF22.

CAPES (Coordination for the Development of Higher Education Personnel) Coordenação de Aperfeiçoamento de Pessoal de Nível Superior. (2019). *Proposta de Aprimoramento da Avaliação da Pós-Graduação Brasileira para o Quadriênio 2021–2024 – Modelo Multidimensional*. Brasília. Retrieved July 25, 2021, from https://www.gov.br/capes/pt-br/centrais-de-conteudo/25052020-relatorio-final-2019-comissao-pnpg-pdf

Cavagnari, G. (1987). A Experiência do Certi. In *Anais do Seminário Internacional de Parques Tecnológicos* (pp. 307–312). Rio de Janeiro (Dez).

Clark, B. R. (1998). *Creating entrepreneurial universities*. Pergamon.

Etzkowitz, H. (1983). Entrepreneurial scientists and entrepreneurial universities in American Academic Science. *Minerva, 21*(2–3), 198–233.
Etzkowitz, H. (1993). Enterprises from science: The origins of science-based regional economic development. *Minerva, 31*(3), 326–360.
Etzkowitz, H. (1998). The norms of entrepreneurial science: Cognitive effects of the new university–industry linkages. *Research Policy, 27*, 823–833.
Etzkowitz, H. (2002). Incubation of incubators: Innovation as a triple helix of university-industry-government networks. *Science and Public Policy, 29*(2), 1–14.
Etzkowitz, H. (2003). Research groups as 'quasi firms': The invention of the entrepreneurial university. *Research Policy, 32*, 109–121.
Etzkowitz, H. (2004). The evolution of the entrepreneurial university. *International Journal of Technology and Globalization, 1*, 64–77.
Etzkowitz, H., & Leydesdorff, L. (1998). The endless transition: A "triple helix" of university-industry-government relations: Introduction. *Minerva, 36*, 203–208.
Etzkowitz, H., & Leydesdorff, L. (2000). The dynamics of innovation: From national systems and 'Mode 2' to a Triple Helix of university–industry–government relations. *Research Policy, 29*(2), 109–123. https://doi.org/10.1016/S0048-7333(99)00055-4
Etzkowitz, H., Mello, J. M. C., & Almeida, M. (2005). Towards "meta-innovation" in Brazil: The evolution of the incubator and the emergence of a triple helix. *Research Policy, 34*(4), 411–424. https://doi.org/10.1016/j.respol.2005.01.011
Etzkowitz, H., Webster, A., Gebhardt, C., & Terra, B. R. C. (2000). The future of the university and the university of the future: Evolution of ivory tower to entrepreneurial paradigm. *Research Policy, 29*(2), 313–330.
Fávero, M. D. L. D. A. (2006). A Universidade no Brasil: das origens à Reforma Universitária de 1968. *Educar em Revista, 28*, 17–36.
Freeman, C. (2002). Continental, national and sub-national innovation systems—Complementarity and economic growth. *Research Policy, 31*, 191–211.
Guerrero, M., & Urbano, D. (2012). The development of an entrepreneurial university. *Journal of Technology Transfer, 37*(1), 43–74.
Herrera, F., Guerrero, M., & Urbano, D. (2018). Entrepreneurship and innovation ecosystem's drivers: The role of higher education organizations. In *Entrepreneurial, innovative and sustainable ecosystems* (pp. 109–128). Springer.
IBGE Instituto Brasileiro de Geografia e Estatística. (2020). *Pesquisa Industrial de Inovação Tecnológica – Pintec – 2017*. IBGE. Retrieved December 20, 2020, from https://biblioteca.ibge.gov.br/index.php/biblioteca-catalogo?view=detalhes&id=2101706
InBIA (International Business Innovation Association). (2016). Numbers of Entrepreneurship Centers (by Type) in US. Accessed February 13, 2022. Available from https://inbia.org/wp-content/uploads/2018/08/NumberofECsimage.jpg?x62369
INEP (Anísio Teixeira National Institute for Educational Studies and Research) Instituto Nacional de Estudos e Pesquisas Educacionais Anísio Teixeira. (2009). *Exame Nacional de Desempenho de Estudantes*. Retrieved January 27, 2017, from http://portal.inep.gov.br/enade/
Jacob, M., Lundqvist, M., & Hellsmark, H. (2003). Entrepreneurial transformations in the Swedish university system: The case of Chalmers University of Technology. *Research Policy, 32*(9), 1555–1568.
Katz, J. A. (2003). The chronology and intellectual trajectory of American entrepreneurship education: 1876–1999. *Journal of Business Venturing, 18*(2), 283–300.
Klofsten, M., & Jones-Evans, D. (2000). Comparing academic entrepreneurship in Europe—The case of Sweden and Ireland. *Small Business Economics, 14*(4), 299–309.
Laredo, P. (2007). Revisiting the third mission of universities: Toward a renewed categorization of university activities? *Higher Education Policy, 20*(4), 441–456.
Leydesdorff, L., & Etzkowitz, H. (1996). Emergence of a triple helix of university—industry—government relations. *Science and Public Policy, 23*(5), 279–286.

Martins, C. B. (2003). Balanço: o papel da CAPES na formação do sistema nacional de pós-graduação. In *CAPES 50 anos: depoimentos ao CPDOC/FGV/Organizadoras: Marieta de Moraes Ferreira & Regina da Luz Moreira* (pp. 294–309). Fundação Getulio Vargas, CPDOC/CAPES. Retrieved November 16, 2021, from https://cpdoc.fgv.br/producao_intelectual/arq/1319_Capes11.pdf

MCTIC. Ministry of Science, Technology, Innovation and Communication/Ministério da Ciência, Tecnologia, Inovação e Comunicação. (2019a). *Relatório Formict 2018: Política de Propriedade Intelectual das Instituições Científicas e Tecnológicas do Brasil.* MCTIC. Retrieved July 25, 2021, from https://gestiona.com.br/wp-content/uploads/2019/12/Relatório-Formict-2019_Ano-Base-2018.pdf

MCTIC. Ministry of Science, Technology, Innovation and Communication/Ministério da Ciência, Tecnologia, Inovação e Comunicação. (2019b). *Indicadores de Parques Tecnológicos. Estudo de Projetos de Alta Complexidade. Fase 2.* MCTIC. Retrieved July 25, 2021, from https://gestiona.com.br/wp-content/uploads/2019/10/MCTIC-UnB-ParquesTecnologicos-Portugues-final.pdf

Miller, K., Cunningham, J., & Lehmann, E. (2021). Extending the university mission and business model: Influences and implications. *Studies in Higher Education, 46*(5), 915–925.

Montesinos, P., Carot, J. M., Martinez, J. M., & Mora, F. (2008). Third mission ranking for world class universities: Beyond teaching and research. *Higher Education in Europe, 33*(2–3), 259–271.

NASSCOM. (2020). *Startup catalysts—Incubators and accelerators 2020.* Retrieved February 13, 2022, from https://nasscom.in/knowledge-center/publications/start-catalysts%2D%2D-incubators-accelerators

Perkmann, M., Tartari, V., McKelvey, M., Autio, E., Broström, A., D'este, P., Fini, R., Geuna, A., Grimaldi, R., Hughes, A., Krabel, S., Kitson, M., Llerena, P., Lissoni, F., Salter, A., & Sobrero, M. (2013). Academic engagement and commercialisation: A review of the literature on university–industry relations. *Research Policy, 42*(2), 423–442.

Póvoa, L. M. C. (2008). *Patentes de universidades e institutos públicos de pesquisa e a transferência de tecnologia para empresas no Brasil* [PhD thesis]. Federal University of Minas Gerais. Retrieved October 14, 2015, from https://repositorio.ufmg.br/bitstream/1843/AMSA-7FBNZ5/1/luciano_p_voa_2008.pdf

Schwartzman, S. (2010). *Space for science: The development of the scientific community in Brazil.* Penn State Press.

Shane, S. A. (2004). *Academic entrepreneurship: University spinoffs and wealth creation.* Edward Elgar Publishing.

Souza, M. C., & Garcia, R. (1999). Sistemas Locais de Inovação em São Paulo. In J. E. Cassiolato & H. M. M. Lastres (Eds.), *Globalização & Inovação Localizada. Capítulo 9* (1st ed.). IBICT.

Xiangfei, Y., Hongcheng, G., & Yanping, L. (2022). Who has greater impact on the performance of TBIs?—A comparative analysis of cities, incubators and incubating enterprises. *Science Research Management, 43*(1), 89.

Entrepreneurial Framework Conditions in Brazil

Esha Thukral and Vanessa Ratten

Abstract Many existing entrepreneurship research suggests that opportunity recognition, an (individual) entrepreneur, and cognitive and behavioral characteristics can all have an impact on business creation and the long-term viability of a business. Traditionally, the focus has been on individual entrepreneurs and enterprises rather than the contextual setting in which they interact. However, in today's interconnected world, a wide range of entities are necessary to function successfully and sustainably. Therefore, this chapter is focusing on Entrepreneurial framework conditions (EFCs) role and status/gaps and its impact on entrepreneurship (in the context of Brazil).

Keywords Brazil · Entrepreneurship · Environment · Institutional barriers · Entrepreneurial framework conditions

1 Introduction

Entrepreneurship is crucial for economic growth, and entrepreneurs both potential and current are influenced by the environmental setting within which entrepreneurs engage, and changes in that environment impact their entrepreneurial activities (Arabi & Abdalla, 2020; Bennett, 2019) because a business is not a stand-alone activity; it is part of a larger ecosystem with which it must engage in order to achieve its goals (Orobia et al., 2020). In the past decade, research on entrepreneurial ecosystem has increased in popularity as one of the most prominent academic topics (Ratten, 2020b). As in today's interconnected world, a wide range of entities are necessary for a business to function successfully and sustainably (Ratten, 2020a) and

E. Thukral
La Trobe University, Melbourne, VIC, Australia

V. Ratten (✉)
Department of Management and Marketing, La Trobe Business School, La Trobe University, Melbourne, VIC, Australia
e-mail: v.ratten@latrobe.edu.au

J. Leitão et al. (eds.), *Brazilian Entrepreneurship*, Studies on Entrepreneurship, Structural Change and Industrial Dynamics,
https://doi.org/10.1007/978-3-031-09392-0_5

a strong ecosystem allows entrepreneur to quickly find knowledge and resources they need to succeed.

The ecosystem is a dynamic network of interconnected systems. The term "system" refers to various institutions that interact with one another to drive the creative performance of national enterprises (Sussan & Acs, 2017; Thukral, 2021). Audretsch and Belitski (2017) define efficient entrepreneurial ecosystems as "a complex system of interactions between agents within various socio-economic, institutional and informational contexts which generate more new businesses and growth" (Audretsch & Belitski, 2017, p. 1045). This can also be backed by institutional theory.

2 Institutional Theory

The institutional theory contends that a society's regulatory environment consists of the fundamental political, social, and legal ground rules that set the basis for manufacturing and distribution, and that organizations must adhere to it in order to gain support and legitimacy. Businesses' viability, profitability, and even longevity are usually dependent on the current institutional environment. This suggests that the nature of structures or institutions within the environment can either aid or hinder the development of the business (Orobia et al., 2020).

Thus, it can be said that numerous elements within the environment like regulatory environment, infrastructure, resources, social and cultural beliefs/norms, etc. are at play that affect entrepreneurship (Thukral, 2022) but only the effective institutions can help entrepreneurship to flourish and grow (Ratten, 2020c). This is in tune with the Global Entrepreneurship Monitor (GEM) proposition that entrepreneurial growth is linked to the environmental conditions also referred to as Entrepreneurial Framework Conditions (EFCs) within which they operate. GEM has identified nine EFCs that drive entrepreneurial activity which include finance, government policy, government entrepreneurship programs, education, R&D transfer, commercial and legal structure, entry regulation, physical infrastructure, and social and cultural norms (Global Entrepreneurship Monitor, 2022; Orobia et al., 2020) (Fig. 1):

- ***Financial resource***—The availability and accessibility of financial resources (debt, equity, subsidies, and grants) allows entrepreneurs to acquire goods and fund other business activities.
- ***Government policy***—Provisions that encourage entrepreneurship (such as taxes and regulations) improve the long-term viability of businesses.
- **Government entrepreneurship programs**—Targeted support programs assist entrepreneurs to run their businesses smoothly by addressing the gaps in their resource and competency requirements.
- ***Education***—Entrepreneurial education improves entrepreneurial capacity, which, when effectively implemented, enhances the chances of success.

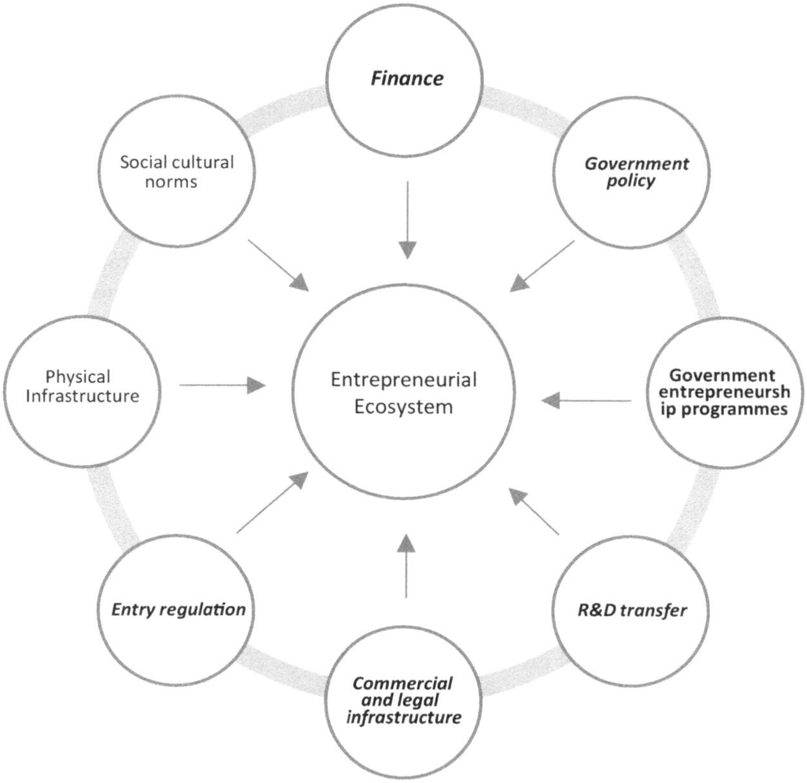

Fig. 1 A conceptual overview of entrepreneurial ecosystems. (Source: Self-created)

- ***R&D transfer***—Awareness and understanding of new technology enhances the capability of the organization to conduct day-to-day operations and allows them to gain a competitive advantage.
- ***Commercial and legal infrastructure***—Business sustainability is aided by the availability and accessibility of property rights, accounting, commercial as well as other legal and assessment services.
- ***Entry regulation***—The convenience with which a company can enter the market has both positive and negative consequences. It is positive in the sense that it fosters new business ventures and detrimental in the sense that it increases competition for the current market and resources. Therefore, only a balanced and controlled entry will favor long-term corporate viability.
- ***Physical infrastructure***—The accessibility to physical resources (utilities, transportation, etc.) facilitates corporate operations and promotes growth.
- ***Social and cultural norms***—The influence of social and cultural norms encourages or permits acts that lead to business success.

Some other models also exist that talk about the different components of entrepreneurial ecosystem. Like Isenberg (2010) presents a range of institutional support systems for entrepreneurs as entrepreneurial ecosystem, including supportive culture ethos, conduce regulatory environment, leadership, financial resource and skilled human capital accessibility, and venture-friendly markets for products (Isenberg, 2010). The report by World Economic Forum together with Stanford University, Ernst and Young, and Endeavor also talks about similar components in the entrepreneurial ecosystem. The eight elements are markets, culture, education and training, university as catalysts, mentors or advisors, regulatory framework and infrastructure, funding and finance, and human capital (World Economic Forum, 2013). The ecosystem, according to Spigel (2017), is a supportive environment that aids in the development of strong economies and innovative initiatives. Economic policies/policy measures, capital investment, sociocultural norms, social networks, and academic institutions are all part of the ecosystem (Spigel, 2017). Market accessibility, geography, cultural norms and beliefs, talent, financial capital, regulatory system and governance, and infrastructure support are all major drivers of a thriving ecosystem (Rolfe, 2020).

Thus, the presence of the above factors or suitable conditions encourages entrepreneurship and enhances the chance of business success. Therefore, numerous efforts must be taken in order to boost entrepreneurship, the first of which is to map and assess the current entrepreneurial environment and remove all obstacles that impede entrepreneurial growth (Arabi & Abdalla, 2020). Entrepreneurship can flourish only if the different elements of the ecosystem are managed together (Arruda et al., 2014). As Firman (2014) points out, that to create a local environment that is suitable for entrepreneurship and economic progress requires numerous public and private organizations to work collaboratively (Firman, 2014).

3 Brazil's Entrepreneurial Framework Conditions Overview

Brazil's start-up ecosystem is made up of various public, semipublic, and private organizations that work collaboratively. On the plus side, Brazil has a well-developed network of business incubators and accelerators, as well as several promising open innovation programs that connect start-ups and small businesses with large corporations in need of specific technological solutions. According to the Brazilian Association of Science Parks and Business Incubators (ANPROTEC) (a non-for-profit organization), Brazil has 369 incubators, approximately 90 technology parks, and 35 accelerators. The business incubator's role is to enable entrepreneurs in developing unique ideas and turning them into viable businesses. To accomplish this, it provides entrepreneurs with infrastructure and management support, as well as advice on business operation, competition, and other critical aspects linked to business development (Tietz et al., 2015).

In addition to that there are various government-sponsored initiatives and programs to support the business environment like The National Program of Incubators and Technology Parks (PNI), which began in 1998 and was revised in 2009, is a network of technology parks and incubators that assists technology-based smaller firms. Open innovation initiatives operated by private sector companies are also a part entrepreneurial ecosystem of Brazil. For example, in 2017, Votorantim Cimentos, the world's fifth largest cement manufacturer, launched an open innovation program focused on cement production and associated technology and in 2017 alone the program received 107 applications (OECD, 2018b).

Despite the above-mentioned entrepreneurial support, institutional/bureaucratic barriers hinder the entrepreneurial environment. On the flipside, a myriad of bureaucratic requirements and plethora of rules and regulations makes it difficult to start and run a business which is also reflected in the TMF's Global Business Complexity Index 2021 and the World Bank's report on Doing Business 2020. According to TMF's Global Business Complexity Index 2021, Brazil is the most challenging/complex jurisdiction. In Brazil, complexity is fostered by a multilayered governance system in which federal, state, and local governments all have strong legislative power; emerging enterprises must register with all three levels of government. Thus, conducting or creating business in Brazil, necessitates a thorough understanding of the country's bureaucratic commercial environment, which is among the world's most complex (TMF Group, 2021) In terms of ease of doing business, Brazil ranks 124 out of 190 countries with a score of 59.1, according to the World Bank's report on Doing Business 2020. The ease of doing business score assesses a country's economic state in terms of a regulatory best practice metric over a set of 41 parameters addressing 10 Doing Business topics. The ten topics relate to "starting a business, dealing with construction permits, getting electricity, registering property, getting credit, protecting minority investors, paying taxes, trading across borders, enforcing contracts, and resolving insolvency" (World Bank Group, 2020). Few of the biggest contributors to Brazil's complexity is its tax environment. At every level of government, different taxes are imposed, resulting in varying tax rates from one city to another and from one state to another (TMF Group, 2021), significant backlog in the patent system, and government R&D tax incentives are largely unavailable to creative start-ups, etc. (OECD, 2018b).

4 Gaps in the Brazilian Entrepreneurial Ecosystem

Despite infrastructural support, there are numerous institutional barriers that affect the entrepreneurial growth. Below are some institutional barriers that exist in Brazil:

Entry regulation One of the reasons why many people chose not to start a business is because of the barriers in setting up a business. The overarching argument is that market entry regulations involve costs in addition to direct compliance and enforcement expenses (if nothing else, it increases the likelihood of bribes that have to be paid), while there may be profound politico-economic interests underlying such regulation that make deregulation impossible, authorities should carefully consider the "excess costs" of entry regulation when making policy decisions (Klapper et al., 2006). Brazil is one of the countries with the most demands and costs when it comes to starting a business. The reform/changes in rules and regulations for establishing and operating a business in Brazil have lagged, posing a number of challenges for businesses. The World Bank's Doing Business report, puts Brazil 124th out of 190 countries in terms of the ease with which one can start a business, obtaining permits, registering property, and paying taxes. In Brazil, starting a firm takes about 11 procedures and 119 working days (Globalization Partners, 2021) whereas it only takes 4 working days to register and start a business in the USA (Monsen, 2020). Streamlining these processes and lowering the costs of starting a business may encourage more people to pursue their dreams of becoming entrepreneurs (Borges et al., 2018). Albeit according to the Global Entrepreneurship Monitor (2020) report highlights that "Ease of entry: market barriers and regulations" improved marginally from 3.9 in 2019 to 4.1 in 2020 (29th overall), which of course is a welcoming improvement for companies looking to break into new markets (Global Entrepreneurship Monitor, 2020), yet there is still a long way to go.

Culture All parts of an entrepreneurial ecosystem are influenced by culture, which has a direct effect on the business start-up and growth (Arruda et al., 2014). Starting a business and its development is influenced by societal and cultural attitudes toward entrepreneurship. Brazil's "Social and cultural norms" score improved from 3.7 in 2019 to 4.8 in 2020, putting it in the top 25 countries. According to data from the Global Entrepreneurship Monitor (GEM) study, approximately one-third (31%) of adults in Brazil (aged 18–64 years) believe that there are good prospects to start a business in their neighborhood, which is lower than the OECD simple average that is 38% and all Latin American countries except Uruguay (29%). National statistics indicate that many Brazilians are currently business owners or are in the process of starting a business owing to the improvement in the ease of market entry and changing attitudes toward entrepreneurship, but most of these enterprises are very tiny and are struggling to grow. This is because of a lack/limited business growth or scale-up opportunity (OECD, 2020). Thus, it can be concluded that Brazil's regulatory environment does not appear to be keeping up with the entrepreneurial drive in Brazil (Arruda et al., 2014). The entrepreneurship can flourish only if the different elements of the ecosystem are managed together (Arruda et al., 2014).

Complex Tax System (part of Government policy) Taxes are recurring costs which reduce the entrepreneurial profits and rewards from innovation. It deters and discourages enterprising entrepreneurs. Higher the tax rates lower the "reward" of bringing a new/innovative product to market, regrettably, if an entrepreneur's idea fails, he or she is still liable and responsible (Darnihamedani et al., 2018). Most of the Brazil's tax revenue comes from value-added taxes (VAT) and corporate tax. Brazil's statutory corporate income tax (CIT) rate is 34%, making it one of the world's highest CIT rates (OECD, 2018b). The tax that firms pay on their taxable income is known as corporate tax. The high corporate tax not only diminishes the reward for innovation but also affects the entrepreneur's ability to further invest in innovation (Darnihamedani et al., 2018).

Brazil's taxation system is burdensome and complex. Compliance cost too is high because of the numerous indirect taxes, which becomes proportionally greater for small enterprises. The Municipal Service Tax (ISS), (the municipal VAT); the Tax on Commerce and Services (ICMS), (the state VAT); the Program of Social Integration (PIS) and the Contribution for Social Security Financing (COFINS); and the tax on industrialized products are the five main taxes on the production and consumption of goods and services in Brazil (IPI). The current proposal recommends combining all five into a single tax: the tax on goods and services (IBS), which is similar to a VAT (Globalization Partners, 2021).

Bureaucracy and Corruption levels The World Bank uses the Worldwide Governance Indicators (WGI) to collect data on governance quality. The six variables are political stability, regulatory quality, governance, rule of law, and voice and accountability. Brazil, as per the report, performs poorly in comparison to other Latin American and emerging economies in the areas of governance and corruption level, while the other indicators show that Brazil's performance is similar to the other countries. Latinobarómetro, a private nonprofit organization that conducts an annual study in Latin American and Caribbean countries (LAC) countries, confirms the low level of trust that people have in the government. Only 7% of Brazilians trust their government, as per to the 2017 edition, which is the lowest of any participating country. Furthermore, Brazilian's regard corruption to be the most serious issue. However, Brazilian government is making efforts to improve its effectiveness, the government, for the most part, has embraced the prospects that digitalization may bring in more inclusive, transparent, and collaborative service delivery. The Digital Governance Strategy 2016–2019 was adopted by the government in 2016, and it was modified in 2018. The focus of the strategy is to help promote the accessibility of government data, elevating the use of digital technologies for openness, improving the delivery and usage of public digital, boosting the participation of the citizens through a digital platform (OECD, 2018b).

Lack of Proper Physical Infrastructure Scholars are becoming increasingly inquisitive about how the environment influences entrepreneurial activity in different regions of the world. One element of the environment that has gotten little attention is investment in physical infrastructure development. Infrastructure development alters the physical environment and makes it more conducive which provides entrepreneurs an opportunity to enter the market (Bennett, 2019). According to the World Economic Forum, Global Competitiveness Index 2017–2018, Brazil's infrastructure ranks 108th out of 137 economies with a score of 3.1 in terms of quality where [1 means highly underdeveloped—the worst in the world; 7 means extensive and efficient—among the best in the world] (World Economic Forum, 2018), which explains the country's high logistical costs. Brazil has huge infrastructure gaps when compared to other members of the BRICS economic bloc (Brazil, Russia, India, China, and South Africa) (Globalization Partners, 2021).

This is due to the relative sluggishness with which infrastructure investments have been implemented in Brazil. The intricate bureaucratic mechanism that has grown generations after generations governing the release of public funds, as well as the authorities' cautious approach in conducting competitive bidding, especially in the realm of novel Public–Private Partnership (PPP) contracts, have been criticized for the infrastructure gaps and delays in implementation (Amann et al., 2016). The federal government in 2016 introduced an Investment Partnership Program (Programa de Parcerias de Investimentos: PPI) to focus on Brazilian infrastructure and strengthen public–private partnership in infrastructure projects. So far, the IPP has yielded remarkable outcomes. In total 193 projects have been approved for the program, with 136 of them currently completed, but there is still a long road ahead (Souza et al., 2019).

Skill Shortage According to the Manpower group survey, one out of every three businesses has trouble filling available positions due to a shortage of applicants with the necessary technical abilities, experience, and soft skills. Talent shortages are limiting firms' capacity to provide value to their customers. Companies in India, Peru, Argentina, Turkey, and Brazil have also been hit hard by skill shortages. All of this has a lot of commercial ramifications. Competing for skills or attracting skilled workers can drive up labor costs, reduce profit margins, and can even halt production. Supply chain interruptions could also be caused by skills shortages at the supplier's end. This can affect the firm's competitiveness in the global market, at the same time, dissatisfaction with high unemployment and rising pay disparity can lead to societal instability, which, can lead to a variety of other risks, including war (Radulovic, 2015). Thus, it is important to address skill shortages.

Knowledge foundation developed in early education is critical for participation in postsecondary education and training throughout one's career. Brazil's educational system faces issues in terms of accessibility and quality. By the age of 25, only 59% of Brazilians are estimated to finish upper secondary school. In comparison to other nations, the percentage of tertiary graduates is also low. Furthermore, even for those who do take up secondary education, quality is not guaranteed. The OECD Programme for International Student Assessment (PISA), which ranks the proficiency of 15-year-old pupils on standardized assessments in reading, maths, and science, shows that children in Brazil fare poorly in all three disciplines (OECD, 2018a). Korn Ferry Institute, Future of Work report has assessed that Brazil by 2030, could suffer skilled worker shortage of approximately 1.7 million (Korn Ferry, 2018). However, there are several initiatives started by the government to address the issue of skill shortage One of which is "Early Childhood Education Care" (ECEC) under which Brazil has made significant progress in expanding the participation in education while continuing to improve quality (OECD, 2021). The percentage of students to finish primary education has increased. Seventeen percent of Brazilians between the ages of 25 and 34 years have completed tertiary education in 2017, as opposed to 10% in 2007 (OECD, 2018b). Nonetheless, there are still numerous obstacles to overcome as with the current pace, Brazil will struggle to achieve the National Education Plan (Plano Nacional de Educaço, PNE) target of at least 50% enrolment for 0–3-year old by 2024. 2018, PISA data highlights that in Brazil, like in other nations, ECEC can have an impact on later educational performance when children attend for 2 years at least. However, in Brazil, the impact was not as beneficial as it was for OECD member nations. Brazil must consequently focus on quality while boosting participation (OECD, 2021).

5 Conclusion

Entrepreneurial activity is generated by interactions between various elements of the socio-economic environment. The overall creation of new businesses may well be hampered by flaws or shortcomings in key components of these "entrepreneurial capital." "Entrepreneurial capital," is defined as local institutions that encourage entrepreneurship. Despite the fact that individual skill and characteristics are important triggers for entrepreneurial behavior, suitable institutional conditions and adequate incentives are essential for maintaining high levels of entrepreneurial activity. In the case of Brazil, it is well recognized that an ineffective regulatory framework poses a structural barrier to entrepreneurial development (Alves et al., 2019). Although efforts are being made to improve the functioning of the entrepreneurial ecosystem, however, there is still a long way before building a diverse portfolio of new profitable ventures. So, for Brazil understanding the above-mentioned issues/gaps are necessary to encourage a more entrepreneurial environment.

References

Alves, A. C., Fischer, B., Schaeffer, P. R., & Queiroz, S. (2019). Determinants of student entrepreneurship An assessment on higher education institutions in Brazil. *Innovation & Management Review, 16*(2), 96–117.

Amann, E., Baer, W., Trebat, T., & Lora, J. V. (2016). Infrastructure and its role in Brazil's development process. *The Quarterly Review of Economics and Finance, 62*(1), 66–73.

Arabi, N. G., & Abdalla, A. M. (2020). The role of ecosystem for entrepreneurship development in Sudan. *World Journal of Entrepreneurship, Management and Sustainable Development, 16*(4), 307–326.

Arruda, C., et al. (2014). The Brazilian entrepreneurial ecosystem of startups: An analysis of entrepreneurship determinants in Brazil and the perceptions around the Brazilian Regulatory Framework. In R. L. L. Rovere & L. d. M. Ozório (Eds.), *Entrepreneurship in BRICS policy and research to support entrepreneurs* (pp. 9–26). Springer.

Audretsch, D. B., & Belitski, M. (2017). Entrepreneurial ecosystems in cities: Establishing the framework conditions. *The Journal of Technology Transfer, 42*(5), 1030–1051.

Bennett, D. L. (2019). Infrastructure investments and entrepreneurial dynamism in the U.S. *Journal of Business Venturing, 34*(5), 105907.

Borges, C., et al. (2018). Entrepreneurship policy in Brazil: Its focus and gaps. *International Journal of Entrepreneurship and Small Business, 34*(2), 184–203.

Darnihamedani, P., Block, J. H., Hessels, J., & Simonyan, A. (2018). Taxes, start-up costs, and innovative entrepreneurship. *Small Business Economics, 51*(2), 355–369.

Firman, J. (2014). Nine strategies to transform community service organizations that assist older adults. *Generations: Journal of the American Society on Aging, 38*(2), 60–66.
Global Entrepreneurship Monitor. (2020). *2020 entrepreneurial activity review*. Retrieved January 20, 2022, from https://www.gemconsortium.org/economy-profiles/brazil-2
Global Entrepreneurship Monitor. (2022). *Global entrepreneurship monitor: What is the National Expert Survey (NES)?*. Retrieved February 6, 2022, from https://www.gemconsortium.org/wiki/1142
Globalization Partners. (2021). *Doing business in Brazil: 7 things you should know*. Retrieved January 19, 2022, from https://www.globalization-partners.com/blog/why-expanding-a-business-to-brazil-is-a-serious-challenge/#gref
Isenberg, D. (2010). *The big idea: How to start an entrepreneurial revolution*. Retrieved February 9, 2022, from https://hbr.org/2010/06/the-big-idea-how-to-start-an-entrepreneurial-revolution
Klapper, L., Laeven, L., & Rajan, R. (2006). Entry regulation as a barrier to entrepreneurship. *Journal of Financial Economics, 82*(3), 591–629.
Korn Ferry. (2018). *Future of work: The Global Talent Crunch*. Retrieved January 20, 2022, from https://focus.kornferry.com/wp-content/uploads/2015/02/The-Global-Talent-Crunch.pdf
Monsen, L. (2020). *In the U.S., it's easy to start a small business*. Retrieved February 9, 2022, from https://share.america.gov/in-u-s-its-easy-to-start-small-business/
OECD. (2018a). *Getting skills right: Brazil (skills needs and skills imbalances)*. Retrieved January 21, 2022, from https://www.oecd-ilibrary.org/sites/9789264309838-5-en/index.html?itemId=/content/component/9789264309838-5-en
OECD. (2018b). *Reviews of national policies for education, rethinking quality assurance for higher education in Brazil: Higher education in Brazil*. Retrieved February 10, 2022, from https://www.oecd-ilibrary.org/sites/9789264309050-6-en/index.html?itemId=/content/component/9789264309050-6-en
OECD. (2020). *The business environment for SMEs and entrepreneurship in Brazil*. Retrieved January 17, 2022, from https://www.oecd-ilibrary.org/sites/2eecb1b7-en/index.html?itemId=/content/component/2eecb1b7-en
OECD. (2021). *Education Policy Outlook Brazil*. Retrieved January 21, 2022, from https://www.oecd.org/education/policy-outlook/country-profile-Brazil-2021-EN.pdf
Orobia, L. A., Tusiime, I., Mwesigwa, R., & Ssekiziyivu, B. (2020). Entrepreneurial framework conditions and business sustainability among the youth and women entrepreneurs. *Asia Pacific Journal of Innovation and Entrepreneurship, 14*(1), 60–75.
Radulovic, D. M. (2015). *Why talent shortages are a risk to global business*. Retrieved January 21, 2022, from https://www.weforum.org/agenda/2015/04/why-talent-shortages-are-a-risk-to-global-business/
Ratten, V. (2020a). Coronavirus and international business: An entrepreneurial ecosystem perspective. *Thunderbird International Business Review, 62*(5), 629–634.
Ratten, V. (2020b). Entrepreneurial ecosystems. *Thunderbird International Business Review, 62*(5), 447–455.
Ratten, V. (2020c). Entrepreneurial ecosystems: The role of accelerators. In V. Ratten (Ed.), *Entrepreneurship as empowerment: Knowledge spillovers and entrepreneurial ecosystems* (pp. 11–22). Emerald Publishing Limited.
Rolfe, D. (2020). *COVID-19: The stand up moment for Australia's startups*. Retrieved February 10, 2022, from https://aicd.companydirectors.com.au/membership/company-director-magazine/2020-back-editions/may/covid-19-the-stand-up-moment-for-australias-startups
Souza, P. B. B. d., Oliveira, R. E. d., & Yukari, C. (2019). *Infrastructure projects in Brazil: The road to partnerships*. Retrieved January 20, 2022, from https://www.financierworldwide.com/infrastructure-projects-in-brazil-the-road-to-partnerships#.YejqAS0Rq8U
Spigel, B. (2017). The relational organization of entrepreneurial ecosystems. *Entrepreneurship Theory and Practice, 41*(1), 49–72.
Sussan, F., & Acs, Z. J. (2017). The digital entrepreneurial ecosystem. *Small Business Economics, 49*(1), 55–73.

Thukral, E. (2021). COVID-19: Small and medium enterprises challenges and responses with creativity, innovation, and entrepreneurship. *Strategic Change, 30*(2), 153–158.

Thukral, E. (2022). Entrepreneurship in Australia: Social values and perception. In V. Ratten (Ed.), *Oceania entrepreneurship* (pp. 127–135). Palgrave Macmillan.

Tietz, G., Anholon, R., Ordonez, R. E. C., & Quelhas, O. L. (2015). Business incubators in Brazil: Main gaps to be explored by academic researchers. *Journal of Technology Management & Innovation, 10*(4), 18–27.

TMF Group. (2021). *Doing business in Brazil: What you should know*. Retrieved January 18, 2022, from https://www.tmf-group.com/en/news-insights/articles/2018/august/doing-business-in-brazil/

World Bank Group. (2020). *Doing business 2020*. Retrieved January 18, 2022, from https://documents1.worldbank.org/curated/en/688761571934946384/pdf/Doing-Business-2020-Comparing-Business-Regulation-in-190-Economies.pdf

World Economic Forum. (2013). *Entrepreneurial ecosystems around the globe and company growth dynamics*. World Economic Forum.

World Economic Forum. (2018). *Quality of overall infrastructure*. Retrieved January 20, 2022, from http://reports.weforum.org/global-competitiveness-index-2017-2018/competitiveness-rankings/#series=EOSQ056

Toward an Entrepreneurial University: Analysis of the Fluminense Federal University Initiatives and Trajectory

Thalyta de Sá Carvalho Velasco, Edilane dos Reis Carraro, and Marcelo Amaral

Abstract This study aims to identify the transformations from the structural and political point of view at the Fluminense Federal University (UFF) toward an Entrepreneurial University. To this end, the degree of UFF's evolution and maturity will be verified as such. We then expect to recommend actions to accelerate the institution's evolution in this direction. The authors carried out exploratory research with a qualitative approach to achieve the defined objectives. A review of the literature was carried out, using bibliometric analysis techniques, in themes like Entrepreneurial University and university-company interaction, based on Web of Science, Scopus, and Scielo publications. Primary data generation was done with a survey forwarded to two groups of people. The first group, formed by UFF's undergraduate courses coordinators, managers of the institution and some of its departments and academic units, and professors who had critical experiences related to the theme, received the research through direct e-mail. The second group responded through a social network platform in a group of university professors to identify structural and political transformations at the University. The analysis of the information collected allowed the application of the model developed by Oliveira and Amaral (Gestão nos Institutos Federais de Educação: experiências e aplicações, PPGA/UFF, 2020) to understand the UFF's evolution stage as an entrepreneurial institution. As a result, the professors of the institution have relatively low knowledge regarding the theme and the mechanisms to support innovation, both at the federal level and at the institution itself, while there is a good performance of interaction activities. With the application of the Oliveira-Amaral maturity assessment model, it was possible to position the institution at level 2 on a scale from 0 to 6, which means a low entrepreneurial positioning. The sampling for the survey was defined by convenience, without a statistical basis. This selection was made to enable the research by sending the survey to a sample of the accessible population. This research takes a picture of the current moment of UFF regarding what would lead to it being

T. de Sá Carvalho Velasco · E. dos Reis Carraro · M. Amaral (✉)
Triple Helix Research Group (THERG-Brazil), Postgraduate Program in Administration, Institute of Human and Social Sciences, Fluminense Federal University, Volta Redonda, RJ, Brazil

J. Leitão et al. (eds.), *Brazilian Entrepreneurship*, Studies on Entrepreneurship, Structural Change and Industrial Dynamics,
https://doi.org/10.1007/978-3-031-09392-0_6

understood as an Entrepreneurial University. According to the Oliveira-Amaral Model, it brings the institution's current needs and, from the application of this model, combined with the poll answered by a sample of the institution's professors, actions are indicated to solve such needs. Furthermore, understanding a lack of knowledge by UFF regarding Federal Laws and Norms to support innovation, two conceptual frameworks on the subject are presented.

Keywords Entrepreneurial University · Maturity model · University–company interaction

1 Introduction

Entrepreneurship can be understood essentially as the creation of new companies, and it has been identified as one of the main trends in the business administration area since the 1990s. However, it is more than just creating companies (Audretsch, 2003). The economic relevance of entrepreneurship is indisputable and institutions are being developed and modified to facilitate such activity, which serves as the underlying driving force for economic growth and prosperity (Wennekers & Thurik, 1999; Shane & Venkataraman, 2000; Acs & Szerb, 2007).

A constant actor in several studies, universities can be considered the central player in both innovation and entrepreneurship (Reinolds & De Negri, 2019). They create the knowledge needed to innovate (Feller, 1990; Fini et al., 2011) and interact with other actors in the innovation system, such as the productive sector and the government, forming a set of bilateral and trilateral relationships that support such activities (Amaral et al., 2020).

Therefore, it is essential to understand the role of the University in the twenty-first-century knowledge society (Etzkowitz & Leydesdorff, 2000). A second academic revolution is underway in which the University incorporates a new mission to participate and lead the process of regional economic development. This University, with missions of education, research, and economic development, is called entrepreneurial (Etzkowitz, 2003, 2004) and the academics are so-called entrepreneurial scientists (Stuart & Ding, 2006).

Brazil is characterized as a late development economy, and implementing a system of science and technology and innovation (S&T&I) was also late (De Negri, 2021). Both academic revolutions, the first and second, have been underway since the 1990s. Important frameworks for the development of university–industry–government interaction were, among others, the approval of Law no. 10,973/2004 (Innovation Law), Law no. 11,196/2005 (Law of Good), and Law no. 13,243/2016 (Legal Framework of S&T&I) (Brasil, 2004, 2016). However, even after nearly 25 years of transition, the helices of goods and services production (knowledge users) and S&T (knowledge creators) are still close to each other (Reinolds & De Negri, 2019).

In this context, it is crucial to study the Brazilian public research university and the transition toward an Entrepreneurial University (as done in Aranha & Garcia,

2013; Dias & Porto, 2013, 2014). The federal and state systems perform more than 90% of the country's research (De Negri, 2021). For this purpose, the largest institution in the federal system is the focus of this chapter, the Fluminense Federal University (Universidade Federal Fluminense—UFF), based in the State of Rio de Janeiro, with about 65,000 students and 3500 faculty body members.

Since 1997, UFF has had initiatives that characterize the incorporation of the third mission (Almeida & Amaral, 2019). Such effort was consolidated in the Institutional Innovation Policy launched in 2020 (UFF, 2020). This policy establishes guidelines, standards, and objectives to manage technological and social innovation at the University, to facilitate interaction with companies, other social organizations, and funding bodies in innovation projects. In addition, the policy defines procedures on several important topics in the establishment of these partnerships.

This study's general and guiding objective is to verify UFF's degree of evolution toward an Entrepreneurial University. We will apply a university–industry–government–society maturity model developed by Oliveira and Amaral (2020) to perform the assessment. The steps corresponding to the specific objectives include (1) Developing a literature review on the subject; (2) Identifying the institutional (structural and political) changes at UFF; (3) Applying the maturity model; and (4) Proposing actions to accelerate the UFF transition toward an Entrepreneurial University.

Oliveira (2019) also highlighted that "it is observed that it is possible to adopt processes to improve their management levels with maturity models." Based on the above mentioned, this research will immerse in the relevant literature about academic themes like Entrepreneurial University and Triple Helix. Besides, a survey was applied to UFF course coordinators and managers to identify changes from a structural and political point of view toward a new university. Finally, the degree of evolution of the institution as an entrepreneur will be verified by applying the maturity model developed in Oliveira's dissertation (2019) and published in Oliveira and Amaral (2020).

This chapter is structured in four parts besides this introduction: theoretical foundation, methodological procedures, presentation of results, and conclusion.

2 Theoretical Foundation

This brief review section is structured in two parts. One deals with the concept of Entrepreneurial University, and the second one presents some ideas of university–industry–government interaction.

2.1 Entrepreneurial University

From World War II onward, the University evolved from Humboldt's model of teaching associated with research to be an essential source of knowledge for a robust

Table 1 Evolution of the university's mission from academic revolutions

Expansion of the University's mission		
Teaching	Research	Entrepreneurial
Preservation and dissemination of knowledge	First academic revolution	Second academic revolution
New missions generate controversy over conflicts of interest	Two missions: teaching and research	Third mission: economic and social development (keeping previous missions)

Source: Etzkowitz (2003)

economic performance of nations (Etzkowitz et al., 2008). Although such a change has increased the importance and significance of the academy in terms of its impact on the economy, it has not significantly altered the University's functions and activities (Lester, 2005; Audretsch, 2012). The first reports that brought an embryonic entrepreneurial academic dynamic emerged in North American universities by the end of the nineteenth century when the lack of a formal research funding system analyzed individual and collective initiatives to obtain resources to support research (Etzkowitz, 2003).

The University's role has evolved considerably by embracing a new mandate for society to directly facilitate entrepreneurial activity to promote economic growth and prosperity (Schulte, 2004; Audretsch, 2014). The so-called second academic revolution is characterized by the inclusion of economic and social development as a new mission in universities, together with teaching and research. The University's ability to transform knowledge into economic activity is the premise of entrepreneurial behavior. Such a university encompasses and expands the teaching and research university, as shown in Table 1 (Etzkowitz, 2003).

Universities assume an entrepreneurial role and identity due to the perception of opportunity, civic duty, and external pressures. The first step toward creating a culture for a new university is increasing sensitivity to the economic potential of knowledge, both scientific and humanistic, followed by a willingness to realize this potential (Kirby, 2005; Kalar & Antoncic, 2015; Etzkowitz, 2016).

For Doutriaux (1987), Chrisman et al. (1995), Clark (1998), Patzelt and Shepherd (2009), and Perkmann et al. (2013), the core of academic entrepreneurship is the process of a professor engaged in entrepreneurial behavior. Thus, an entrepreneurial institution can be defined as a university that adopts a coherent strategy to leverage research and teaching in its third mission. This institution also considers and coordinates the efforts for academic entrepreneurship, technology transfer, start-ups and spin-offs, entrepreneurial education (curricular or co-curricular), industry collaboration, and regional and economic development policy (Rothaermel et al., 2007). This third mission can be defined as a "commercial engagement" (Vorley & Nelles, 2009) and as "contributing to innovation and social change" (Gulbrandsen & Slipersaeter, 2007, p. 112).

A central premise for entrepreneurship research and the broader management field is that value creation through entrepreneurship and innovation are key drivers for countries' economic growth (Wennekers & Thurik, 1999).

2.2 University–Industry–Government Interaction

The interaction between a University and industry has played a significant role in technological innovations, consequently contributing to the country's economic development (Rosa et al., 2018). Governments, universities, and companies are constantly interacting to stimulate economic growth and create value in their regions.

The conceptual frameworks that capture this collective quest to promote value-creating activities include the so-called Triple Helix model (Etzkowitz & Leydesdorff, 2000). As well as other approaches such as information systems clustering (Porter, 2000; Engel, 2015), regional innovation projects (Cooke, 2001), innovation districts (Albino et al., 1998), and entrepreneurial ecosystems (Isenberg, 2010; Stam, 2015; Cavallo et al., 2018).

In the constant effort to create products, services, and technological processes, universities and research centers are essential structures for an innovation system to promote economic development (Faria et al., 2013). In the university–industry interaction study, it is necessary to analyze it considering the motivations and obstacles of each actor in this process, as suggested in Fig. 1, developed by Bonaccorsi and Piccaluga (1994).

The dynamics of innovation are linked to the integration processes between organizations and agents that allow the generation, reproduction, and feedback of learning processes and help convert them into innovative activity (Mota, 1999). Among the University's roles, it is possible to find the provision of human resources (as in the case of consultancy), scientific discoveries, creation of new businesses through spin-offs and start-ups. It is up to companies to play a role in managing assets, taxes, research, development, and capital venture investments, in addition to making suggestions about industrial needs (Wu et al., 2018).

Since 2004, in the Brazilian scenery, new perspectives and possibilities have emerged for S&T&I, with the creation of laws, special regimes, and incentive programs according to the legislation summarized in Table 2 (Oliveira, 2019).

3 Research Design and Procedures

The present research effort was built on information collected and organized in two parts: (1) Construction of literature review, and (2) Applied field research. The references collection was focused on exploring the issues of university–industry interaction and Entrepreneurial University literature, considering the research base and the key theme. The applied research uses data collected through a survey addressed to the UFF faculty body, split into groups like managers, leaders of departments and academic units, and professors who have had critical experiences related to the topic.

In the systematic literature review, the documents collected from academic databases Web of Science (WOS), Scopus, and Scielo were organized in a Microsoft

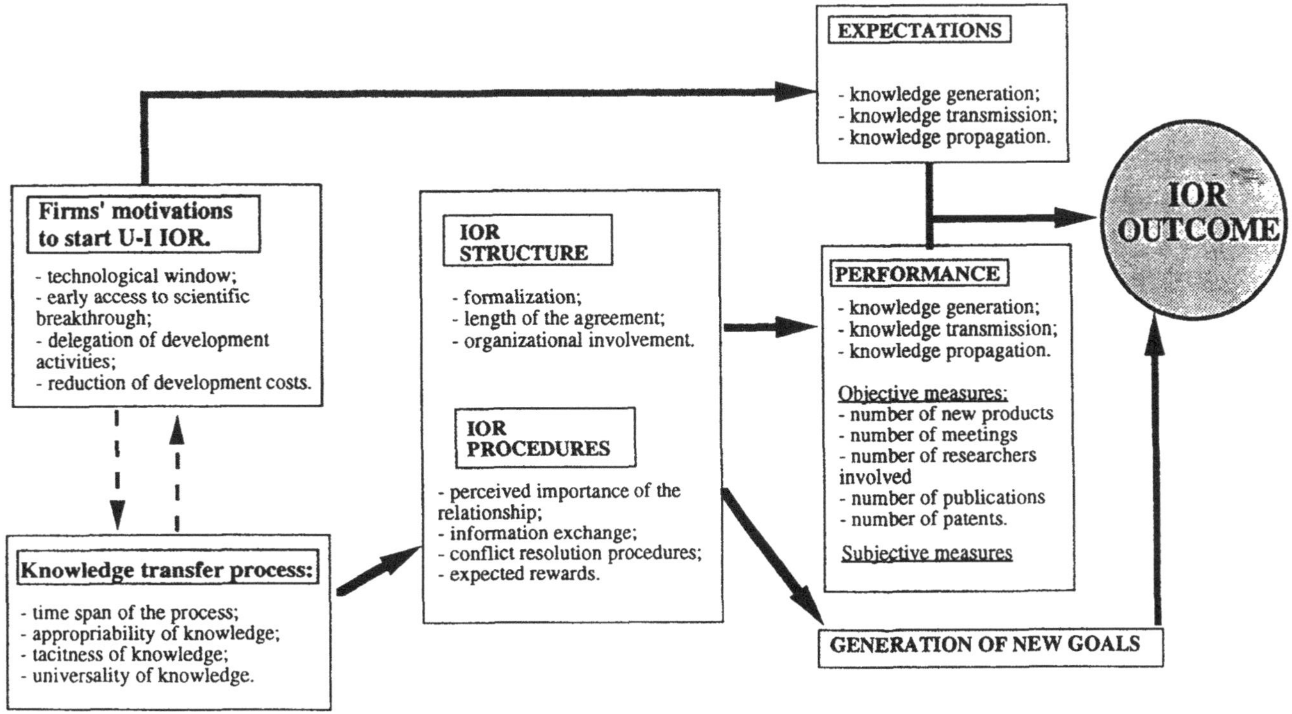

Fig. 1 University–company interaction. (Source: Bonaccorsi and Piccaluga 1994)

Table 2 Innovation supporting legislation

Law Nr. 9279/1996	Rights and obligations related to the industrial property (IP)
Innovation Law (Nr. 10,973/2004)	Encourages innovation and scientific and technological research in the business environment and the participation of researchers from public academic institutions in research projects in partnership with companies (De Negri, 2021).
Law of Good (Nr. 11,196/2005)	Creates tax incentives for technological innovation, the special regimes of taxation for the information technology services export, and the Digital Inclusion Program (Zucoloto et al., 2017).
S&T&I Framework (Nr. 13,243/2016)	Amendments to the Innovation Law allow the possibility of direct funding by foundations to support research, scientific and technological training, and innovation (Rauen & Turchi, 2017).
Law Nr. 13,674/2018 and Law Nr. 3969/2019	Provides industrial policy (financial credit) for the information and communication technology sector and the semiconductor sector (Brasil, 2018, 2019).
Law Nr. 13,800/2019	Creates endowment funds in the country, providing the preservation of the main value, consisting of donations received.

Source: Developed by the authors based on Oliveira (2019)

Excel spreadsheet. In this process, the academic papers were classified by the number of citations, number of documents published per country, journals where they were published, authors, temporal evolution, and abstract. Table 3 details the process search and the results obtained.

The applied research was guided by developing a questionnaire based on the Oliveira-Amaral maturity model, published in 2020, which was proposed and validated in a case study in another public research institution. The questionnaire was divided into four parts, with complementary targets, namely:

- Collect the profile of respondents.
- Explore the familiarity of the faculty body with academic discussions and models on Entrepreneurial University and university–industry–government relationship.
- Identify the perception of the faculty body about the interaction with internal innovation support bodies at UFF.
- Collect information about the participation of faculty members in activities of generation, appropriation, and dissemination of technical-scientific knowledge.

The information collection was conducted from May 2019 to July 2020. The study intended to conduct other interviews, which was impossible due to the COVID-19 pandemic.

In order to apply the model, a chart of maturity levels was built, with indicators (Table 4). So, they could be individually assessed if present at UFF. Indicators were classified as "Yes" for those identified in the institution, "No" for those that were not performed, and "Partial" for those who are not fully present in the organization.

As for the limitations, the sample selection for survey responses should be mentioned, which, in this research, was defined by convenience, without a statistical basis. This selection was made to make the study feasible by sending the survey to a

Table 3 Platform search strategy

Topic	Basis	University–industry interaction	Entrepreneurial university
Search Strategy	WoS	TOPIC: ("universit* business collaborat*") OR TÓPICO: ("universit* industr* collaborat*")	TOPIC: "entreprene* university"
	Scopus	TITLE-ABS-KEY ("universit* business collaborat*" OR "universit* industr* collaborat*")	TITLE-ABS-KEY ("entreprene* university")
	Scielo	"University-company interaction" (all indexes)	"Entrepreneurial university" (all indexes)
Documents	WoS	815	634
	Scopus	937	889
	Scielo	21	10
Articles × others	WoS	465 × 350	416 × 218
	Scopus	579 × 358	618 × 271
	Scielo	21 × 0	10 × 0
Main authors	WoS	Igartua, J. (13); Fernandes, G. (11); Ganzarain, J. (11)	Etzkowitz, H. (18); Guerrero, M. (16); Urbano, D. (15)
	Scopus	Fernandes, G. (14); Machado, R. J. (11); Pinto, E.B. (10)	Etzkowitz, H. (27); Guerrero, M. (25); Urbano, D. (25)
	Scielo	Alves, A. (1); Pimenta-Bueno, J. (1); Garcia, R (1)	Volles, B. (1); Gomes, G. (1); Parisotto, I. (1)
Main titles/ journals	WoS	Inted Proceedings (54); Journal of Technology Transfer (37); Edulearn Proceedings (22)	Journal of Technology Transfer (27); Industry and Higher Education (17); Technological Forecasting and Social Change (16)
	Scopus	Journal of Technology Transfer (45); Industry and Higher Education (32); Research Policy (20)	Industry and Higher Education (45); Journal of Technology Transfer (28); Technological Forecasting and Social Change (19)
	Scielo	Production (3); EBAPE.BR supplements (2); Economic Studies (2)	EBAPE.BR supplements; REAd—Electronic Administration Magazine; society and state
Main countries	WoS	United States (101); England (85); Brazil (18)	United States (82); England (72); Brazil (24)
	Scopus	United States (131); United Kingdom (125); Brazil (16)	United Kingdom (139); United States (124); Brazil (30)
	Scielo	Brazil (20)	Brazil (9); Uruguay (1)

Source: Developed by the authors

sample of the accessible population and within the compatibility criteria of the research's target audience. Interviews can clarify some points of the information collected; however, face-to-face activities at the university were suspended in March

Table 4 Levels and indicators of Oliveira-Amaral Maturity Assessment Model

Indicator/metrics	Level
• Lack of decision by the Superior Council to create the technology transfer unit (Núcleo de Inovação—NIT)	0[a]
• Lack of Innovation Policy document	
• Absent from the institution's organizational chart	
• Non-existence of capitalization and use of financial resources	
• A decision of the Superior Council for the creation of NIT	1
• Innovation Policy Regulation	
• Presence in the institution's organizational chart and structure	
• Industrial Property Regulation (PIND)	
• Disseminate the culture of innovation	
• All from level 1+	2
• Mapping of research groups, laboratories, and potential technologies	
• PIND Catalog	
• All from level 2+	3
• Capitalization and use of financial resources	
• Number of contracts (or accesses in the case of open social technologies) and licensing revenue	
• Economic impact measures (decrease production cost, jobs creation, taxes, etc.)	
• Social impact measures (number of people served or benefited)	
• All from level 3+	4
• Structured management system or procedures	
• All from level 4+	5
• Revenue and volume of research and extension investment	
• All from level 5+	6
• Social contract	

Source: Oliveira and Amaral (2020). Adapted by the authors
[a] Except for Level 0, which must be identified as "No" in other levels, the element must be identified with "Yes" when present

2020. In the return of activities, there was a considerable accumulation of tasks. So, we decided to proceed with the collection of information.

4 Analysis of Results

4.1 Research Environment Characterization

Fluminense Federal University (UFF) was founded on December 18, 1960, by Law no. 3848. UFF received an economic development mission for the State Rio de Janeiro region (UFF, 2017). It has physical, academic units outside the headquarters, in Niterói, spread in ten municipalities in Rio de Janeiro and Pará. The organizational structure is based on 125 teaching departments, which offers 125 on-site undergraduate courses and 7 distance undergraduate courses, 133 *stricto* sensu postgraduate courses (64 academic master courses, 18 professional master courses, 51 doctoral courses), and 213 *lato* sensu postgraduate courses (156 specialization courses and 57 residency programs) (UFF, 2021).

UFF has 3543 faculty members, and the administrative staff has around 4662 people. The Institution offer education for 56,000 undergrad students and 9000 graduate students. The University identifies itself as having an innovation policy based on promoting interaction and learning between entities from the academic, business, and governmental institutional spheres (UFF, 2021). According to Service Bulletin nr. 189/2020, by the end of 2020, the institution took another step toward a more Entrepreneurial behavior by launching its Institutional Innovation Policy (IIP).

In recent decades, several actions were performed to align UFF with academic trends and spread a more entrepreneurial culture. It is possible to mention the creation of several mechanisms, courses, and sectors (Almeida & Amaral, 2019), like:

- The Technology-Based Business Incubator, in 1997.
- The Technology Commercialization Office (ETCO), in 2000.
- The Triple Helix Research Group (THERG-Brazil), in 2008.
- The Agency of Innovation, in 2009.
- The undergraduate course in Entrepreneurship and Innovation, in 2009.
- The Department of Entrepreneurship and Management, in 2013.

Table 5 presents some of the leading frameworks in regulating innovation activities at UFF.

Table 5 UFF innovation policies

Service Standard Nr. 518/2001	Provides rules on technology transfer and regulation of industrial property and computer programs.
Service Standard Nr. 529/2003	Creates the Knowledge Transfer Office (Escritório de Transferência de Conhecimento—ETCO).
Service Standard Nr. 603/2009	Provides procedures to be adopted in the relationship between UFF and its supporting foundations.
Service Standard Nr. 604/2009	Creates the Innovation Agency (AGIR), which focuses on disseminating the culture of innovation.
Institutional Innovation Policy (UFF, 2020)	Establishes a strategic institutional framework of guidelines, norms, and objectives regarding technological and social innovation at the University. The articles follow the priorities of the National Science, Technology, and Innovation Policy and the National Industrial and Technological Policy. The proposal facilitates UFF's interaction with companies, other civil society organizations, and funding agencies in innovation projects.

Source: Developed by the authors based on UFF (2020)

Table 6 Institutional time of professors at UFF

Item	Classifier	
Training	Doctorate	
Time at the institution	10 years or more	21
	From 5 to 10 years	8
	Less than 5 years	7
Career level	Adjunct professors	53%
	Associate professors	36%
	Full professors	11%
Management/leadership positions at UFF	Occupy or have occupied	56%
	Never occupied	44%

Source: Developed by the authors

4.2 Description of Results

The first two parts of the survey aimed to identify the profile and training of the 36 respondents, identifying the faculty profile. The division of time at the institution by the groups can be seen in Table 6.

Respondents are familiar, not as expected but familiar, with academic discussions and models about Entrepreneurial University and the university–industry–government relationship. On the other hand, there was a marked lack of knowledge regarding Quadruple Helix, followed by expertise regarding Triple Helix. The discussion about university–company collaboration was the largest one in the professors' responses, as shown in Fig. 2.

Regarding the perception of the institution's position as to Entrepreneurial University discussion, 51% of the valid responses indicated that UFF has some areas and groups with an entrepreneurial profile, but that they are specific dynamics that do not affect the entire institution. Such respondents believe that the issue is relevant but not a priority, as there are other emerging issues (in the context of the crisis in recent years) (Fig. 3).

Another important factor when discussing the relationship between research professors and the bodies responsible for innovation activities within UFF is identifying the limitations to executing concrete actions. The respondents mentioned three reasons. First, the internal bureaucracy. Second, the lack of resources (financial, specialized people, and working structure). And, finally, the lack of dissemination/clarification about the legal implications of the university–industry–government interactions (the faculty body has a 40 h per week exclusive dedication to the University and as a civil servant they cannot participate in activities outside UFF). The improvements required to enhance the collaboration involve (1) the improvement of the disclosure of internal support bodies; (2) the development of an innovation-oriented institutional agenda; (3) the clarification and education of the academic community about inherent regulatory aspects, such as laws and internal regulation; and (4) the creation of legal and institutional assistance dynamics to

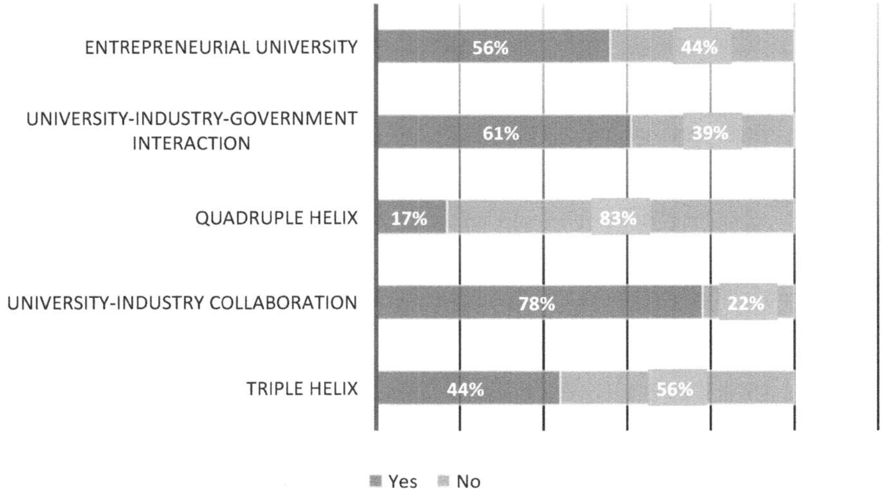

Fig. 2 Prior knowledge of U–I–G interaction. (Source: Developed by the authors)

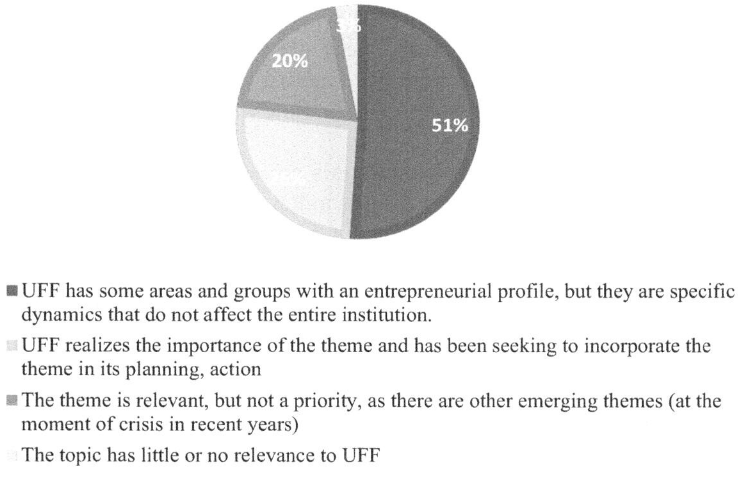

Fig. 3 Professors' perception of entrepreneurship at UFF. (Source: Developed by the authors)

remove part of the managerial burden from the faculty, due to the number of activities that are required.

The results showed a low percentage of knowledge about legal instruments and mechanisms. Also, the survey shows a low level of knowledge about internal UFF's regulations or initiatives to support innovation and the low use of these internal instruments. Only 12.2% of all surveyed faculty know and have applied the internal rules in some way, and, in some topics, the rate of total ignorance of service rules reaches 80.3%. Another point observed is that activities in partnership with NGOs (third sector) are the ones that figured least among those carried out. On the other hand, the activity of formalizing "umbrella" agreements for research, carried out in partnership with government agencies, was predominantly mentioned as known and performed by professors who already occupy or have occupied leadership or management positions. Related to other activities, like individual consultancy (paid or free), lectures, participation in events, seminars, technical visits, and research and extension projects without contract/development agreement, both groups (managers and non-managers) know and use the procedures. However, the number of contracts is more significant among professors who have never held positions in the university structure.

4.3 Application of the Maturity Assessment Model

Based on the responses and the documents about UFF, all the indicators present in the Oliveira-Amaral maturity assessment model were analyzed. Some of the indicators at levels 3, 4, and 5 were identified as being carried out within the institution. However, to reach these levels, all activities at the individual level of the scale need to be achieved.

In the current assessment of the institution, it is possible to see that UFF is at Level 2, with possibilities to migrate to Level 3. The university needs to act on the "capitalization and use of resources," via the Agency of Innovation, and in measures on the economic and social impact to reach the next level.

Table 7 presents the indicators one by one according to their identification in the university structure, being: "Yes," for those identified in the institution, "No," for those that were not identified, and "Partial" for those that have not been implemented yet.

The need for better detailing or exemplifying some activities was observed by applying the model. Different universities have different structures, cultures, and strategies. In terms of legal requirements, according to the Integrated Management Report (UFF, 2021, 2020), the University approved an Institutional Innovation Policy in 2020. This policy establishes a strategic institutional framework of guidelines, norms, and objectives for technological and social innovation in the University. The approach also facilitates interaction with companies, other civil society organizations, and funding bodies in innovation projects. The policy implementation is the basis for further development.

4.4 Analysis

To analyze the results arising from the survey and the application of the Oliveira-Amaral maturity assessment model, we used Clark's (1998) research. In a study of

Table 7 Application of Oliveira-Amaral Model at UFF

Indicator/metrics	Identified	Level
• Lack of decision by the Superior Council to create NIT	No	0
• Lack of Innovation Policy document	No	
• Absence on the institution's organizational chart	No	
• Non-existence of capitalization and use of financial resources	Yes	
• A decision of the Superior Council for the creation of NIT	Yes	1
• Innovation Policy Regulation	Yes	
• Presence in the institution's organizational chart and structure	Yes	
• PIND regulation	Yes	
• Disseminate the culture of innovation	Partial	
• Mapping research groups, laboratories, and potential technologies	Partial	2
• PIND Catalog	Yes	
• Mapping research groups and potential technologies	Partial	3
• PIND Catalog	Yes	
• Capitalization and use of resources	No	
• Number of contracts (or accesses in the case of open social technologies) and licensing revenue	Yes	
• Economic impact measures (decrease production cost, jobs creation, taxes, etc.)	No	
• Social impact measures (number of people served or benefited)	No	
• Mapping research groups and potential technologies	Partial	4
• PIND Catalogs	Yes	
• Number of contracts (or accesses in the case of open social technologies) and licensing revenue	Yes	
• Economic impact measures (decrease production cost, jobs creation, taxes, etc.)	No	
• Social impact measures (number of people served or benefited)	No	
• Structured management system or procedures	No	
• Mapping research groups and potential technologies	Partial	5
• PIND Catalogs	Yes	
• No contracts (or access in the case of open social technologies) and licensing revenue	Yes	
• Revenue and volume of research and extension investment	No	
• Economic impact measures (decrease production cost, jobs creation, taxes, etc.)	No	
• Social impact measures (number of people served or benefited)	No	
• Structured management system or procedures	No	
• Social contract	No	6
• Mapping research groups and potential technologies	Partial	
• PIND Catalogs	Yes	
• Number of contracts (or accesses in the case of open social technologies) and licensing revenue	Yes	
• Revenue and volume of research and extension investment	No	
• Economic impact measures (decrease production cost, jobs creation, taxes, etc.)	No	

(continued)

Table 7 (continued)

Indicator/metrics	Identified	Level
• Social impact measures (number of people served or benefited)	No	
• Structured management system or procedures	No	

Source: Developed by the authors

five different universities that were in the process of change, this author identified a set of predominant elements in these organizations. At UFF, it is essential to emphasize that several respondents stated that the institution has some areas and groups with an entrepreneurial profile. Still, these are specific dynamics that do not correspond to the entire faculty body. The lack of knowledge or distancing from the themes was also reflected in the professors' low-level identification of the concepts closely linked to Entrepreneurial University, such as university–industry relationship and the Triple and Quadruple Helix models.

As a counterpoint to the lack of knowledge or distancing from the discussion about this new University's role, there is an intense insertion in the surroundings, by activities such as individual consultancy and offering lectures, conducting academic research, with the participation of professors from other departments and institutions. Regarding the activities of creation, appropriation, and dissemination of technical-scientific knowledge, we could observe the involvement of external partners. We can highlight partnerships with other universities and companies and business entities (including the National Service of Industrial Training—SENAI, Brazilian Micro and Small Business Support Service—SEBRAE, and similar ones) and government agencies, in detriment to NGOs and other kinds of organizations.

In general, significant advances were being and were designed from the publication of the Institutional Development Plan 2018–2022 and the Institutional Innovation Policy. However, they are not yet disseminated in the organization's culture, which would elevate the University to more advanced levels while entrepreneurial player. The excess of missions (teaching, research, and extension) combined with the emergence of social themes linked to minorities (like diversity, gender, social inclusion, among others) has left the theme of innovation and entrepreneurship in the low-level priority in the organization's discourse and practice.

5 Conclusion

In the current socio-economic scenario, it is possible to verify that the evolution of a society is directly linked to the capacity to structure investments in S&T&I in a reliable way. In this context, the University assumes a central role in economic development—besides teaching, research, and extension vocation—by forming alliances with external players, such as companies and government agencies. This proposal gives universities the challenge of aligning with this new reality in developing an entrepreneurial profile. Thus, it is necessary to understand the moment in which the institution is currently prepared to start a transition plan.

Based on the scenario of transformation of the University's role worldwide, this research had as a general and guiding objective to verify UFF's degree of evolution as an entrepreneurial university. The study was developed based on applying the maturity assessment model developed by Oliveira and Amaral (2020). In order to achieve it, bibliographical research was carried out to expand applied theoretical and exploratory knowledge. Then, to enter the study environment, UFF's structural and political aspects were analyzed, mainly through its internal rules and formal plans. The Oliveira-Amaral model was carried out and the consequent understanding of the gaps in the institution about entrepreneurial evolution.

As a final part of the work, it is possible to recommend actions to accelerate UFF's evolution toward entrepreneurial status. It seems urgent to produce a map of the institution's research groups to be accessible to possible external users. There is already an initiative along with social technologies, but without renouncing traditional technologies. In addition, the University needs to find a legal and simple way to provide technological services, obtain resources from services and licensing, and have an autonomous budget at the Agency of Innovation. We found initiatives to work closely with a private nonprofit foundation, but the process is complex and has several transaction costs.

As for the limitations of the research, we can discuss two aspects. First, the method of selecting the respondents' sample in the survey brought a limitation to the study. Then, we faced research difficulties due to the uncertainties created by the COVID-19 pandemics in 2020 and 2021. Second, regarding the assessment model used, the need to improve the description of activities of each level was observed. The order of how some activities are developed may be different at different institutions. One of the suggestions for change is to open the chart of levels for identifying or not of each of the activities/indicators, making it easier to visualize the steps already taken, to be carried out, or even that is already partially carried out.

For future studies, the survey can be expanded and replicated at UFF, supplemented with interviews and case studies. The reapplication of the model in 5 or 10-years horizons will verify the advances toward an Entrepreneurial University. Extending the maturity assessment model to other institutions will test and bring more robustness to the model, allowing a comparison between the results found.

References

Acs, Z. J., & Szerb, L. (2007). Entrepreneurship, economic growth and public policy. *Small Business Economics, 28*(2), 109–122. https://doi.org/10.1007/s11187-006-9012-3

Albino, V., Garavelli, A. C., & Schiuma, G. (1998). Knowledge transfer and inter-firm relationships in industrial districts: The role of the leader firm. *Technovation, 19*(1), 53–63. https://doi.org/10.1016/S0166-4972(98)00078-9

Almeida, F., & Amaral, M. (2019). Conceptual Framework for Assessment Entrepreneurial Education. *International Journal of Knowledge, Innovation and Entrepreneurship.*

Amaral, M., Faria, A., & Schocair, M. (2020). Assessing the innovation environment of the research triangle region. *Revista de Administração, Sociedade e Inovação, 6*(2), 90–111. https://doi.org/10.20401/rasi.6.2.386
Aranha, E., & Garcia, N. (2013). A Análise da Universidade Empreendedora no Contexto Brasileiro. *Revista da Faculdade de Administração e Economia (ReFAE), 5*(1), 101–126. https://doi.org/10.15603/2176-9583/refae.v5n1p101-126
Audretsch, D. B. (2003). *Entrepreneurship: A survey of the literature*. Office for Official Publications of the European Communities.
Audretsch, D. B. (2012). Entrepreneurship research. *Management Decision, 50*(5), 755–764. https://doi.org/10.1108/00251741211227384
Audretsch, D. B. (2014). From the entrepreneurial university to the university for the entrepreneurial society. *The Journal of Technology Transfer, 39*(3), 313–321. https://doi.org/10.1007/s10961-012-9288-1
Bonaccorsi, A., & Piccaluga, A. (1994). A theoretical framework for the evaluation of university-industry relationships. *R&D Management, 24*(3), 229–247. https://doi.org/10.1111/j.1467-9310.1994.tb00876.x
Brasil. (2004). *Lei. 10.973, de 02 de dezembro de 2004*. Dispõe sobre incentivos à inovação e à pesquisa científica e tecnológica no ambiente produtivo e dá outras providências. Diário Oficial da União
Brasil. (2016). *Lei. 13.243, de 11 de janeiro de 2016*. Dispõe sobre estímulos ao desenvolvimento científico, à pesquisa, à capacitação científica e tecnológica e à inovação e altera a Lei n° 10.973, de 2 de dezembro de 2004. Diário Oficial da União
Brasil. (2018). Lei 13,674 de 11 de junho de 2018. Dispõe sobre benefícios fiscais para as empresas de desenvolvimento ou produção de bens e serviços de tecnologias da informação e comunicação que investirem em atividades de pesquisa, desenvolvimento e inovação. Diário Oficial da União.
Brasil. (2019). Lei 13,800 de 4 de janeiro de 2019. Dispõe sobre a constituição de fundos patrimoniais com o objetivo de arrecadar, gerir e destinar doações de pessoas físicas e jurídicas privadas para programas, projetos e demais finalidades de interesse público. Diário Oficial da União.
Cavallo, A., Ghezzi, A., & Balocco, R. (2018). Entrepreneurial ecosystem research: Present debates and future directions. *International Entrepreneurship and Management Journal, 15*(3), 1–24. https://doi.org/10.1007/s11365-018-0526-3
Chrisman, J. J., Hynes, T., & Fraser, S. (1995). Faculty entrepreneurship and economic development: The case of the University of Calgary. *Journal of Business Venturing, 10*(4), 267–281. https://doi.org/10.1016/0883-9026(95)00015-Z
Clark, B. R. (1998). *Creating entrepreneurial universities: Organizational pathways of transformation. Issues in higher education*. International Association of Universities.
Cooke, P. (2001). Regional innovation systems, clusters, and the knowledge economy. *Industrial and Corporate Change, 10*(4), 945–974. https://doi.org/10.1093/ICC/10.4.945
De Negri, F. (2021). *New pathways for innovation in Brazil*. IPEA - Instituto de Pesquisas Avançadas.
Dias, A. A., & Porto, G. S. (2013). Gestão de transferência de tecnologia na Inova Unicamp. *Revista de Administração Contemporânea (RAC), 17*(3). https://doi.org/10.1590/S1415-65552013000300002
Dias, A. A., & Porto, G. S. (2014). Como a USP transfere tecnologia? *Organizações & Sociedade, 21*(70), 489–507. https://doi.org/10.1590/S1984-92302014000300008
Doutriaux, J. (1987). Growth pattern of academic entrepreneurial firms. *Journal of Business Venturing, 2*(4), 285–297. https://doi.org/10.1016/0883-9026(87)90022-X
Engel, J. S. (2015). Global clusters of innovation: Lessons from Silicon Valley. *California Management Review, 57*(2), 36–65. https://doi.org/10.1525/cmr.2015.57.2.36

Etzkowitz, H. (2003). Innovation in innovation: The triple helix of university-industry-government relations. *Social Science Information, 42*(3), 293–337. https://doi.org/10.1177/05390184030423002

Etzkowitz, H. (2004). The evolution of the entrepreneurial university. *International Journal of Technology and Globalization, 1*(1), 64–77. https://doi.org/10.1504/IJTG.2004.004551

Etzkowitz, H. (2016). The entrepreneurial university: Vision and metrics. *Industry and Higher Education, 30*(2), 83–97. https://doi.org/10.5367/ihe.2016.0303

Etzkowitz, H., & Leydesdorff, L. (2000). The dynamics of innovation: From National Systems and "Mode 2" to a Triple Helix of university–industry–government relations. *Research Policy, 29*(2), 109–123. https://doi.org/10.1016/S0048-7333(99)00055-4

Etzkowitz, H., Ranga, M., Benner, M., Guaranys, L., Maculan, A. M., & Kneller, R. (2008). Pathways to the entrepreneurial university: Towards a global convergence. *Science and Public Policy, 35*(9), 681–695. https://doi.org/10.3152/030234208X389701

Faria, A., Suzuki, J., Almeida, A., Rodrigues, M., Vidigal, C., Ferreira, N., & Mendonça, P. (2013). Promoção da interação universidade-empresa: estudo de caso do CenTev/UFV. In *ALTEC - Congresso Latino e Ibero Americano de Gestão da Inovação,* Porto.

Feller, I. (1990). Universities as engines of R&D-based economic growth: They think they can. *Research Policy, 19*(4), 335–348.

Fini, R., Grimaldi, R., Santoni, S., & Sobrero, M. (2011). Complements or substitutes? The role of universities and local context in supporting the creation of academic spin-offs. *Research Policy, 40*(8), 1113–1127.

Gulbrandsen, M., & Slipersaeter, S. (2007). The third mission and the entrepreneurial university model. In C. D. A. Bonaccorsi (Ed.), *Universities and strategic knowledge creation: Specialization and performance in Europe* (pp. 112–143). Edward Elgar Publishing.

Isenberg, D. J. (2010). How to start an entrepreneurial revolution. *Harvard business review, 88*(6), 40–50.

Kalar, B., & Antoncic, B. (2015). The entrepreneurial university, academic activities and technology and knowledge transfer in four European countries. *Technovation, 36-37*(2–3), 1–11. https://doi.org/10.1016/j.technovation.2014.11.002

Kirby, D. A. (2005). Creating entrepreneurial universities in the UK: Applying entrepreneurship theory to practice. *Journal of Technology Transfer, 31*(5), 599–603. https://doi.org/10.1007/s10961-006-9061-4

Lester, R. K. (2005). *Universities, innovation, and the competitiveness of local economies: A summary report from the Local Innovation Systems Project* (Working paper 05-010). MIT - Industrial Performance Center.

Mota, T. (1999). Interação universidade-empresa na sociedade do conhecimento: reflexões e realidade. *Ciência da Informação, 28*(1), 79–86. https://doi.org/10.1590/S0100-19651999000100011

Oliveira, J. (2019). *Um instituto federal como universidade empreendedora*: um estudo sobre a maturidade nas interações universidade-empresa-governo-sociedade-sustentabilidade. Dissertação de Mestrado Profissional em Administração - Universidade Federal Fluminense, 272 f.

Oliveira, J., & Amaral, M. (2020). *O modelo Oliveira-Amaral de maturidade das interações da academia com os demais atores da hélice quádrupla.* In M. A. Oliveira & M. M. Abdalla (Eds.), *Gestão nos Institutos Federais de Educação: experiências e aplicações* (pp. 263–290). PPGA/UFF.

Patzelt, H., & Shepherd, D. A. (2009). Strategic entrepreneurship at universities: Academic entrepreneurs' assessment of policy programs. *Entrepreneurship Theory and Practice, 33*(1), 319–340. https://doi.org/10.1111/j.1540-6520.2008.00291.x

Perkmann, M., Tartari, V., Mckelvey, M., Autio, E., Broström, A., D'Este, P., & Sobrero, M. (2013). Academic engagement and commercialization: A review of the literature on university–industry relations. *Research Policy, 42*(2), 423–442. https://doi.org/10.1016/j.respol.2012.09.007

Porter, M. E. (2000). Location, competition, and economic development: Local clusters in a global economy. *Economic Development Quarterly, 14*(1), 15–34. https://doi.org/10.1177/089124240001400105

Rauen, C., & Turchi, L. (2017). *Apoio à Inovação por Institutos Públicos de Pesquisa: limites e possibilidades legais na interação ICT - Empresa*. Políticas de apoio à inovação tecnológica no Brasil – avanços recentes e propostas de ações, IPEA.

Reinolds, E., & De Negri, F. (org) (2019). Universities as engines of innovation. The context for tech transfer in case studies from Brazil and the U.S. In E. Reynolds, B. Schneider, & E. Zylberberg (org), *Innovation in Brazil—Advancing development in the 21st century* (1st ed.). Routledge

Rosa, R., Vicente, A., Pinheiro, L., Jr., & Frega, J. (2018). Cooperação universidade-empresa: um estudo bibliométrico e sociométrico em periódicos científicos brasileiros de administração. *Revista de Administração da UNIMEP, 16*(1). https://doi.org/10.15600/rau.v16i1.1083

Rothaermel, F. T., Agung, S. D., & Jiang, L. (2007). University entrepreneurship: A taxonomy of the literature. *Industrial and Corporate Change, 16*(4), 691–791. https://doi.org/10.1093/icc/dtm023

Schulte, P. (2004). The entrepreneurial university: A strategy for institutional development. *Higher Education in Europe, 29*(2), 187–191. https://doi.org/10.1080/0379772042000234811

Shane, S., & Venkataraman, S. (2000). The promise of entrepreneurship as a field of research. *Academy of Management Review, 25*(1), 217–226. https://doi.org/10.5465/amr.2000.2791611

Stam, E. (2015). Entrepreneurial ecosystems and regional policy: A sympathetic critique. *European Planning Studies, 23*(9), 1759–1769. https://doi.org/10.1080/09654313.2015.1061484

Stuart, T. E., & Ding, W. W. (2006). When do scientists become entrepreneurs? The social structural antecedents of commercial activity in the academic life sciences. *American Journal of Sociology, 112*(1), 97–144. https://doi.org/10.1086/502691

UFF. (2017). *Plano de Desenvolvimento Institucional* PDI UFF 2018–2022. Disponível em: <http://pdi.sites.uff.br/wp-content/uploads/sites/196/2018/06/PDI_2018-2022_aprovado-CUV_30-05-2018.pdf>

UFF. (2020). *Política Institucional de Inovação*. Disponível em: http://agir.uff.br/wp-content/uploads/sites/351/2021/01/197-20-RETIFICADO.pdf

UFF. (2021). *Relatório Integrado de Gestão 2020*. Disponível em: <http://www.uff.br/?q=tags/relatorios-de-gestao>

Vorley, T., & Nelles, J. (2009). Building entrepreneurial architectures: A conceptual interpretation of the third mission. *Policy Futures in Education, 7*(3), 284–296. https://doi.org/10.2304/pfie.2009.7.3.284

Wennekers, S., & Thurik, R. (1999). Linking entrepreneurship and economic growth. *Small Business Economics, 13*(1), 27–56. https://doi.org/10.1023/A:1008063200484

Wu, M., Siswanto, I., & Arifin, Z. (2018). Fostering telecommunication industry development through collaboration among university, industry, and government—Elevating triple helix model of collaboration in Indonesia. *International Journal of Engineering & Technology, 7*(2–5), 4–8. https://doi.org/10.14419/ijet.v7i2.5.10044

Zucoloto, G. F., Santana, B. G., Veloso, L. J. P., & Kannebley Junior, S. (2017). *Lei do Bem e produtividade das firmas industriais brasileiras. Em Políticas de apoio à inovação tecnológica no Brasil: avanços recentes, limitações e propostas de ações*. Ipea.

Celta: Knowledge Building Model for Business Incubators

Andreia de Bem Machado and Maria José Sousa

Abstract A country's ability to innovate can be used to gauge its progress. One of the environments that support the generation of knowledge is the so-called "innovation habitat," which is defined by a large number of knowledge assets. In this innovation scenario, incubators stand out as the study's focus since they are locations that enable the production of knowledge. This construction is aided by the use of a management model. Incubators of ideas enable technology-based businesses in their early stages of development, resulting in new jobs that contribute to economic growth. As a result, the goal of this paper is to suggest a model for verifying knowledge construction in business incubators for the generation of successful creative firms, leveraging new jobs routinely and frequently, and delivering solutions to Brazil's economic strategy. As a result, an integrated evaluation of the literature was conducted utilizing the Scopus database and rules, as well as international and national papers and data collected from Brazilian incubators. As a result, CELTA (Business Center for Advanced Technologies) is provided as a model for confirming knowledge construction in incubators, which implies and encourages the incubator's ability to prospect and pick strong ideas sequentially, and then turn them into successful and lucrative companies. This model is based on five axes: entrepreneur, capital, management, market, and technology. It comprises 21 criteria. It can be used to determine the level of knowledge maturity in incubators and other Innovation Habitats.

Keywords Celta · Brazil · Inclusion · Systematic review · Incubators · Business model

A. de Bem Machado (✉)
Department of Engineering and Knowledge Management, Universidade Federal de Santa Catarina, Florianópolis, Brazil
e-mail: andreia.bem@ufsc.br

M. J. Sousa
Political Science and Public Policy Department, ISCTE – Instituto Universitário de Lisboa, Lisbon, Portugal
e-mail: maria.jose.sousa@ISCTE-IUL.pt

J. Leitão et al. (eds.), *Brazilian Entrepreneurship*, Studies on Entrepreneurship, Structural Change and Industrial Dynamics,
https://doi.org/10.1007/978-3-031-09392-0_7

1 Introduction

Innovation is pervasive in today's knowledge-based society. The ability to innovate, or the ability to use and transform scientific Knowledge of how to improve and/or create new products, processes, or services, as well as how to innovate existing ones, enables the development of new products, processes, and services of foundations for the promotion of competitiveness and quality required for nation-building.

It should be mentioned that the ability to innovate is linked to global economic and social development. Technology-based entrepreneurship and innovation have an impact on external relations. It is also worth noting that collaborations between universities, firms, and governments, all of which are considered agents of innovation, contribute to expanding entrepreneurship and innovation culture in economically developed countries. By sharing their resources and capabilities of knowledge with other regions in joint P&D partnerships, promoting innovative and entrepreneurial systems, developing smart solutions, and promulgating Triple Helix relationships involving businesses, universities, and government, business ecosystems can enhance their strengths, combine skills, and create diverse applications for newly discovered solutions (Ferreira & Teixeira, 2018).

In this context, as of the 1990s, the world economy heated up with innovations that marked this decade, among them the advent of the internet. There has been an increase in economic development in Brazil, which, together with policies centered on the building of a national framework of innovation, has supported a stronger focus on small and medium firms as job creators and income increasers (Drucker, 2012).

The importance of innovation, which was underlined in Brazil in the 1990s, was directly tied to global economic and social development. The triple helix, a partnership that incorporates universities, companies, and government, three divisions considered agents of innovation, is said to disseminate the culture of entrepreneurship and innovation in economically developed countries (Leite & Moraes, 2015). In this context, Brazil has advanced in terms of innovation policies and the regulatory framework for technological development. There has been a diversification of the spectrum of innovation support mechanisms, from the creation of Sector Funds in 1999, to the return of industrial policies with the Industrial, Technological, and Foreign Trade Policy (PITCE) and the Innovation Law in 2004, to more recent programs, such as Inova Empresa in 2013 (Freire et al., 2017).

When it comes to innovative entrepreneurship it was no different. Different programs have been created that directly or indirectly contribute to the development of startups and small companies that wish to innovate. These actions have been making the environment for innovative entrepreneurship in Brazil more complex and diverse. As in other countries, policy makers for innovation and startups (Freire et al., 2017). need to consider in their list of concerns not only the issue of investment and capitalization of companies but also a set of actors and governance mechanisms that make up these networks of organizations and institutions: entrepreneurs, investors, researchers in science and technology institutions, large companies, as well as associations, incubators, accelerators, and mentors.

Knowledge as a resource for generating innovation in products or services throughout the early years of an enterprise's life cycle is not about facts or specific contents, but rather about contexts; it is placed and applied knowledge. This information, in turn, generates solutions, solves issues, and, when implemented into a product or service, alters, generates utility, and adds value (Teece, 2010). It is critical to gain new skills and knowledge in order to stay up with the fierce economic competition, which necessitates enhancing the company's ability to turn learning into a competitive advantage. Knowledge becomes a vital ingredient for innovation to occur in this context of competitiveness. As a result, the process of invention is an interactive one, involving multiple individuals with various forms of information and knowledge.

Knowledge, according to Nonaka and Takeuchi (1997), is true belief justified, and it is a dynamic process in which a human being justifies personal views in pursuit of truth and tacit knowledge.

As a result, tacit knowledge may be demonstrated to be based on a human's subjective understanding, which is difficult to express in words, phrases, numbers, or formulae. Cognitive talents such as beliefs, images, intuition, and mental models, as well as technical abilities such as crafts, are included. Acts, debates, and explanations by humans demonstrate explicit knowledge (Nonaka, 1994).

Knowledge can be developed in a variety of methods and in many forms in an organization, but its value is revealed by the variety of capabilities that the company has as a result of that knowledge. As a result, most of an organization's information is based on each member's expertise and experience. The company, in turn, provides a physical, social, and cultural setting in which this knowledge can be practiced and grown in order to gain meaning and purpose.

Organizations develop knowledge continually, according to Nonaka (1994), by reconfiguring the synergy of the four main processes of knowledge transformation. Organizations, in other words, are centers of knowledge formation in a process of internalizing and externalizing, according to the author.

One of the support mechanisms for entrepreneurs in the early phases of their business is organizational knowledge; however, another resource is also essential, as a lack of these leads to a high probability of company death. As a result, it is critical to develop tools to assist entrepreneurs during this vulnerable and uncertain early stage of their business. This is how business incubators come into being.

The purpose of the incubator is to incubate an idea or to foster the formation of a company from the ground up by providing infrastructure and conditions for the development of technical, managerial, and administrative abilities. Incubators are thus knowledge-intensive environments, as they provide variables that develop incubates' skills and knowledge during the incubation process, as well as assist the enterprise's future once it graduates from the incubator.

The success of the incubation process is aided by the knowledge-building process, which leads to learning. Incubation programs can thus be thought of as learning networks in which connections between incubated and incubated, incubated and incubator, incubator and incubated, and incubator and incubated can aid in the development of information, which leads to learning (Chang et al., 2004; Hadjimanolis & Dickson, 2000).

In recent years, Brazil has been highlighted in the area of innovative ventures, according to studies conducted by Anprotec in partnership with the Ministry of Science, Technology and Innovation (MCTI). According to the figures obtained, the number of ventures increased from 2640 in 2011 to 6255 in 2013. In 2011, the 384 incubators in operation housed 2640 companies, generating 16,394 jobs; in 2013, these 384 incubators housed 45,605 companies and generated 32,237 jobs. By 2011, such incubators had graduated 2509 enterprises, with revenues of R$4.1 billion and 29,205 people employed in 2011. In 2013, there was a significant growth of 6255 graduated and incubated enterprises and 939 installed enterprises, with a turnover of R$533 million for incubated and associated companies and R$4.1 billion for graduated companies (ANPROTEC, 2016).

The incubation program and its operationalization are linked to the resources needed to implement successful incubators. Among these, we can discuss support infrastructure, management services to assist technological initiatives, such as incubated enterprises, collaboration with universities and research centers, networking acquisition, and the incubator's organizational technology infrastructure.

There are numerous management approaches for business incubators that can help improve the incubation process. There are around 17 of them in the international scenario (Machado et al., 2018). In Brazil, there are two management models: In Brazil, there are two management models: the Genesis Institute in Rio de Janeiro and the CERNE Model.

The CERNE Model (Reference Center to Support New Ventures), which is the focus of this study, attempts to provide a platform of solutions in order to increase an incubator's potential to consistently develop successful creative businesses (ANPROTEC, 2016). The incubator, according to this paradigm, must act in three distinct and complementary enterprise, process, and incubator (Machado et al., 2018). This management strategy has proven to be effective in the incubation process as well as in the creation of successful technology firms following the incubation period.

Incubators incubate the ideas generated by their incubators, therefore are innovative in the production of new products. Due to the amount of processes to be completed in the management of the same and its complexity, CERNE was structured according to the Incubator Maturity Model in the incubator in order to build successful ventures methodically. As a result of the intersection of this CERNE Model and the SECI Model (Nonaka, 1994), empirical inspiration for the implementation of economic policy solutions in Brazil in the area of technology-based firms related to incubators was supplied. As a result, the goal of this paper is to provide a model for the verification of knowledge construction in business incubators for the generation of successful creative firms, leveraging new jobs routinely and frequently, and delivering solutions to Brazil's economic strategy. How might a model of knowledge construction in incubators be proposed for the generation of innovative enterprises with economic policy consequences in Brazil?

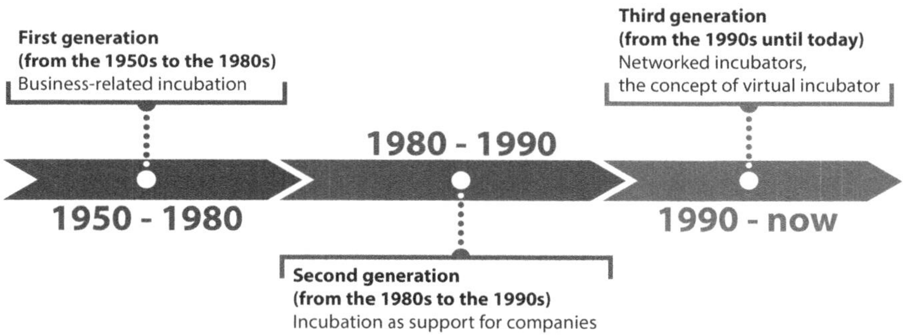

Fig. 1 Generations of incubation concepts

2 Technology-Based Entrepreneurship Incubators

In the context of innovation, Innovation Habitats are critical for regional development and economic progress because they serve as a conduit for information, productive practices, and connections between businesses, universities, and government officials. However, creating a structure for organizations to gain the knowledge essential for their growth and survival in a competitive market is one of the major problems of the innovation environment.

Business incubators are a type of innovation habitat that provides physical, technological, and service infrastructure to support the creation and development of new businesses. The use of business incubation as a tool or instrument to support the creation and development of businesses is growing rapidly. As a result, the existence of incubation programs creates opportunities for access to the business function as well as the formation of businesses, thereby encouraging entrepreneurship. In addition to small businesses that are creative and technology-based, we are confronted with the so-called New Technology-Based Companies (NTBC), which are critical to the country's economic growth as representations of technical entrepreneurship. The convergence of business incubation and entrepreneurship has been highlighted in a recent study, identifying the notion of entrepreneurship based on the establishment of especially technology-based enterprises and stressing the role of business incubators in encouraging business entrepreneurship.

In this setting, business incubators exist, which assist entrepreneurs in identifying and selecting chances for the creation of new, creative, and successful firms.

The progression of the notion in three generations may be observed in Fig. 1's historical line (Bruneel et al., 2012).

- The first generation (around 1950–1980) saw the birth and development of the notion of incubation, which was related to infrastructure and economies of scale.
- Second generation (from 1980 to 1990): Expansion and development of the incubation idea, connected to company assistance and learning curve acceleration.

- Third generation (from 1990 to now): Industrial maturity and new technological breakthroughs. The incubator is related to networks and value chains during this time period.

The word "incubation" is linked to business in the first generation. The incubator, according to Chinsomboon (2000), was a controlled environment that supported care, growth, and protection throughout the early stages of a venture's development before it was ready for the market.

Incubators of the second generation were founded on the need for economic growth in the United States. They have been bolstered by the federal government's support for innovation and the creation of university-based research initiatives. With support for the formation of new technological enterprises, investment banks have become a popular instrument for economic development (Lewis, 2001). Government organizations and colleges have come to recognize that entrepreneurship and innovation are engines of economic progress.

In 1990, the third generation began with the growth of the Internet. Tim Bernes-Lee, an English engineer, created the World Wide Web (www) during that decade, enabling the use of visual connectivity and the creation of websites. The incubator design became connected with networking in this way.

Incubators help businesses whose main goal is to create new products or services. "A business incubator is an economic development tool, designed to accelerate the growth and success of entrepreneurial companies through a wide range of resources and services to support new business, developed or organized by the incubator management team and companies and their network," according to the National Business Incubation Association (NBIA) (2004). This is the notion that will be used in this chapter.

The aim of ANPROTEC, the National Association of Entities Promoting Enterprises in Brazil, is to be recognized as a vital actor in creative entrepreneurship via leadership of the Network of Innovation Environments and the economic and societal consequences created. By strengthening innovation ecosystems that promote social, environmental, and economic development, the country will be transformed into an entrepreneurial society. It oversees and researches innovation ecosystems, which include incubators.

Also according to Anprotec (2016), Brazil has 369 incubators in operation, which house 2310 incubated companies and 2815 graduated companies, generating 53,280 jobs. The turnover of companies supported by incubators exceeds R$15 billion. As for the type of activity, 55% of Brazilian business incubators are technological, 19% are traditional, 18% are mixed, and 8% are of other types. In the year 2017, Brazil had 405 incubators, of which 363 demonstrated activity in the last 3 years (2017–2019) and had 3694 incubated companies that were responsible for generating 14,457 jobs and jointly invoiced R$551 million (ANPROTEC, 2019) (Fig. 2).

In light of the expansion in business incubation over the last 10 years, the fact is that half of the Brazilian incubators are under the age of eight, with a concentration of 3–5 years and revenue from management and public organizations.

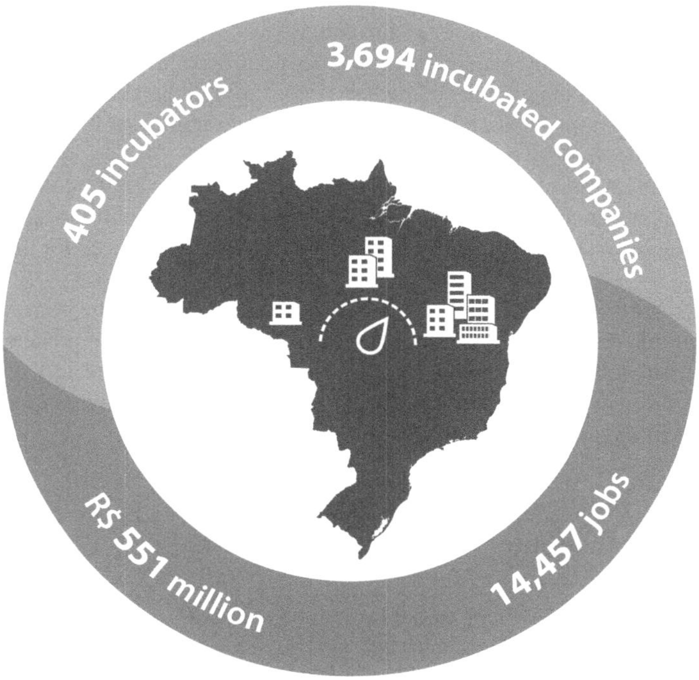

Fig. 2 Brazilian business incubators (2019)

The internal functions of incubators are diverse and numerous, emphasizing the importance of a taxonomy based on functions, strategies, and objectives (ANPROTEC, 2016).

It was discovered that the biggest issue in Brazilian incubators is a lack of qualification among the professionals responsible for the incubator's administration and support of incubated firms, which has made funding difficult as well as a lack of harmony with the region's innovation ecosystems. The biggest problems facing new knowledge-based companies in the startup phase that use public incubators, according to Grimaldi and Grandi (2005), are access to advanced technological knowledge, access to finance and risk capital, lack of contacts with universities, lack of advanced management knowledge, and lack of economic and financial skills.

Since 1990, it has been seen that the mobility of incubators in Brazil has increased dramatically. This is due to the work of ANPROTEC, which, via partnerships, implements projects that promote incubator planning, manager training, and the establishment of reference centers with the goal of building management models for business incubators.

As a consequence of these characteristics in the Brazilian context, ANPROTEC developed the CERNE (Center of Reference for Support to New Ventures) reference management model for business incubators in 2006, with the goal of improving the quality and quantitative outcomes of incubators.

This concept of strong management practices corresponds to what is known as a "third-generation Incubator." From the late 1950s through the 1980s, first-generation incubators stressed physical and technological infrastructure as a means of assisting the growth of new, creative companies.

This management reference model's principles and values are founded on quality management systems, and it encourages all of its members to participate in order to achieve long-term success via customer satisfaction and advantages for the firm and society.

Management models for incubators have to be aligned with the context of each country, in this research we will show the CERNE Model, as a reference model of business incubators, is a national model, based on the reality and in the Brazilian context, it will serve as inspiration for the composition of guidelines for building knowledge in incubators.

3 Business Incubator Management Models

The first business management model for incubators dates from 1985, 26 years after the creation of the world's first incubator, in Batavia, New York, United States. This began in 1959, when Massey Ferguson liquidated some of its tractors and agricultural products operations, laying off numerous people. According to the authors Machado et al. (2018), there are now 17 management models for business incubators across the world.

Campbell et al. (1985) established the first management model for business incubators, which advocated that the incubator serves as the primary business development instrument, transforming a concept into a viable firm.

Smilor presented the second model in 1987 to enhance Campbell, Kendrick, and Samuelson's model. Smilor created a model that outlined the incubator's primary functions, as well as the support system and the incubation process's key outcomes. The focus is on the requirements of the entrepreneur, who is a stakeholder in the incubation process.

Malecki and Nijkamp developed the third model in 1988, based on two criteria: the existence of venture capital in the community and business networks with an entrepreneurial basis, and financial sources—local government, universities, and the private sector.

Carter and Jones-Evans introduced the fourth model in 2000, with a five-stage incubation phase. This approach is organized and focused on the needs of the incubated, and it is supported by the incubators' services during the incubation phase. In the same year, Nowak and Grantham introduced the fifth virtual incubation model, which is built on network innovation and connects technical and business excellence or management centers electronically. In the year 2000, Booz, Allen, and

Hamilton introduced the sixth model, stressing the notion of business incubation and applying it to the demands of a firm engaged in continuous innovation.

Lazarowich and Wojciechowski created the seventh model in 2002, which aimed to define an incubator for a new economy. Costa-David, Malan, and Lalkaka developed the eighth model in the same year, based on an incubator benchmarking research, suggesting a generic incubation model based on incubation size surveys. According to these writers, incubation consists of three stages: preincubation, incubation, and a stage of care.

The ninth model, built by Wiggins and Gibson in 2003, adds a technical dimension to the previous versions. The authors suggested that capital and know-how networks are more important building blocks than secretarial services and basic business knowledge when it comes to support systems.

Sahay developed the eleventh model in 2004. In this situation, the business incubator's purpose is to help entrepreneurs turn their ideas into profitable businesses. In the same year, Hackett and Dilts proposed the eleventh model. According to this paradigm, if an incubator is properly organized and given the right raw materials, it can only develop profitable and inventive companies, or at the very least boost their chances of survival. In the same year, Hackett and Dilts produced the twelfth model, which aimed to describe fundamental processes in the structure of an incubator.

The thirteenth model, developed by Bergek and Norrman in 2008, is a management model for business incubators that examines an incubator's performance in relation to particular goals and outcomes.

The fourteenth model, InfoDev (2009), was suggested in 2009. It is a strong and well-known World Bank model that encourages innovation all across the world. This model posits a relationship between the corporate life cycle and the incubation process, demonstrating strong ties between the two.

Jones' approach, which interconnects time with the behaviors that incubators use to foster entrepreneurship throughout their life cycle in the incubation process, was introduced in 2010.

The sixteenth model of Chandra and Chao appeared in 2011, modeling the flow of resources among the primary players associated to business incubators in the innovation ecosystem.

The seventeenth model, Metibtikar (GADEA, 2016), was developed in 2012 and evaluates the incubation process of firms based on the demands of entrepreneurs.

UBI Index, a nonprofit organization based in the United Kingdom, studies incubator management. The chosen standard is founded on principles that attempt to assess the incubator's efficiency and competitiveness throughout the world. The following metrics were used: the incubator's profile, a performance index, and a historical assessment of the success of graduating enterprises.

There are few references on management models for business incubators in Brazil. We can discuss two of the existing models: the management model used at the Instituto Genesis in Rio de Janeiro and the CERNE Model. We will look at the CERNE Model in this chapter, which will be detailed in the next section.

4 CERNE: Model

Anprotec (National Association of Entities Promoting Innovative Enterprises) established and promoted the CERNE Model in collaboration with the Brazilian Service of Support to Micro and Small Enterprises (SEBRAE). It uses a technique to determine the systems, elements, and important behaviors that must be implemented by an incubator in order to develop successful ventures. It is a business support reference model that intends to encourage a quantitative–qualitative leap for business incubators in many domains (ANPROTEC, 2016) and to help incubators reach a level of maturity that allows them to systematically develop profitable ventures (ANPROTEC, 2016).

The incubator must function in three separate and complementary dimensions, according to this model: development, process, and incubator (Machado et al., 2018).

The first dimension, entrepreneurship, encompasses processes directly related to the creation and growth of businesses, with a focus on practices that aid in the improvement of products, services, and technologies, as well as access to capital, market participation, effective management, and personal development of entrepreneurs.

The second component, Process, focuses on the methods that allow ideas to become businesses.

Third dimension—Incubator: concentrate on the administration of the incubator as a business and the expansion of its boundaries, i.e., processes involving finances, people, and the incubator's connection with the environment.

The CERNE Model suggests four stages of maturation, each with its own focus (Machado et al., 2018):

- CERNE 1—Enterprise Development: At this level, all procedures and practices are directly tied to the enterprise's development. In this view, activities directly related to incubator administration, such as financial management and management of physical and technological infrastructure, were included in addition to procedures such as planning, qualification, consultation, selection, and monitoring. The incubator displays its capacity to prospect and pick strong ideas and convert them into successful creative enterprises in a systematic and repeatable manner by deploying this stage.
- CERNE 2—Incubator: The goal of this level is to guarantee that the incubator as a whole is well-managed. As a result, the incubator must develop mechanisms that allow for strategic management, the expansion of services supplied and target audiences, as well as the assessment of its outcomes and impacts.
- CERNE 3—Network of Partners: The goal of this level is to consolidate a network of partners with the goal of improving performance by developing capable and effective distance incubation tools. As a result, the incubator's performance as one of the "us" of the network of players participating in the process of encouraging innovation is reinforced at this level.

- CERNE 4—Internationalization: At this level, the incubator has the maturity to cement its international positioning, implementing methods that help enterprises incubated or graduated in the internationalization process, based on the framework created at previous levels.

Each maturity level has a series of critical processes that aim to guarantee that the incubator is following all best practices for that maturity level (ANPROTEC, 2016). This system is founded on eight principles: Focus on processes, Responsibility, Transparent and participative management, Human development, Sustainability, Ethic, Focus on initiatives, Continuous improvement, in addition to the dimensions and stages of maturity.

All incubators that utilize CERNE adhere to these principles, ensuring that the model is implemented in a consistent manner (ANPROTEC, 2016). The principles are aspects that pervade the main processes, coordinate and mature the incubator's recommended action, and give rise to the key practices known as initial practice, defined practice, established practice, and systematized practice (ANPROTEC, 2016).

During the early practice, the incubator employs instruments to capture the acts taken at the moment, so documenting the practice. The incubator organizes the actions for a year as part of the stated practice. The incubator, as is customary, creates an indicator to compare the outcomes to the efficacy of the suggested activity. The incubator suggests sessions for review and enhancement of this essential practice in the systematized practice, depending on the outcomes of the specified practice (ANPROTEC, 2016).

The CERNE Model is applied by these techniques. Implementation is a continuous and dynamic process that evolves in response to the fulfillment of requirements.

CERNE 1, which contains eight key processes and 33 key practices, is where implementation begins; preparation for the execution of these key practices is essential. The eight main procedures are: prospecting and increasing awareness, selection, planning, qualification, advising, monitoring, graduation and contact with graduates, and basic management.[1] Each key process contains key practices that must be executed, each with a different level of progressions, such as beginning practice, specified practice, and practice.

[1] We have the following important practices in the main process of Sensitization and Prospecting: Potential entrepreneurs are sensitized, prospected, and qualified. These are the important practices in key-process selection: Proposals are accepted, evaluated, and hired. These key practices are used in the Key Planning process: The entrepreneur's development strategy, the technological plan, the capital plan, the market plan, and the management plan. The following are essential practices in the

5 Knowledge Construction Mode

The dispute over knowledge creation and management procedures is nothing new. The debate began in the 1990s over concerns of corporate strategy, which considers knowledge as a source of intangible value in firms (Ponchirolli & Fialho, 2015). Knowledge management, according to Shinyashiki et al. (2003), is constantly created and rearranged, therefore understanding and internalizing its actions, possibilities, and impacts take time.

Knowledge building is a process that occurs as a result of the management of knowledge, which leads to learning. Some definitions of knowledge management are tied to knowledge building, such as talks based on the sequential transmission of tacit to explicit knowledge and vice versa. In this scenario, Nonaka and Takeuchi (1997) proposed the knowledge spiral.

The knowledge spiral will be used to represent the process of knowledge production in this essay. As a result, existing knowledge in an organization evolves via the mediation of individuals with tacit and explicit knowledge, as well as a variety of theme knowledge (Nonaka & Takeuchi, 1997).

Other writers (Nonaka & Takeuchi, 1997) have examined Nonaka's (1994) knowledge spiral model, which depicts the dynamics of knowledge that produces innovation. The authors define knowledge formation as a movement between the subjective (tacit knowledge) and the objective (knowledge) (explicit knowledge).

Nonaka and Takeuchi (1997) present four knowledge conversion processes that are created in four different ways, which the authors refer to as Model SECI—Socialization, Externalization, Combination, and Internalization:

- Socialization: When one person shares tacit information, such as mental models, experiences, and practices, with another person. It can happen in the course of normal business interactions.
- Externalization is a type of knowledge generation that is sparked by individual contemplation and debate. Knowledge is articulated in a tangible form through books, paperwork, articles, worksheets, models, and metaphors, all of which are regarded as key externalization methods.
- Combination: When explicit information is rethought, re-articulated, and combined again, a new notion or practice emerges. It is the bringing together of

key qualifying process: Entrepreneurial qualification, technological qualification, capital qualification, market qualification, and managerial qualification. Advisory/consultancy to the entrepreneur, advisory/Technology Consulting, advisory/consulting in capital, Advisory/Consulting in market, and Advisory/Consulting in management are among the important processes. The following key practices are found in the key-process: monitoring: Entrepreneurial monitoring, technological monitoring, capital monitoring, market monitoring, and management monitoring are all examples of monitoring. When it comes to key-processes, Graduation and relationships with graduates are two of the most important practices. In addition, in the key-process: The key practice in basic management is: Financial management and sustainability, physical and technology infrastructure, operational services, and communication and marketing.

various types of explicit information through a communication network with the goal of improving things.
- Internalization: Transition from explicit to tacit knowledge. This process is linked to "learning by doing," in which individuals create their own mental models of documents (Nonaka & Takeuchi, 1997).

Individuals are said to understand the dynamics of a company's workflow to the point where they know-how to carry out their tasks without having to ask for information. When this occurs, the person has turned explicit information into tacit knowledge, organizing concepts into operational knowledge.

Some writers (Probst et al., 2002) suggest that techniques including blogging, wikis, coffee knowledge, group discussions, knowledge clusters, collaborative virtual spaces, lessons learned, and collaborative face-to-face spaces may be utilized to develop knowledge. They are some methods of knowledge sharing that strive to provide collaborators autonomy in the creation of new knowledge.

In the dynamics between tacit and explicit knowledge, the spiral of knowledge is a cycle of knowledge that begins with an individual and flows through the group and organization. It is believed that there is a relationship between knowledge and education that is formed by the learning that is planned and accomplished in that environment, as well as by the subject of knowledge creation accountable for the production and appropriation of knowledge (Yorks, 2000).

The relationships between subject and object are embedded in the labor process, according to the spiral of knowledge. Individuals discover the new in this way, whether it is a problem situation that arises or an individual hunt for innovation aided by information sharing. Some writers (Elkjaer, 2001) claim that this learning process happens in companies and is influenced by social behaviors. Learning, in this perspective, is a factor associated to individual interactions in their work setting, i.e., it is situated learning (Elkjaer, 2001).

Learning in the workplace normally takes place through practice, with the goal of determining what to do, when to do it, and how to do it utilizing routines and elements; it is a technique that takes place in a group, between and through individuals (Gherardi et al., 1998). This learning process starts with the individual and is internalized through the organization's absorption of concepts.

The process of accumulating information that leads to learning becomes a tool for innovation in the incubator. The incubator, using the CERNE Model, encourages moments of socializing, externalization, and knowledge combination in this context. However, we were unable to locate scenarios in which internalization is quantified, which is necessary for learning in the incubator.

The SECI Model-based building of knowledge provides for a dynamic interaction in which knowledge is constantly transformed and built among persons. This process may be viewed as a continuous, dynamic, swirling knowledge process (Nonaka & Takeuchi, 1997), allowing the value of information to be traded among the individuals and groups in the incubator in this research. As a result, knowledge is created and developed as it moves through the organization at various levels and between individuals and groups. In the context of innovation, the value of knowledge is produced through collaboration between the incubated and the incubator. Learning becomes necessary in an era of tumultuous economy and rapid technological development, whether it is to gain know-how to address basic issues, that is, to build new premises, paradigms, or other models.

The execution of knowledge building connects the modalities of knowledge conversion and the activities established in its processes, according to the SECI Model's conception.

One of the reasons for developing a plan to check the level of maturity of knowledge construction in incubators might be the confluence of SECI processes and CERNE key activities. Based on the cyclical spiral between tacit and explicit knowledge, as well as socialization and internalization movements, this study investigates this concept.

An incubator is a company that exists to care for a business, product, or service that is incubated in this setting until it is ready to graduate. One of the requirements for graduating from the incubator is knowledge of effective company management. The incubator considers knowledge to be the most important component of innovation. In the business sector, innovation may provide a significant competitive edge to the entrepreneur, assuring long-term viability and competitiveness.

Incubators in Brazil still lack a more effective plan for ensuring that businesses reach a level of growth that allows them to compete in a global market. Analyzing the findings of the literature review, the capabilities of the CERNE Model in conjunction with the SECI Model, the concepts of knowledge assets and their construction processes, and the concepts of knowledge assets and their construction processes, it is clear that a model for knowledge construction in incubated companies is required for the systematic generation of innovative enterprises that will result in the creation of new jobs and have an impact on Brazil's economic solutions.

6 Methodology

The purpose of this study is to examine the inductive technique. It is a way of thinking in which "a truth is inferred in a broad or universal meaning from private material that has been suitably confirmed". Thus, it evolves ontologically, in the interpretationist model, and epistemologically, in the actual constructivism approach and the inductive technique, with empirical inspiration. The interpretive approach views reality as something dynamic, produced for a certain purpose, no more, no less true, but as it manifests itself. The interpretative paradigm takes a more subjective approach, claiming that reality is socially produced via human interactions.

The empirical inspiration allowed for the establishment of relationships between the CERNE Model and the SECI model in the documentary collection, allowing for the verification of intersections between the two documents using a framework of relations. Data was gathered using CERNE's documentary analysis, which revealed the confluence of critical practices and the SECI Model. Each SECI word was evaluated by intersecting each key practice with Nonaka and Takeuchi's (1997) knowledge spiral:

- Socialization: Encounters, courses, conferences, face-to-face meetings, workshops, events, and exchanges with professionals help to socialize knowledge.
- Externalization: Plans and techniques for assessment and monitoring of important practices are used to communicate and apply information.
- Combination: Since it adopts a notion to enhance important processes, it distributes, applies, and converts knowledge.
- Internalization: Individuals develop their own mental models of documents as a result of their learning by doing.

In this work, I show an example of the result of the intersection construct between a CERNE Model process and the SECI model.[2]

This intersection took place in the other seven important processes and key practices that were previously discussed. Because no adherence to the SECI model was verified in the basic key management process, in practical key physical infrastructure and technology, and in practical key operating services, no adherence to the model was verified in what concerns the understanding of the key practices, cumulative and progressive the initial practice intersected to the SECI model.

There is no time of internalization and two instances where CERNE does not comply with SECI at this junction of CERNE and SECI, according to the findings. It was confirmed that there are 19 times of socialization, 76 of externalization, 35 of combination, and two without specified practice, which are not obedient to SECI, among the 132 essential practices estimated cumulatively and progressively. In the CERNE Model, there is no internalization.

These data helped to build the theoretical foundation and understanding of a management model for business incubators, as well as the research techniques utilized in the field study, which were implemented in two phases with the goal of gathering data via an online form and a semi-structured interview. Both the online form and the semi-structured interview are data collection tools, but they have distinct characteristics: the online form is a tool with assertions developed by the researcher, whereas the semi-structured interview is conducted through a meeting between two people with the goal of obtaining information about a specific subject.

In this essay, I report the findings of a study on knowledge verification in incubators that was conducted in Brazilian incubators. A reduction was made from the 369 incubators in use to apply to 81 incubators that are in the process of implementing the CERNE Management Model. Incubators that are in the process of implementing the CERNE management model, as well as those that have previously adopted CERNE 1, will be subjected to interviews and questionnaires.

The structured questionnaires were created by combining CERNE 1 and SECI, and the claims were created using the Dialogical Problematizing Matrix. The main

[2]Machado's research for his PhD thesis (2018). According to the sources below, Innovation Habitat: Knowledge Construction in Incubators.

processes and key practices were combined in the matrix to define the stage of evolution of the practice in the incubator. Through the DPM's basic notion, these factors were linked to times of socialization, externalization, and knowledge combination. The 5W2H technique was used to develop the essential aspects of the evolution phases of major practices. As a result, these claims were created using the answers to the following questions: What? (Main Objective), Who? (involving actors), When? (How often), Where are you? How are you going to do it (space, region)? (methodology), How much does it cost? (Pricing was not employed because it is not the emphasis of this incubator management approach for startups.) The responses to these questions gave rise to the primary idea and the statements that comprised the online form.

As a result, a web-based and online-administered instrument was developed to test the process of knowledge internalization in incubators that are employing CERNE 1. This tool was built using a five-point Likert scale. The questionnaire had 21 claims and was available for 17 days online to receive the responses. According to an Anprotec (2016) study, it was given to 81 incubators that are in the process of adopting CERNE 1 (2016). Being that out of the 81, 69 responded and 12 did not, resulting in an overall response rate of 85 percent. We came up with criteria for verifying the internalization process of CERNE 1, which has five axes, after applying and evaluating the data from the web form (entrepreneurial, technological, capital, market, and management). The model prototype was made based on this decisive study.

Following the submission of the online form, a semi-structured interview was developed, allowing the interviewee to express themselves freely while the interviewer maintains objectivity in the research emphasis. The incubators that earned the CERNE 1 accreditation were subjected to a semi-structured interview. The interview was designed around the fundamental notion of key practice progression (initial, defined, systematized, and established) intersecting with the SECI Model, which was explored throughout the development of the online form. As a result, depending on the online form, six questions were organized for the interview: Question 1 was derived from the form's assertions 1, 2, and 3; question 2 was derived from assertions 4, 6, 7, and 8; question 3 was derived from assertive 5; question 4 was derived from assertions 9, 10, 11, 12, 13, 14, 15, and 16; question 5 was derived from assertions 17, 18, and 19; and question 6 was derived from assertions 20 and 21. The goal of the interview was to figure out what factors led to CERNE 1 certification. According to statistics from Anprotec (2016), it was applied to all 15 incubators that got CERNE 1 accreditation in 2016 and 2017, until the research deadline. Within 15 days, the collection was completed over Skype. The goal was to have a representative and qualitative sample for the development of a model to validate knowledge construction in company incubators for the CERNE 1 certification, which was the study's ultimate subject.

The semi-structured interview, like the online version, has five categories/axes for knowledge construction: entrepreneur, technology, capital, market, and management.

In this chapter, I will present the findings of this study, which were conducted in Brazilian incubators and can be empirically applied in Portuguese incubators because it raises a lot of information about the organization of incubators and incubated companies, as well as maturity verification processes. It also acts as a check on the model's applicability, which will be discussed later.

7 Model for Incubator Knowledge Construction Verification

A model is a schematic depiction of a given reality, whether literal, symbolic, figurative, or wholly conventional, or a formal abstraction that may be altered, changed, and recomposed in numerous ways (Santaella, 2010; Bunge, 2013).

A model, according to Bunge (2013), might be physical, mathematical, or conceptual. Formulas and/or graphs are used to depict the physical and/or mathematical model. The conceptual model, on the other hand, is equivalent to an object model, which is defined as "a schematic depiction of an item or situation, actual or imagined as such" (Bunge, 2013, p. 16).

According to Bunge (2013), the conceptual model used is determined by the researcher's goal. The theoretical-conceptual model was defined as acceptable in this chapter, with the acceptance of three concepts:

- People, procedures, and technology are the three essential pillars of the management paradigm for business incubators. It identifies key skills, external agent interactions that drive performance, and action plan. The latter, in turn, has as its primary goal the development of ideas into viable businesses (Machado et al., 2018).
- Knowledge construction: Based on Nonaka and Takeuchi's (1997) four quadrants, which lead to the learning of each key practice and, as a result, of CERNE 1's key process through the synergy of the four basic processes of knowledge construction.
- A directive; a plan of action; an outline of a plan, a project, or a road; a guideline is a line that expresses/determines the tracing of a path; a directive; a plan of action; an outline of a plan, a project, or a road. Guidelines can also be utilized in the social environment to aid a country's growth. Innovation is one of the variables that influence growth. Emphasis is paid to innovation because of the recognition of its importance for a company's, region's, or country's economic growth; hence, various attempts are made to quantify it. As the number of business incubators in Brazil grows, it is important to have guidelines that measure the process of knowledge construction for the generation of innovative enterprises, and such guidelines should contribute to the knowledge society as well as the growth and development of entrepreneurs.

Incubators are creative spaces that foster social and economic growth by methodically generating successful businesses. As a result, the construction of this model is based on guidelines for evaluating knowledge construction and, as a result, allowing the learning of such processes for incubator management, which will lead to the ability to prospect and select good ideas, transforming them into enterprise innovators, systematically and repeatedly.

Twenty-one assertions were organized from the intersection of the CERNE and SECI models, as well as the inferences of the respondents of the online form and the semi-structured interview, for the construction of the model, which evaluates the cycle of knowledge construction in business incubators so that they are prepared to leverage innovative ventures and can guarantee their stability in the competitive market after the incubation period. These facts guided the development of the conceptual model, which is detailed below:

1. At least one yearly event (including lectures, seminars, entrepreneurship and innovation workshops, business meetings, and a company ideas contest) that promotes entrepreneurship in the local community to potential entrepreneurs is required. These activities must take place in accordance with the incubator's requirements. At least one to five occurrences are anticipated to occur each year.
2. In the incubator's and/or partners' space, the incubator must design an annual sensibilization, prospecting, and qualification strategy aimed at future entrepreneurs and the promotion of the talent pool. Meetings, study groups, and concept workshops should be used to carry out such initiatives.
3. It is crucial to execute activities every year based on a critical analysis targeted at enhancing key behaviors such as raising awareness, prospecting, and qualifying new entrepreneurs. Through a bank of possibilities and the establishment of promotional campaigns to produce outcomes, these activities may be established at the incubator's space, universities, and partner institutions.
4. Annually, protocols for receiving proposals from potential entrepreneurs must be defined at the incubator. A proposal submission and assessment model should be used to codify these procedures. According to the setting in which the incubator is placed, such a model must be given to the incubator by potential entrepreneurs and must consider the following axes: Entrepreneur, Technology, Capital, Market, and Management.
5. It is crucial to encourage, every year, at the incubator, initiatives that aim to enhance key procedures such as proposal receipt, appraisal, and employment of potential entrepreneurs, based on a critical analysis. These steps should be carried out with the help of external and internal experts, as well as the management team.
6. An yearly orientation at the incubator is required in order to build several strategies (developmental, technological, capital, market, and management) for the incubator's entrepreneurs. This activity may be carried out by the use of a formal document, report, and the development of plans, goals, and activities, and it must be done on a biannual basis.

7. An yearly orientation at the incubator is required in order to build several strategies (developmental, technological, capital, market, and management) for entrepreneurs. This activity may be carried out through the establishment of plans, goals, and actions for the management of companies, as well as the planning of the evolution of solutions.
8. It is necessary to carry out activities at the incubator space each year, based on a critical analysis, with the goal of enhancing the core practices of the enterprises: entrepreneur development plan, technology plan, capital plan, market plan, and management plan.
9. The incubator must carry out operations in its space on an annual basis that spread the solutions accessible to clients, boost fundraising, and work the entrepreneurs' commercial and management abilities. Courses, seminars, conferences, face-to-face meetings, trainings, and business rounds can all be used to encourage these behaviors.
10. It is critical to implement the entrepreneurs' certification annually in the incubator space, or through partners (entrepreneurial, technological, capital, market, and management qualification). This qualification may be obtained through the company's commercial management and marketing strategy.
11. Based on a critical analysis, it is necessary to implement activities at the incubator each year to strengthen key practices such as entrepreneur qualification, technology qualification, capital qualification, market qualification, and management qualification.
12. At the incubator, it is required to foster the development of the following entrepreneurial competences on an annual basis, either by the incubator or by partners: entrepreneurial skills, technology skills, capital skills, market knowledge, and managerial skills. These measures can be carried out through advisory/consultancy, providing customers with solutions (technology, product, service), fundraising and financial leverage, commercial development, and the administration of business operations and vital functions.
13. It is critical to undertake yearly consulting at the incubator in the areas of entrepreneurship, technology, financing, market, and management. These steps can be carried out through a consulting strategy for businesses that are tailored to the incubator's needs.
14. It is necessary to promote improvements for the following key practices at the incubator, based on a critical analysis and annual frequency: advisory/consultancy to the entrepreneur, technical advisory/consultancy, capital advisory/consultancy, market advisory/consultancy, and advisory/consultancy in enterprise management.
15. It is vital to verify the incubator entrepreneurs' graduation maturity on an annual basis. This activity must be carried out using a defined periodic review instrument that takes into account the following factors: customer solution (technology, goods, and services), financial health, commercial development, and management. The baby should be examined on a regular basis until it is ready to graduate.

16. It is crucial to carry out measures targeted at enhancing the following core practices at the incubator each year, based on a critical analysis: monitoring the entrepreneur, technology monitoring, capital monitoring, market monitoring, project management monitoring. This type of monitoring should be done on a regular basis; it is anticipated that it should be done every semester.
17. It is critical to follow annual processes at the incubator to transition from "incubated company" to "graduated enterprise" status. These steps can be carried out through an Annual Graduation Plan, which includes monitoring the progression of the graduating firms' development.
18. It is necessary to perform yearly activities at the incubator, based on a critical analysis, to enhance the following core practices: Graduation; connection with the entrepreneurs' clientele.
19. It is vital to do an annual review of the quality of the suppliers at the incubator, shortly after delivery and on a biennial or quarterly basis.
20. Documents proving the formation and operation of the incubators, as well as the relationship with the maintainers, must be authorized by the management organization at the incubator. An institutional model, the development and updating of the cash flow, a sustainability strategy, and communication material may all be used to represent these documents.
21. It is critical to carry out actions at the incubator every year, based on a critical analysis, with the goal of improving key entrepreneurial practices: institutional model, financial management and sustainability, physical and technological infrastructure, operational services, communication and marketing. For entrepreneurs, such acts should be followed up on a regular basis, frequently quarterly.

Key Ideas were extracted based on the parameters. Because some of them were integrated into various axes, as well as the constant necessity for development during the incubators' maturation process, it was decided that the guidelines model should be represented by a spiral and dynamic movement.

The researcher termed this model CELTA, which was inspired by the Celtic people's spiral emblem, which represents movement and dynamism. The Celts are a group of people that originated in Europe and are credited with being the inventors of metallurgy, or the "entrepreneurs of Antiquity."

The Celta Model was based on 21 guidelines and five axes: entrepreneurial, technological, market, capital, and management, as shown in Fig. 3.

The Celta Model has 21 directions and five axes, including entrepreneur, technology, market, capital, and management. These axes do not exist in isolation; the entrepreneurial axis connects them, and the other axes outlined below cross them.

Entrepreneurial axis: It identifies the mechanisms that encourage the formation and growth of innovative businesses. With the help of the incubator, the number of individuals interested in the venture may be raised by promoting and preparing events, plans, models, bank chances, and talent banks, among other things. This is the model's integrating axis.

Fig. 3 Celta Model

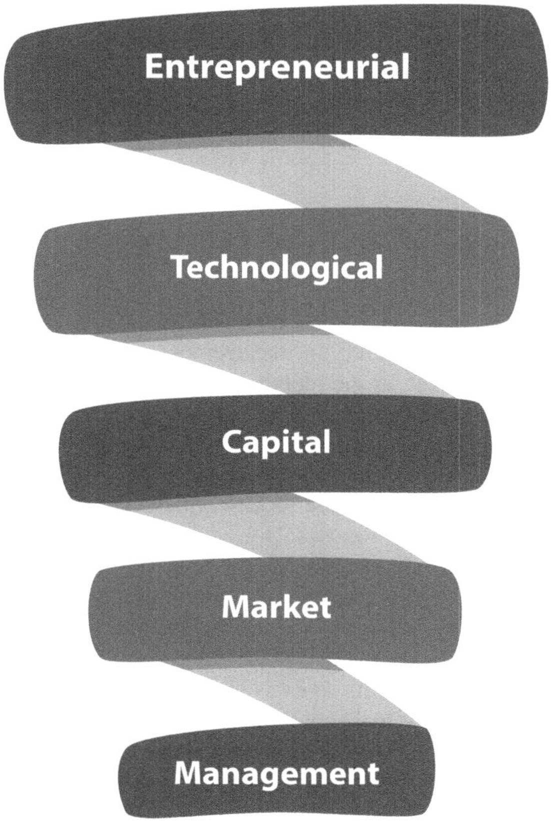

Technological axis: It denotes the procedures that require new technical solutions in order for businesses to succeed. It is linked to the entrepreneurial axis as well as the other axes.

Capital axis: It refers to the planning and development of actions and models with the goal of increasing the enterprise's financial leverage and ensuring its long-term viability. It is linked to the entrepreneurial axis as well as the other axes.

Market axis: Refers to the development of business models, strategies, and plans to help the company grow commercially. It is the procedures and aspects that commercial issues must consider for the enterprise's competitiveness and long-term viability in the setting in which it operates. It is linked to the entrepreneurial axis as well as the other axes.

Management axis: Refers to the financial management, resources, infrastructure, people, and technology required for the enterprise's growth. Its goal is to ensure that good ideas become successful businesses by assuring the execution of quality-generating actions in the organizations it supports. It is linked to the entrepreneurial axis as well as the other axes.

The model's spiral has linked axes. The 21 guidelines are linked to the entrepreneurial axis and intersect with the market, capital, management, and technological axes, resulting in knowledge construction in business incubators, which implies and promotes the incubator's ability to identify and select good ideas and turn them into successful and profitable businesses.

8 Final Considerations

To address the issue raised in this study, we began with empirical research, conducting a search for management models in incubators and knowledge management models. In the global scenario, we choose a model that has previously been successfully deployed in Brazil. As a result of the junction of these two models, as well as field research conducted in Brazilian incubators, the CELTA Model was born. The Entrepreneur, Technological, Market, Capital, and Management Axes were used to create the Model, which consisted of 21 directives and five axes.

This model proposes 21 guidelines for confirming the construction of innovative knowledge (knowledge that would have been added to the incubated tools for survival in the competitive market after the incubation period), implying and promoting the incubator's ability to prospect and select good ideas sequentially, and then turn them into successful and profitable ventures.

The goal of this study is to serve as a starting point for discussions and experiences in Portugal, so that this model can be used to generate innovative and profitable ventures, thereby increasing the number of jobs and increasing the likelihood of new businesses surviving, resulting in growth in the Portuguese scenario.

This research does not conclude with the CELTA Model proposal since this is a complicated issue that requires development in the economic and social situation in which the incubator is inserted. In the Portuguese context, we propose continuity studies with the validation of the CELTA Model for practical use of the CELTA Model for quantitative verification of the incubator's degree of maturity in the development of successful ventures.

As a result, it is thought that there is a need for incubators and researchers of this theme to continue their studies and research so that innovation and knowledge are linked in order to promote local, regional, and national development provided by this innovation habitat, the incubator, both economically and non-economically.

References

Anprotec. (2016). *Estudo de impacto econômico: segmento de incubadoras de empresas do Brasil*. Anprotec; Sebrae.

Anprotec. (2019). Mapeamento dos Mecanismos de Empreendimentos Inovadores-Brasília, DF: Anprotec; Sebrae. Disponível em: https://informativo.anprotec.org.br/mapeamento-dos-mecanismos-de-geracao-de-empreendimentos-inovadores

Bruneel, J., et al. (2012). The evolution of business incubators: Comparing demand and supply of business incubation services across different incubator generations. *Technovation, 32*, 110–121.
Bunge, M. (2013). *Teoria e realidade*. Perspectiva.
Campbell, C., Kendrick, R., & Samuelson, D. (1985). Stalking the latent entrepreneur. *Economic Development Review, 3*(2), 43–48.
Chang, P. L., Shih, C., & Hsu, C. W. (2004). *The innovation systems of Taiwan and China: A comparative analysis*. Technovation (pp. 529–539). Disponível em: Acesso em: 8 jan 2022, from http://www.sciencedirect.com/science/article/pii/S0166497202001177
Chinsomboon, O. M. (2000). Incubators in the new economy: An academic thesis submitted to the Sloan School of Management.
Drucker, P. F. (2012). *Post-capitalist society*. Harper Business.
Elkjaer, B. (2001). *Em busca de uma teoria de aprendizagem social*. In M. Easterby-Smith, J. Burgoyne, & L. Araujo (Eds.), *Aprendizagem organizacional e organização de aprendizagem: desenvolvimento na teoria e na prática*. Atlas.
Ferreira, J., & Teixeira, A. A. C. (2018). Open innovation and knowledge for fostering business ecosystems. *Journal of Innovation & Knowledge* (forthcoming).
Freire, C. T., Massami Maruyama, F., & Polli, M. (2017). Inovação e Empreendedorismo: Políticas Públicas e Ações Privadas. *Novos estudos CEBRAP, 36*(3), 51–78. https://doi.org/10.25091/s01013300201700030004
Gadea, E. S. (2016). *Rentabilidad económica y social de los viveros de empresas de la Comunidad Valenciana: durante el periodo* 2004-2014. 2016. 675 f. Thesis (Doctorate). Curso de Facultad de Económicas, Departamento de Organización de Empresas, Universidad de Alicante, Spain. Accessed January 9, 2022, from https://rua.ua.es/dspace/bitstream/10045/55627/1/tesis_eloy_sentana_gadea.pdf
Gherardi, S., Nicolini, D., & Odella, F. (1998). Toward a social understanding of how people learn in organizations: The notion of situated curriculum. *Management Learning, 29*(3), 273–297.
Grimaldi, R., & Grandi, A. (2005). Business incubators and new venture creation: An assessment of incubating models. *Technovation, 25*(2), 111–121.
Hadjimanolis, A., & Dickson, K. (2000). Innovation strategies of SMEs in Cyprus, a small developing country. *International Small Business Journal*. Acesso em: 8 de jan. 2022, from http://isb.sagepub.com/content/18/4/62.short
Infodev. InfoDev. (2009). *Annual Report is published*. InfoDev, 30 jun. 2010. Acesso em: 8 de jan. 2022, from http://www.infodev.org/highlights/infodev-2009-annual-report-published
Leite, Y. V. P., & Moraes, W. F. A. (2015). *The ability to innovate in international entrepreneurship*. Rev. Adm. (São Paulo) [online], v. 50, n. 4, 2015, p. 447–459.
Lewis, D. A. (2001). *Does technology incubation work: A critical review of the evidence*. U.S. Department of Commerce Economic Development Administration.
Machado, A. B. (2018). *Habitat De Inovação: Construção Do Conhecimento Em Incubadoras*. 266 F. Thesis (Doctorate) - Postgraduate in Engineering and Knowledge Management, Universidade Federal De Santa Catarina, Florianópolis.
Machado, A. B., Catapan, A. H., & Sousa, M. J. (2018). *Incubators management models*. In G. L. Jamil, J. J. P. Ferreira, M. M. Pinto, C. R. M. Pessoa, & A. Xavier (Org.), *Handbook of research on strategic innovation management for improved competitive advantage* (Vol. 2, pp. 200–230, 2 Vols., 1st ed.). IGI Global.
Nonaka, I. (1994). A dynamic theory of organisational knowledge creation. *Organisational Science, 5*(1), 14–37.
Nonaka, I., & Takeuchi, H. (1997). *The knowledge creating company*. Oxford University Press, 301 p.
Ponchirolli, O., & Fialho, F. A. P. (2015). Gestão estratégica do conhecimento como parte da estratégia empresarial. Revista da FAE. *Curitiba, 8*(1), 2005, 127–138. Accessed February 14, 2015, from http://goo.gl/saiHb1
Probst, G., Raub, S., & Romhardt, K. (2002). *Gestão do conhecimento: os elementos construtivos do sucesso* (p. 2002). Bookman.

Santaella, L. (2010). *Comunicação e pesquisa: projetos para mestrado e doutorado* (144 p, 2nd ed.). Bluecom.

Shinyashiki, G. T., Trevizan, M. A., & Mendes, I. A. C. (2003). Sobre a criação e a gestão do conhecimento organizacional. *Revista Latino-Americana de Enfermagem, Ribeirão Preto, 11*(4), 499–506.

Teece, D. J. (2010). Business models, business strategy and innovation. *Long Range Planning, 43*(2010), 172–194.

Yorks, L. (2000). The emergence of action learning. *Training & Development*.

Entrepreneurship in Brazil: Geography and History

Vanessa Ratten

Abstract Entrepreneurship in Brazil varies greatly from state to state. Despite this difference, there is a tendency to generalise entrepreneurship as being the same. This assumption needs to change due to the realisation that each state in Brazil has its own unique heritage and culture that differentiates it from other states. The aim of this chapter is to provide an overview of each state in Brazil in terms of land area and population as well as history. Important cultural characteristics of each state in Brazil are stated that help to provide a broader overview of Brazilian entrepreneurship.

Keywords Brazil · Culture · Entrepreneurship · Geography · History · Latin America

1 Introduction

The study of entrepreneurship in Brazil as it pertains to business management offers great potential (Coelho et al., 2018). It is a topic of immense interest due to the position Brazil plays in the global economy (Beekun et al., 2003). The concept of Brazilian entrepreneurship draws on the sociology and management fields as well as other areas of inquiry (Ratten et al., 2016). This makes the area very fertile for theoretical advancement as well as practical understanding of entrepreneurship in a specific country context (Ratten et al., 2019).

The range of topics within the concept of Brazilian entrepreneurship is immense and includes areas such as corporate entrepreneurship, diversity management, ethnic studies, and technological change (Soares et al., 2021). This raises some important questions about what exactly Brazilian entrepreneurship is and how it relates to the broader entrepreneurship literature (Mendonça & Alves, 2012). For example, what is the role of Brazilian policy initiatives in fostering entrepreneurship? How does the

V. Ratten (✉)
La Trobe University, Melbourne, VIC, Australia
e-mail: v.ratten@latrobe.edu.au

J. Leitão et al. (eds.), *Brazilian Entrepreneurship*, Studies on Entrepreneurship, Structural Change and Industrial Dynamics,
https://doi.org/10.1007/978-3-031-09392-0_8

Brazilian diaspora facilitate innovation? To what extent should the focus be on leadership within Brazilian entrepreneurship studies?

This chapter provides an overview of the main states in Brazil that can provide a basis for understanding the broader context of Brazilian entrepreneurship. As there are 26 states in Brazil there is a range of ways entrepreneurship can occur. Whilst I focus on the general concept of Brazilian entrepreneurship, it is still important to consider the state variations in entrepreneurship. This will help to determine how location and culture influence entrepreneurial activity.

The study of entrepreneurship is about innovation and business activity (Ratten & Ferreira, 2017). The term 'Brazil' denotes a country whilst the word 'entrepreneurship' refers to a process. Entrepreneurship in the wider sense includes all elements of business activity that involve proactive innovation (Ratten & Dana, 2019). This can include the development of an idea for the marketing of a service. Therefore, the concept of entrepreneurship is contextually based (Ferreira & Ratten, 2017).

The challenge for researchers and practitioners of entrepreneurship in Brazil is to build a theory around the practice of Brazilian entrepreneurship. Whether they want to do this is debatable as some prefer to focus on the wider entrepreneurship context whilst others like to emphasise country differences. The study of Brazilian entrepreneurship needs to include a focus on history and culture (Canever et al., 2010; Fischer et al., 2018)). The next section will discuss this in more detail by providing an overview of each state in Brazil.

2 Overview of States in Brazil

The states in Brazil are grouped into five large regions (Grandes Regioes): North (Norte), Northeast (Nordeste), Central-West (Centro-Oeste), Southeast (Sudeste) and South (Sul). There are 26 states in Brazil that have a certain degree of autonomy regarding government and regulation. This means each state has their own rules and policies that are based on historical conventions (de Oliveira et al., 2018). Table 1 states each state in Brazil in terms of its capital city, area, and population.

3 Acre

Acre state is a small-sized region in the northwest Brazil. It is bordered by Bolivia and Peru. Its largest city is Rio Branco, which is also its capital. Most of the state is within the forest part of the Amazon river basin and is covered by tropical rainforest. Due to its geographic position and remoteness the area was later in being explored. This meant that there were few settlements in the area. The region was part of Bolivia from 1867 due to the Treaty of Ayacucho. In 1903 Acre again became part of Brazil due to the Treaty of Petropolis. In 1962 Acre became a formal state of Brazil.

Table 1 States of Brazil

State	Capital city	Area	Population
Acre	Rio Branco	152,581 km^2	900,000
Alagoas	Macapa	27,767 km^2	3 million
Amapa	Maceió	142,814 km^2	800,000
Amazonas	Manuas	1,570,745 km^2	3 million
Bahia	Salvador	565,733 km^2	15 million
Ceara	Fortaleza	146,348 km^2	9 million
Distrito Federal	Brasilia	5802 km^2	3 million
Espirito	Santo Vitoria	46,077 km^2	4 million
Goias	Gloania	340,086 km^2	7 million
Maranhao	Sao Luis	331,983 lm2	7 million
Mato Grosso	Cuiaba	903,357 km^2	3 million
Mato Grosso do Sul	Campo Grande	357,124 km^2	2 million
Minas Gerais	Belo Horizonte	586,528 km^2	20 million
Para	Belem	1,247,689 km^2	8 million
Paraiba	Joao Pessoa	56,584 km^2	4 million
Parana	Curitiba	199,298 km^2	12 million
Pernambuco	Recife	98,311 km^2	10 million
Piaui	Teresina	251,529 km^2	3 million
Rio de Janeiro	Rio de Janeiro	43,696 km^2	17 million
Rio Grande do Norte	Natal	52,796 km^2	4 million
Rio Grande do Sul	Porto Alegre	281,707 km^2	11 million
Rondonia	Porto Velho	237,576 km^2	2 million
Roraima	Boa Vista	223,644 km^2	700,000
Santa Catarina	Florianopolis	95,730 km^2	7 million
Sao Paulo	Sao Paulo	248,222 km^2	47 million
Sergipe	Aracaju	21,910 km^2	2 million
Tocantins	Palmas	277,620 km^2	2 million

Source: Author's own, estimated numbers as of 3/3/2022, population is estimated (other consulted sources Britannica, 2022)

In the Acre region many of the trees are rubber meaning that it is one of its main industries. The wildlife in the area include capybaras, which are rodents with partly webbed feet and Peccaries, which are piglike animals. There are still a number of Indigenous tribes in the area but there is also a large number of immigrants. Most of the population lives in urban areas. In the 18th century, the area was colonised by the Spanish and became part of Peru. After the Wars of Independence, Bolivia became an independent country and the area was part of its territory. Due to the importance of rubber to the global economy, Acre produced rubber during World War II when the rubber plantations in Malaysia were under Japanese control. There have been discoveries in the area indicating ancient practices.

4 Alagoas

Alagoas is one of the smallest states in Brazil and is located in the Northeast of the country. It was named due to the large number of lakes in the area, which are called lagoas. The state has a coastline on the Atlantic Ocean. The area was colonised by Portugal in the 16th century but in the seventeenth century the Dutch colonised some areas but then left. In 1889 it formally became a state.

Lakes in the region include Lagoa Mundau or Lagoa do Norte (Lake of the north), Lagoa Manguaba or Lagoa do Sul (Lake of the South). Mountain ranges in the area include the Serra da Borborema (Borborema mountain range). Due to the poverty in the region, Alagoas has a high emigration rate. The main agricultural products in the region include sugarcane, cotton, and tobacco. There is also iron smelting and textile production. The tourism industry in the region has grown due to the beaches.

5 Amapa

Amapa is a state in the north and borders Suriname. It is one of the least populous states in Brazil. Most of the region is within the Amazon rainforest making the area difficult to enter. The Tumucumaque Mountains National Park is located in the state and is the world's largest tropical forest. It was created in 2002 and covers part of the Amapa biodiversity corridor. The Treaty of Utrecht in 1713 established a boundary in the area between Brazil and French Guiana. It became a state in 1990. The main industries in the state involve wood, medicinal plants, and fish. The resources in the area include gold, iron ore, and manganese.

6 Amazonas

Amazonas is a large state in the northwest of Brazil. Due to most of the region being within the Amazon river basin it does not have a large population compared to other states in Brazil. It shares border with Colombia and Venezuela. Spanish explorers passed through the region but it was Portuguese explorers who built the first buildings in the area. In 1891, it officially became a state of Brazil. Large parts of the state are uninhabited and there is a growing ecotourism industry. The state produces guarana, which is a climbing shrub that includes tannin and coffee, which is used in soft drinks. Other products grown in the area include bananas, nuts and timber.

7 Bahia

Bahia is a state located in the east of Brazil that has a coastline along the Atlantic ocean. Its capital is Salvador, which is located at the southern tip of a bay that is connected to the Atlantic Ocean. Most of the population lives in the eastern coastal area. Cities in the state include Salvador, Itabuna and Alagoinhas. Many people in Bahia practice spiritualism with the rituals of Candomble popular. Whilst there has been an increase in tourism most of the economy is still based on agriculture. There is cotton, corn, soy and sugarcane grown in the region. Bahia has a number of natural resources including marble, amethyst, manganese and copper. Capoeira which is a martial art was cultivated in Bahia.

8 Ceara

Ceara is a state in the northeast of Brazil. The state has a highland as well as coastal area. Initially, the state was settled by the Portuguese who managed sugar plantations in the area. In 1884 Ceara was the first state in Brazil to give emancipation to slaves. The economy is still based on sugar but also on cotton as it is one of the largest producers in the country. There is also many cattle ranches in the areas as well as other fruits and vegetables.

9 Federal District

The federal district is located in the central-west region of Brazil and is one of the smaller states. Its capital is Brasilia is where the government of Brazil is located. The federal district was part of Goias state before its creation. Brasilia was designated a UNESCO world heritage site in 1987 due to its architecture and landscape. The layout of Brasilia is shaped like a bird or airplane. The city was designed by Lucio Costa and many of the buildings by Oscar Niemeyer.

10 Espirito Santo

Espirito Santo is a small state in the southeast of Brazil. It has a coastline with beaches and ports. It is relatively small compared to other states. The capital of the state is on an island. The state was originally part of Bahia but was made a province in 1814. The economy is based on coffee, sugarcane and tourism. Within the state are the volcanic islands of Trindade and Martim Vaz.

11 Goias

Goias is a state in south-central Brazil and incorporates the country's capital city of Brasilia. In 1682 Bartolomeu Bueno da Silva discovered gold in the Araguaia river. This then led to more exploration of the area by the Portuguese. The state is within the Brazilian highlands meaning it is more than 750 m above sea level. The state has one of the fastest-growing population rates mostly due to Brazil's capital city being located in the state. There is a high level of agricultural activity in the state including cattle ranches, sugarcane and rice. There are also mineral resources such as diamonds and titanium in the area.

12 Maranhao

Maranhao is a state in the north of Brazil that has a coastline on the Atlantic Ocean. It is located close to the equator. The Portuguese established land grants in the area in 1534. In 1612 the French established a presence on Sao Luis Island but were expelled in 1615. The Dutch then held Sao Luis Island from 1641 to 1644 before the Portuguese regained control. The state was settled by Jesuit missionaries who influenced the religious practices and way of life for citizens in the area. The state is still mostly underdeveloped and based on agriculture. There are aluminium smelting and steel manufacturing in the area.

13 Mato Grosso

Mato Grosso is a large inland state of Brazil. Its name means 'thick bush' meaning that it is still mostly uninhabited and densely forested in some areas. The state is the third largest by area but is not as populated as other states. The area was largely settled by miners searching for valuable minerals. The main cities in the state are Cuiaba, Cacares and Rondonopolis.

14 Mato Grosso do Sul

Mato Grosso do Sul is a state in the Midwest. It shares a border with Bolivia and Paraguay. It has a small percentage of Brazil's overall population largely due to its natural environment. It was previously part of the Mato Grosso state before it became its own state. The state is one of the world's largest producers of oilseeds and sugarcane. It also is a major exporter of beef and maize.

15 Minas Gerais

Minas Gerais is a large inland state that is close to coastal cities such as Rio de Janeiro and Sao Paulo. It is the fourth largest state by size and has the second largest population. Thereby making it one of the most economically active states in Brazil. Its name translated to English means General Mines, which indicates the mineral reserves found in the state.

16 Para

Para is a state in the north of Brazil that has a coastline along the Atlantic Ocean. It is the second-largest state by size in Brazil. Its capital city is Belem, which was founded in 1615 by the Portuguese. The Spanish also founded settlements in the area but were expelled by the Portuguese in 1710. The state has a large forest with rubber trees and an abundance of natural resources including gold. The Amazon river crosses the state and influences the biodiversity of the area. Forest products including malvas (a herb) and medicinal herbs are harvested from the forest. There has been considerable mining in the area for iron ore and other minerals.

17 Paraiba

Paraiba is a state in northeast Brazil that is relatively small compared to neighbouring states. The state has a small coastline and its capital city Joao Pessoa is near the Atlantic ocean. Originally the state capital was called Paraiba, which means arm of the river but was changed to honour a former governor of the state. The state had large sugarcane plantations and cotton fields. The economic structure of the state has been changing with more emphasis on manufacturing in particular clothing and shoes.

18 Parana

Parana is a state in the south of Brazil that shares a border with Argentina and Paraguay. The state was settled by Spanish and Portuguese explorers. It was recognised as being part of Portuguese territory and became a state in 1891. The main rivers in the state are the Iguacu, Ivan and Tibagi. There is a dense tropical rainforest covering parts of the state. There are large coffee plantations in the area as well as tea. Other products grown in the state include cotton and wheat. Fruit and vegetables including potatoes, pineapple, oranges and bananas are grown in the state. There are also dairy farms and cattle ranches in the area.

19 Pernambuco

Pernambuco is a state in the east of Brazil. Its capital is Recife. The first main European settlement of the area was in 1535 at Olinda. Parts of the state were occupied by the Dutch from 1630 to 1654 until the Portuguese started to rule the state. In 1827 Recife was made the capital of the state due to its strategic position. The state was a place where there were unsuccessful uprisings against Portuguese rule. It became a state in 1889. Most of the population lives near the coast. There are a number of food products grown in the area including corn, rice and onions.

20 Piaui

Piaui is a state in the north of Brazil. It has a very small coastline on the Atlantic Ocean. It became a state in 1889. The land in the area has scrub woodland as well as forests The state is sparsely populated compared to other states. The main economic activities of the state include livestock farming.

21 Rio de Janeiro

Rio de Janeiro is one of the most well known states in Brazil because of its capital city, which it shares the same name. Explorers from Portugal named the city because they mistook the bay for a river (Rio meaning river and Janeiro meaning January in Portuguese). It was the capital of the country until 1960 when Brasilia was built as the new capital. The city is considered Brazil's cultural capital. It is located on Guanabara Bay.

22 Rio Grande do Norte

Rio Grande do Norte is a state in the northeast whose name can be translated to the great northern river. It occupies a strategic position due to its coastline. There are petroleum producers and mineral production in the state as well as agricultural production. The world's largest cashew tree is located in the state. The state has a relatively small population and economic activity compared to other states.

23 Rio Grande do Sul

Rio Grande do Sul means the great river of the south. It is located in the south of Brazil and is amongst the most populous states. Porto Alegre is the capital of the state. People in the state have a high standard of living and the longest life expectancy in Brazil. There are two lagoons—the Lagoa dos Patos and Lagoa Mirim—that are separated from the ocean in the state. The state has a number of tourist attractions including Yacuma Falls, which are the second widest in the world.

24 Rondonia

Rondonia is an inland state in Brazil that is landlocked. Due to its geographic position, it is not as populated as other states. The main economic activities involve agriculture, food production and livestock. There are coffee, cocoa, soybean and maize grown in the state.

25 Roraima

Roraima is a landlocked state in the north of Brazil. It is bordered by Guyana and Venezuela. It is one of the least populated states due to its location. The Branco river is in the state and was used by colonialists to settle the area. There is a large number of protected areas in the state due to the existence of forested areas and the Branco river basin.

26 Santa Catarina

Santa Catarina is a state in the south of Brazil that borders the Atlantic ocean. It is one of the oldest states in Brazil that was created to extend Portuguese interest in the country. In the early nineteenth century, there was a large number of immigrants to the state from Austria and Germany. Other European immigrants also settled in the area and created many small family farms.

27 Sao Paulo

Sao Paulo is a state in the south of Brazil named after the Saint Paul of Tarsus. It is a wealthy state due to the industrialisation in the region. Many people in the state have Italian ancestry due to immigration in the nineteenth century. It is a major agricultural producer. Sao Paulo the state capital is one of the world's largest cities.

28 Sergipe

Sergipe is a small state in the north of Brazil. It has a coastline and tropical rainforest. Aracaju is the state's capital and is located near the coast of the Cotinguiba river. One of the cities in the state (Sao Cristavao) was where the Portuguese first settled in Brazil. The state was invaded by the Dutch and French before coming under Portuguese rule.

29 Tocantins

Tocantins is a landlocked state in Brazil. It is the youngest state having been established in 1988. There are hydropower resources in the state that has attracted new residents. The state is named after the Tocantines river that exists in the state. Originally the state was part of Goias state before its creation as its own state. The economy is dependent on agriculture, in particular beef, rice and soybean.

30 Summary of States in Brazil

In summary, the 26 states in Brazil are all different and need to be studied in order to provide a better overview of entrepreneurship. Each state has its own culture and history that is reflected in the type of entrepreneurial activities that are pursued. The previous section stated all the states in Brazil in terms of their main features. Thereby providing a good overview of the history of the state and how an understanding of history can help in entrepreneurship research. Table 2 states each state in Brazil in terms of its motto, anthem and demonym.

Table 2 States in Brazil

State	Motto	Anthem	Demonym
Acre	I do not shine differently from the others	Hino do Acre	Acriano(a)
Alagoas	For which is good and for prosperity	Hino de Alagoas	Alagoano(a)
Amapa	–	Hino do Amapa	Amapaense
Amazonas	–	Hino de Amazonas	Amazonense
Bahia	I rise through the hardship	Hino da Bahia	Baiano
Ceara	Land of the light	Hino do Ceara	Cearense
Federal district	To the coming winds		Brasiliense
Espirito Santo	Work and trust	Hino do Espirito Santo	Espirito Santense
Goias	–	Hino de Goias	Goiano
Maranhao	–	Hino do Maranhao	Maranhense
Mato Grosso	By virtue more than by gold	Hino de Mato Grosso	Mato grossense
Mato Grosso do Sul	–	Hino de Mato Grosso do Sul	Mato-grossesne-do-sul
Minas Gerais	Freedom albeit late	Hino de Minas Gerais	Mineiro
Para	Let us progress under the law	Hino do Para	Paraense
Paraiba	–	Hino da Paraiba	Paraibano
Parana	–	Hino do Parana	Paranaense
Pernambuco	–	Hino de Parnambuco	Pernambucan
Piaui	Wounded and undaunted amid the ruins	Hino do Piaui	Piauiense
Rio de Janeiro	Conduct the affairs of the public with righteousness	Hino 15 de Novembro	Fluminense
Rio Grande do Norte			Norte-Rio-Grandense
Rio Grande do Sul	Liberty, equality, humanity	Hino Rio-Grandense	Rio Grandense
Rondonia	–	Hino de Rondonia	Rondoniense
Roraima	The Amazon- Brazilian's heritage	Hino de Roraima	Roraimense
Santa Catarina	–	Hino do Estado de Santa Catarina	Catarinense
Sao Paulo	Let great things be done for Brazil	Bandeirantes anthem	Paulista
Sergipe	Liberty under the law	Hino de Sergipe	Sergipano
Tocantins	This land is ours.	Hino do Tocantins	Tocantinense

Source: Author's own

31 Conclusion

To conclude, I discuss a number of reflective thoughts that will influence the study of Brazilian entrepreneurship. First, due to the COVID-19 pandemic there has been a resurgence in interest in national rather than international interests. Due to supply chain issues and stay-at-home requirements citizens around the world have been restricted to their local areas. This has resulted in more interest in local products that relate to culture. Therefore, I call on researchers to take into account the COVID-19 pandemic when designing studies on Brazilian entrepreneurship.

Second, although the focus of this chapter is on Brazil, such a focus might be broadened to the South American context. Or alternatively, the Latin American context in which many countries share the same culture and history. Therefore, when we talk about Brazilian entrepreneurship we can also include other country contexts.

Finally, I encourage forward-looking research into Brazilian entrepreneurship. Specifically focusing on both low- and high-tech contexts. The low-tech context includes artisan and cultural production that has occurred over time. The high-tech context refers to the use of artificial intelligence and other emerging technologies.

In summary, this chapter was written with the aim of guiding researchers on Brazilian entrepreneurship as to how they can research the Brazilian state contexts. This will improve their overall research by considering each state in Brazil as a unique research setting. In doing so, I presented a brief overview of the states in Brazil and highlighted important cultural facts. This provides an interesting way to discover the rich insights to be gained from Brazilian entrepreneurship research.

References

Beekun, R. I., Stedham, Y., & Yamamura, J. H. (2003). Business ethics in Brazil and the US: A comparative investigation. *Journal of Business Ethics, 42*(3), 267–279.

Britannica. (2022). Accessed August 4, 2022, from https://www.britannica.com/place/Brazil

Canever, M. D., Carraro, A., Kohls, V. K., & Teles, M. Y. O. (2010). Entrepreneurship in the Rio Grande do Sul, Brazil: The determinants and consequences for the municipal development. *Revista de Economia e Sociologia Rural, 48*(1), 85–108.

Coelho, F. J. M., Marques, C., Loureiro, A., & Ratten, V. (2018). Evaluation of the impact of an entrepreneurship training program in Recife, Brazil. *Journal of Entrepreneurship in Emerging Economies, 10*(3), 472–488.

de Oliveira, J. A. S., Basso, L. F. C., Kimura, H., & Sobreiro, V. A. (2018). Innovation and financial performance of companies doing business in Brazil. *International Journal of Innovation Studies, 2*(4), 153–164.

Ferreira, J., & Ratten, V. (2017). Competitiveness of locations: The effects of regional innovation and entrepreneurial practices. *Competitiveness Review: An International Business Journal, 28*(1), 2–5.

Fischer, B. B., Queiroz, S., & Vonortas, N. S. (2018). On the location of knowledge-intensive entrepreneurship in developing countries: Lessons from São Paulo, Brazil. *Entrepreneurship & Regional Development, 30*(5–6), 612–638.

Mendonça, P. M. E., & Alves, M. A. (2012). Institutional entrepreneurship and professionalization of the rural development of the sisal region in Brazil. *Revista de Administração, 47*(3), 489–499.

Ratten, V., & Dana, L. P. (2019). *Societal entrepreneurship and competitiveness*. Emerald Publishing Limited.

Ratten, V., & Ferreira, J. (2017). Future research directions for innovation and entrepreneurial networks. *International Journal of Business and Globalisation, 18*(1), 1–8.

Ratten, V., Ferreira, J., & Fernandes, C. (2016). Social entrepreneurship and fashion innovation in Brazil: A case study of crafty women (Mulheres Arteiras) and Rede Asta. In *Routledge handbook of entrepreneurship in developing economies* (pp. 266–274). Routledge.

Ratten, V., Jones, P., Braga, V., & Marques, C. S. (2019). Sustainable entrepreneurship: The role of collaboration in the global economy. In *Sustainable entrepreneurship* (pp. 1–7). Springer.

Soares, G. G., da Silva Braga, V. L., da Encarnação Marques, C. S., & Ratten, V. (2021). Corporate entrepreneurship education's impact on family business sustainability: A case study in Brazil. *The International Journal of Management Education, 19*(1), 100424.

Wine Tourism Entrepreneurship in Brazil

Paul Strickland and Vanessa Ratten

Abstract Wine tourism is one of the most popular forms of tourism due to the way it integrates culture, history and consumption patterns. The aim of this chapter is to focus on wine tourism entrepreneurship from a Brazilian context. Thereby highlighting how the wine industry in Brazil has grown based on its innovative and entrepreneurial characteristics. Brazil is considered a new wine country compared to the old wine countries that have been producing wine for some time. This means it provides an interesting context as to how wine tourism develops in an entrepreneurial way. Suggestions for future research and practice regarding wine tourism entrepreneurship in Brazil are stated in this chapter.

Keywords Brazil · Culture · Destination marketing · Entrepreneurship · Tourism · Wine entrepreneurship · Winemaking

1 Introduction

Tourism is an important economic driver and influences the quality of life for many people around the world. Brazil is one of the largest countries in the world in terms of landmass and population size, which has meant that it has a variety of tourism activities occurring within the country. Most of the tourism attention has focused on well-known attractions, particularly around the sea and surf but there are also popular tourist places in the interior of the country. Rural and regional tourism has become particularly important in Brazil as a way of distinguishing between different states in the country. As a result, each state in Brazil has its own tourism marketing in terms of highlighting unique places to visit.

Wine tourism is a popular form of tourism activity as it incorporates rural tourism with cultural tourism. The rural tourism component is due to most wine regions being in the country and having beautiful landscapes. This means people go to the

P. Strickland · V. Ratten (✉)
La Trobe University, Melbourne, VIC, Australia
e-mail: v.ratten@latrobe.edu.au

J. Leitão et al. (eds.), *Brazilian Entrepreneurship*, Studies on Entrepreneurship, Structural Change and Industrial Dynamics,
https://doi.org/10.1007/978-3-031-09392-0_9

country for sightseeing reasons but also because of the lifestyle. Moreover, because of pollution and crowding in city centres, rural areas provide a change of scenery. They normally are more quiet and less busy than city areas and offer a refreshing change to those who live in the city. In the past, wineries were thought of as mostly production centres in terms of making and producing wine. This meant they were normally confined to the people who worked or lived in the area. This has changed with more people interested in how the wine is made and seeing first hand the production process.

In Brazil, there is a high reliance on agricultural activity and in particular the wine industry. Wine is exported from Brazil to many countries around the world and the wine is more well known now due to marketing efforts. As a result, people are travelling to Brazil to visit vineyards and to experience rural tourism.

The aim of this chapter is to discuss the role of wine tourism entrepreneurship in Brazil. To do this, the Brazilian context of wine tourism is highlighted as a unique cultural context. This means focusing on the wine regions in Brazil in terms of their geography and uniqueness together with the context of Brazilian wine. Future research suggestions and managerial implications are stated.

2 Brazilian Context

Brazil is the largest country in South America and covers most of the eastern part of the continent. It is also one of the world's largest countries by land mass and population size. Most people in Brazil speak Portuguese due to Portugal previously colonising the country. This makes it different from other South American countries where the main language is Spanish. Brazil was first discovered in the sixteenth century by Europeans with Portugal then beginning to claim it as part of their Kingdom. Brazil shares border with most countries in South America except for Ecuador and Chile. This means it has an influential role in the economic and political climate of the region. Brazil is well known as a tourism destination due to its beach lifestyle and abundance of natural resources. The world's largest carnival is held in Rio de Janeiro in the first week of March. Brazil is also famous for its football stars with the sport being the most popular in the country. The motto of Brazil is 'order and progress'. The oldest city in Brazil is Sao Vincente, which is located near Sao Paolo. It was established by the Portuguese in 1532. The capital of Brazil is Brasilia, which was built in 1960. The previous capital was Rio de Janeiro. Brazil is one of the world's largest exporters of coffee.

There is a high level of inequality in Brazil between the rich and poor. As a result, there has been large shanty towns (favelas) located near big cities. Brazil is one of the most biodiverse countries in the world, largely due to the Amazon forest being located in the country. The main mountain ranges in Brazil are the Serra do Mar and the Serra do Espinhaco. The landscape in Brazil varies from wetlands, rainforests to coastal plains. A majority of people in Brazil live in Sao Paolo and Rio de Janeiro. In Brazil, people are mostly descendants from Indigenous, European and African cultures but there was a large number of immigrants from Japan and other countries that came to the country.

3 Wine Regions in Brazil

Wine cultivation in Brazil can be traced back to 1532 with the European colonisation by the Portuguese (André Wurz et al., 2017). During the mid-nineteenth century (circa 1875), Italian immigrants introduced an American grape variety named 'Isabel' which rapidly dominated over other European grape varieties (Botelho & Pires, 2009). With the support of the Brazilian federal government, wine regions were established throughout the southern areas and other American grape varieties were introduced as it was the most lucrative agricultural industry at the time. More recently, three more wine regions were established in the South-East and Eastern Brazil (Table 1).

Table 1 Wine regions and grape varieties of Brazil

Wine region	Grape varieties cultivated
Vale do Sao Francisco	Alicante Bouschet, Syrah, Tempranillo, Touriga Nacional, Cabernet Sauvignon, Chardonnay, Chenin Blanc, Malvasia, Moscato, Charmat—for sparkling wine
Sul de Minas	Ancelota, Alicante Bouschet, Barbera, Gamay, Malbec, Marselan, Merlot, Periquita, Syrah, Tempranillo, Teroldego, Touriga Nacional, Malvasia, Riesling
Sao Roque	Ancelota, Alicante Bouschet, Barbera, Gamay, Malbec, Marselan, Merlot, Periquita, Syrah, Tempranillo, Teroldego, Touriga Nacional, Malvasia, Riesling
Cacador	Cabernet Sauvignon, Tannat, Touriga Nacional, Tempranillo, Merlot, Pinot Noir, Chardonnay, Sauvignon, Pinot Gris, Gewurztraminer
Sao Joaquim	Ancelota, Alicante Bouschet, Barbera, Gamay, Malbec, Marselan, Merlot, Periquita, Syrah, Tempranillo, Teroldego, Touriga Nacional, Malvasia, Riesling
Serra Gaûcha	Merlot, Tempranillo, Malbec, Tannat, Pinot Noir, Chardonnay, Charmat, Moscato
Serra do Sudeste	Ancelota, Alicante Bouschet, Barbera, Gamay, Malbec, Marselan, Periquita, Syrah, Teroldego, Touriga Nacional, Malvasia, Riesling
Campanha	Cabernet Sauvignon, Tannat, Touriga Nacional, Tempranillo, Merlot, Pinot Noir, Chardonnay, Sauvignon, Pinot Gris, Gewurztraminer
Campos de Cima das Serra	Cabernet Sauvignon, Tannat, Touriga Nacional, Tempranillo, Merlot, Pinot Noir, Chardonnay, Sauvignon, Pinot Gris, Gewurztraminer
Campus Novas	Cabernet Sauvignon, Tannat, Touriga Nacional, Tempranillo, Merlot, Pinot Noir, Chardonnay, Sauvignon, Pinot Gris, Gewurztraminer
Planalto Catarinense	Cabernet, Merlot, Pinot Noir, Chardonnay, Sauvignon, Riesling and potentially ice wine in the future
Pinto Bandeira	Charmat and Chardonnay for only sparkling wines

Source: Author's own but adapted from Statista Research Department (2022)

Brazil is a very large country located in South America (continent) and also referred to as in Latin America which are countries with languages (Portuguese, French and Spanish) derived from Latin including Brazil, Argentina, Bolivia, Chile and Colombia (Campbell, 2021). Brazil contains diverse climates, contrasting landscapes and unique terroirs which allows for varying qualities of grape cultivation and winemaking (Dutra et al., 2011). There are nine main wine producing regions in Brazil which include: Vale do Sao Francisco, Sul de Minas, Sao Roque, Cacador, Sao Joaquim, Serra Gaûcha, Serra do Sudeste, Campanha, Campos de Cima das Serra and Campus Novas with more recently added, Planalto Catarinense and Pinto Bandeira (both GI coded). The mountainous areas in the state of Rio Grande do Sul produce 90% of the domestic wine production mainly in Serra Gaúcha (Dutra et al., 2011).

Similar to other countries, Brazilian wines are segmented by Geographical Indicators (GI) as well as grape varieties. This highlights the geographical location of individual grape cultivation and is often known for certain grape varieties such as Merlot or Riesling. Brazil also has two sub-groups that assist in determining the quality of the brand based on indications or origin (IO) and denominations of origin (DO). IO's analyse the reputation and quality of the wines and DO's strive to determine the peculiarities of the wine region and the overall wine production process (Castro & Giraldi, 2018), which the French term 'terroir' denotes.

4 Brazilian Wines

Typically, the global wine market is segmented by colour; most notably red, rosé, and white wine. Other wine products also exist such as sparkling, still, dessert, and fortified wines. (Conway, 2021). Another way of segmenting wine products is by reputation, brand recognition, quality, availability, sense of occasion and price of wine. As there are many wine regions showcasing different and unique grape characteristics creating a variety of wine products, wine regions must differentiate themselves for competitive advantage. Most vineyards start with the grape variety best suited to their geographical location and/or terroir. The main wine regions and grape varieties which Brazil's wine industry produce are represented in Table 1.

Table 1 highlights that array of differing grape varieties cultivated in Brazil and the value of unique terroirs for different wine regions. It is important to establish the positive attributes in which the grape cultivation and winemaking process can bring to a rural and regional area. This is best illustrated through wine tourism as it is increasing in importance from an economic and social perspective (Kantenholz & Lane, 2021).

5 Wine Tourism in Brazil

Wine tourism occurred in three phases in Brazil. The first phase was the arrival of Italian immigrants from 1875 to establishing vineyards and family houses which continued until the mid-1960s. The second phase was the expansion of wine tourism (1970–1990) and introduces wine events and festivals and the beginning of attracting visitors to wineries to sample wines. The third phase (1990–2004) is the consolidation of assets which saw large wine complexes and estates, accommodation, food, and wine visitation coming together by organised marketing and promotional strategies including designated wine routes on tourist maps (de Oliveira & Colchete Filho, 2016).

As the definition of wine tourism has developed and expanded over the last few decades, studies in the field of wine tourism have increased as well as the importance of attracting visitors to wine regions. In 2004, Carlsen wrote:

> Many wine regions and tourism destinations have realised that the benefits of wine tourism extend well beyond the cellar door to virtually all areas of the regional economy and into the urban areas that generate the majority of wine tourists. Wine, food, tourism, and the arts collectively comprise the core elements of the wine tourism product and provide the lifestyle package that wine tourists aspire to and seek to experience (p. 5).

These words have remained relevant with wine festivals, wine events and the use of technologies being added to have a more encompassing understanding of wine tourism. It is necessary then, to explore wine tourism in Brazil through facilities, services and wine products and how complementary businesses can benefit from wine tourism and winery visitation.

According to Ibravin, in 2016 approximately 600 vineyards were operating in Brazil and 150 of these wineries were actively involved with wine tourism. The entire country's wine industry has been based on the protection of small vineyards through cooperatives, territorial certifications, introduction of GI's and 'the proximity to the direct marketing of production allows an economic reproduction of the short chain while the consumer feedback allows the entrepreneurs to establish a virtuous circle of innovation from the new demands' (Salvagni et al., 2020). This is due to many multinational companies wanting to purchase small farms and are not representative of local culture. For competitive advantage, wine tourism distinguishes each wine region through wine products (starting with grape varieties cultivated), offering wine experiences and developing marketing strategies that attract visitors.

Most of the wine produced in Brazil is still consumed domestically therefore wine regions must cater for their needs. Brazil does provide the typical wine tourism offerings other wine producing countries offer. These include wine tasting at wineries, restaurants, café's, gift shops, winery tours and art exhibitions. Promotional material also encourages tourists to visit local town squares, shops, nearby cathedrals, nature trails, adventure parks, sample local produce, eat local dishes and of course, stay overnight in a variety of accommodation offerings (Winetourism.com, 2022).

However, Salvagni et al. (2020) argue that as Brazil's wine tourism strategy is still in its infancy (phase four), there is an opportunity to focus on Tyler's (1871) concept of culture which encompasses knowledge, beliefs, morals, laws, arts customs or any habits that assist with their goals and apply it to cultural tourism. This will ensure the preservation of entire wine regions including heritage, cultural events, local cuisine, customs and social habits will remain. It has also been put forward that wine tourism attracts tourist as they have a 'quest for knowledge about wine cultivation, production and tasting' which has fostered the growth of wine tourism and hedonic, enjoyable social wine experiences with family and friends which should be encouraged.

6 Global Wine Industry Versus the Brazilian Wine Sector

The ten largest global wine producing countries are Italy, France, Spain, the United States, and Australia Argentina, China, South Africa, Chile and Germany (Conway, 2021). Countries located in Europe, Middle East and Northern Africa are known as 'old world wineries' where countries colonised in the last few centuries including New Zealand, Australia, South Africa, Chile and Brazil are known as 'new world wineries' (Strickland et al., 2013).

The significance of a countries wine production can also be calculated by market share value against the US dollar. The means the countries wine value in percentages is 'France (30%), Italy (19%), Spain (10%), Chile (6%), Australia (5%), the United States (4%), Germany (4%), New Zealand (3%), Portugal (3%), and Argentina (3%)' (Wine Population Review, 2022).

Worldwide wine consumption in 2020 was estimated at 234 million hectolitres (Conway, 2021). Argentina was the largest wine-consuming country in Latin America, amounting to 9.4 million hectolitres, followed by Brazil, the second-largest wine-consuming market in the region with 4.3 million hectolitres (Trenda, 2022). The most popular wines were red varietals, specifically Malbec and Cabernet Sauvignon and Chardonnay and Sauvignon Blanc the most preferred white wine varietals in Brazil. Additionally, fortified wines used in mulled wine during traditional June festivities ('Festas Juninas') are still popular amongst Brazilians.

Brazil's global exports and quality of wine are increasing as a response to locals consuming more foreign wines in the last decade after placing pressure on the wine industry (Campbell, 2021). However, comparatively, Brazil is an emerging global market in the wine industry. Brazil is the largest Latin American economy and has an estimated population more than 210 million people, of which 150 million are over the legal alcohol consuming age of 20. It is also estimated that about 39 million consumers consumed wine at least once per month in Brazil which compares with other wine producing nations on average (Statista Research Department, 2022).

7 Managerial Implications

Managers of wineries need to consider how new winemaking countries like Brazil are innovating and being entrepreneurial in their business practices. This is important to know as the wine industry is competitive and any kind of new successful business practice that is implemented can have an effect on the company's success. This means it is important for managers to stay up to date with regards to what is happening in overseas marketplaces and to consider different strategic directions. Brazil has become a very successful winemaking country and has transformed the expectations about what it is to be a winemaker. Thus, managers of wineries and other food producing companies such as cheese makers need to consider new ways of thinking regarding marketing and production techniques.

As this chapter has discussed entrepreneurship and innovation in a winery can occur in a number of different ways. Therefore, managers should consider incremental as well as radical forms of innovation in terms of how it can be applied to winemaking companies. Incremental forms of innovation can involve minor changes such as a change in logo or branding. It can involve the addition of new product sizes or alterations in the way wine is shipped to consumers. Radical forms of innovation take a more substantive change and include introducing new types of wine into the marketplace that require time in terms of development. To do this managers need to keep up to date about changing tastes and preferences of consumers in order to anticipate future needs. This will help them in predicting growth trends and what needs to be done at the current point of time in order to fulfill future demands. This is a complex task and requires managers to spend time reading and researching new trends. Some trends will be able to predict based on current usages such as an increase in organic farming practices or healthier alternatives whilst other trends or events such as the COVID-19 pandemic are harder to predict. Therefore, there needs to be some flexibility with how wine managers anticipate and predict change. To do this requires winemakers to have a calm mind and think in a holistic way about possibilities. This will enable them to outcompete their competitors and obtain a better position in the marketplace.

8 Suggestions for Future Research

Other broad topics may include investigating gamification and other hedonic wine tourism experiences including virtual reality or the implementation of robots and drones serving wine, younger wine-consuming demographics such as Gen Z or people with disabilities. These may also include online master classes for wine connoisseurs, food and wine pairing hampers or access to celebrity chefs with matching wine with certain foods at affordable prices. Therefore, there is still so much to know regarding wine tourism in the Brazilian context. Whilst we have suggested some interesting topics there are more topics requiring attention. Thus, it is important to encourage more research on wine tourism in Brazil and in particular how it is entrepreneurial and innovative.

References

Botelho, R. V., & Pires, E. J. P. (2009). Viticultura como opção de desenvolvimento para os Campos Gerais. *Anais Encontro de Fruticultura dos Campos Gerais, 1*, 40–54. https://doi.org/10.5380/rsa.v12i3.34088

Campbell, L. (2021). Middle American languages. In L. Campbell & M. Mithun (Eds.), *The languages of native America: Historical and comparative assessment* (pp. 902–1000). University of Texas Press. https://doi.org/10.7560/746244-018

Carlsen, P. J. (2004). A review of global wine tourism research. *Journal of Wine Research, 15*(1), 5–13. https://doi.org/10.1080/0957126042000300281

Castro, V. A., & Giraldi, J. d. M. E. (2018). Shared brands and sustainable competitive advantage in the Brazilian wine sector. *International Journal of Wine Business Research, 30*(2), 243–259. https://doi.org/10.1108/IJWBR-04-2017-0019

Conway, J. (2021). *Global wine consumption 2000–2020*. Retrieved February 8, 2022 from https://www.statista.com/statistics/232937/volume-of-global-wine-consumption/

de Oliveira, D. M., & Colchete Filho, A. F. (2016). *City, architecture and wine: Wine tourism in the contemporary society*. In BIO web of conferences (Vol. 7, p. 03026). EDP Sciences. https://doi.org/10.1051/bioconf/20160703026.

Dutra, S. V., Adami, L., Marcon, A. R., Carnieli, G. J., Roani, C. A., Spinelli, F. R., Leonardelli, S., Ducatti, C., Moreira, Z., & Vanderlinde, R. (2011). Determination of the geographical origin of Brazilian wines by isotope and mineral analysis. *Analytical and Bioanalytical Chemistry, 401*(5), 1571–1576. https://doi.org/10.1007/s00216-011-5181-2

Ibravin. (2016). *Instituto Brasileiro do Vinho*. Retrieved February 9, 2022 from https://www.ibravin.org.br/Dados-Estatisticos

Kantenholz, E., & Lane, B. (2021). Delivering appealing and competitive rural wine tourism experiences. In R. Sharpley (Ed.), *Routledge handbook of the tourist experience*. Taylor & Francis Group, ProQuest Ebook Central. https://ebookcentral-proquest-com.ez.library.latrobe.edu.au/lib/latrobe/detail.action?docID=6727115

Salvagni, J., Nodari, C. H., & Valduga, V. (2020). Cooperation, innovation and tourism in the grape and wine region, Brazil. *Cuadernos de Desarrollo Rural, 17*. https://doi.org/10.11144/Javeriana.cdr17.citg

Statista Research Department. (2022). *Statista Research Department*. Retrieved 8 February, 2022 from https://www.statista.com/topics/5228/wine-industry-in-brazil/

Strickland, P., Smith-Maguire, J., & Frost, W. (2013). Using family heritage to market wines: A case study of three 'New World' wineries in Victoria, Australia. *International Journal of Wine Business Research, 25*(2), 125–137.

Trenda, E. (2022). *Largest wine markets in Latin America by consumption 2019–2020*. Retrieved February 8, 2022 from https://www.statista.com/statistics/982347/wine-consumption-latin-america-country/

Tyler, E. B. (1871). *Primitive culture: Researches into the development of mythology, philosophy, religion, art and custom* (Vol. 2). J. Murray.
Wine Population Review. (2022). *Wine Producing Countries 2022*. Retrieved February 8, from https://worldpopulationreview.com/country-rankings/wine-producing-countries
Winetourism.com. (2022). *Brazilian Wine Regions – country Brazil*. Retrieved February 9, 2022 from https://www.winetourism.com/wine-country/brazil/
Wurz, D. A., de Bem, B. P., Allebrandt, R., Bonin, B., Dalmolin, L. G., Canossa, A. T., Rufato, L. & Kretzschmar, A. A. (2017). *New wine-growing regions of Brazil and their importance in the evolution of Brazilian wine*. In BIO web of conferences (Vol. 9, p. 01025). EDP Sciences. https://doi.org/10.1051/bioconf/20170901025

Brazilian Entrepreneurship: Implications for ASEAN Countries

Mercedes Barrachina Fernández, María del Carmen García Centeno, and Carmen Calderón Patier

Abstract This chapter sheds light on the main characteristics of Brazil as an entrepreneurial ecosystem, by providing an up-to-date review of the status of the Brazilian entrepreneurship ecosystem, as well as identifying several challenges Brazil has to overcome, in order to foster the opportunities for the companies that are born in its territory and their growing possibilities. Several cities focused on entrepreneurial activities, such as São Paulo, Rio de Janeiro, Belo Horizonte, or Porto Alegre, are characterized in terms of their entrepreneurial ecosystems. Several research avenues are made available to the readers.

Keywords Entrepreneurial ecosystems · Cities · Brazil

1 Background

Brazil is one of the countries located in Latin America, Brazil is characterized as being the longest country in the world. Its capital is Brasilia and some of the biggest cities in this country are: Sao Paulo, Rio de Janeiro, or Salvador. Its main language is Portuguese, a difference from most of the Latin American countries whose main language is Spanish (Fig. 1).

Spain and Portugal have a strong connection with Brazil from 1494 to 1834, the Brazilian territory was ruled by one of those countries. It was not until 1834, when Spain recognized the independence of Brazil. According to information from the Spanish Ministry of Foreign Affairs, 15 million people living in Brazil are descendants of Spanish people.

M. B. Fernández (✉)
Departamento de Métodos Cuantitativos, Facultad de Ciencias Económicas y Empresariales, Universidad Pontificia de Comillas, Madrid, Spain
e-mail: mar.barrachina.ce@ceindo.ceu.es

M. del Carmen García Centeno · C. C. Patier
CEU University, Madrid, Spain

J. Leitão et al. (eds.), *Brazilian Entrepreneurship*, Studies on Entrepreneurship, Structural Change and Industrial Dynamics,
https://doi.org/10.1007/978-3-031-09392-0_10

Fig. 1 Brazil location in South America. Source: Authors' own

The report "Doing Business" is a specific business report designed and created by the World Bank (2020) and it tries to evaluate how difficult is to start a business in a specific country. It considers different variables, such as the needed time to create an officially create a company, the ease of getting a loan, the amount of taxes related to a corporation or the regulations that affect the different businesses. In this rank, Brazil is ranked in the position 124th, being New Zealand, the country located in first position and Somalia the country situated in the last one (190th).

In relation to the time to create a business in Brazil, it is interesting to mention that the average time to create a company is 17 days, according to data from 2019 (World Bank, 2020). However, there are countries in which this time is considerably lower, such as New Zealand or Georgia, in which it is possible to create a company in only 1 day.

Another interesting indicator to evaluate how is the entrepreneurial environment is the cost procedure for funding a company. According to data from the World Bank Database (World Bank, 2019), creating a company in Brazil has an average procedure cost of 4.2% of the GNI (Gross National Income). It is critical to mention that these procedures have zero cost in countries such as the United Kingdom or Slovenia.

Brazil can be considered an unlimited potential region for entrepreneurs and it is the third-largest entrepreneurship community (behind China and the United States). The country itself has several amazing areas and traditions, such as the Amazon, the surprising beach area in Rio, and the tradition of the Carnival. Brazil can be considered an entrepreneurial country, as one in six adults is involved in creating a business (GEM, 2014). Moreover, Brazil has experimented a continuous growth during the last 20 years, which caused an increase in the living standards decreasing the inequality between the population. Most of the Brazilian entrepreneurial companies evaluate the business models that succeeds in the United States and try to replicate them in their own country. This way of working is highlighted as related to the e-commerce companies or tech-based companies. Moreover, even though education is a huge barrier in Brazil, a huge effort is being performed by the educational institutions to foster entrepreneurship and one example of this can be exposed with the fact that 70% of the Brazilian universities have at least one course related to entrepreneurship. Another important point is that Brazil has transitioned in the past 40 years from an authoritarian military regime to a globalized democracy (Booker, 2013). Brazil's governments created an appropriate environment for flourishing startups, solving the challenges found during the process, little by little. Those figures can be utilized for countries (for example, the ASEAN countries) with the objective of being an entrepreneurship pole, showing the way to become, step by step, and with a strong collaboration between the different institutions, an entrepreneurial region.

2 Analysis

The main purpose of this section is to introduce relevant information about the Brazilian entrepreneurial ecosystem. This information will be focused on, first of all, an overview of the relevant characteristics of the country and second, interesting information about Brazil as an entrepreneurial ecosystem. Then, a subsection related to policies and tax benefits when creating a company is included. After that, relevant female entrepreneurship information is highlighted to understand if there are relevant differences between male and female entrepreneurial activities. A subsection related to social enterprise is also included to identify which is the importance of this type of entrepreneurship in Brazil. Finally, a subsection related to investors is incorporated in this section.

2.1 Overview

Brazil is the country with the highest number of entrepreneurs. According to the survey of respondents provided by the GEM (2014), around 34.5% of Brazilians have a company or are involved in the creation of a new business. This key fact is really important, as Brazil is ahead of countries such as China, the United States, or Japan.

Entrepreneurship in Brazil started in 1990 with the support of the Brazilian Service to Support Micro and Small Enterprises (SEBRAE for the name in Portuguese) of the Brazilian Society for Software Export (SOFTEX). Those organizations have the main purpose of providing help and support to entrepreneurs to give them the appropriate resource to create a business.

Of the almost 50 million Brazilians who have become entrepreneurs, 59.4% decided to create their own business because of the opportunity, meanwhile, 39.9% of them create a company due to necessity, according to information provided by the SEBRAE (2017).

2.2 Entrepreneurial Ecosystem

The entrepreneurial ecosystem is an essential element when developing ideas and funding new companies, having big cities as the main entrepreneurship areas as they attract talent and offer opportunities to have professional careers. Interestingly, most of the startups in Brazil are headquartered in the South-Eastern region. The most relevant cities in Brazil related to entrepreneurship are São Paulo, Rio de Janeiro, Belo Horizonte, and Porto Alegre. Below some significant information about each of those entrepreneurial cities are detailed:

- *São Paulo*: It is one of the best cities in Latin America for doing business. The main advantage of São Paulo is the access to capital, in comparison with the other Brazilian cities. Population in this city is around 15 million people, and it is responsible for almost 20% of the Brazilian's GDP (Gross Domestic Product) (World Bank, 2020).
- *Rio de Janeiro*: This is the second largest city in Brazil and a very popular destination among tourists. The culture of this city has changed dramatically in the last decade transforming into a pole of entrepreneurship and attracting investors from around the world. Social entrepreneurship, especially those affecting women, is transforming the work and the support to the community (Pioneer, 2020).
- *Belo Horizonte*: This city is the sixth largest city in Brazil, is located in the state of Minas Gerais and it is also known as "San Pedro Valley." It is the headquarters for different startups, and this place has become an important player in the local entrepreneurship ecosystem. This area is famous for having four Universities that serve as a tech hub for the creation of new companies based on technology. There

are multiple examples of companies with their origin in Belo Horizonte, such as Sympla, Smarttbot, and Mercado de Residuos.

- *Porto Alegre*: In this city, the startup community is rising extremely quickly. All the entrepreneurs who work in the area have three factors in common: they are young, they are innovative, and they want a better future for Brazil. The ideas built around this hub are focused on technology, education, and also in social entrepreneurship.

2.3 Policies and Tax Benefits

The main objective of this subsection is to present the most suitable details about the fiscal and legal environment that support entrepreneurship in Brazil.

Sometimes, the entrepreneurial ecosystems face different challenges or barriers, as a consequence of the market behavior, the institutional behavior, or the lack of resources. Policies are useful to reduce the barriers and secure the economic and social benefits created by the entrepreneurship (Stinchcombe, 1965).

According to Ferreira et al. (2018), there are 94 federal government public entrepreneurship policies and the following table categorizes those policies according to the focused area:

- Promotion of entrepreneurship
- Education in entrepreneurship
- Reduce barriers to entry/exit
- Financial support
- General support
- Infrastructure
- Technology and innovation

In the literature, there are several studies that justify the importance of entrepreneurship and the critical factor of having policy support to foster those activities. In Brazil, the lack of support from the government, especially for the social entrepreneurship is remarkable.

2.4 Female Entrepreneurship

It is important to start this section by highlighting that, according to a report from the Brazilian Federal Government, 75% of Brazilian households are headed by women (financially).

Startups in Brazil are led by women only in 10% of the cases, according to the female founder's report of 2021 (Distrito, 2021), meanwhile, traditional companies are found in a 46% by women.

There are different fears faced by women when thinking about becoming entrepreneurs, mainly related to uncertainty about the future, the instability in the sector, or the financial concerns (Camargo et al. 2018).

2.5 SME in Brazil

The information published by the OECD (2020a) indicates that the micro-sized enterprises and the small-sized companies are key in Brazil's economy, representing 98.5% of the existing companies, and producing 27% of Brazil's GDP. The employment provided by those companies is around 62% of the total employment.

Even though, the mentioned companies are key in the Brazilian economy, they do not have appropriate access to credit, limiting the expansion possibilities. According to the SEBRAE (*Serviço Brasileiro de Apoio às Micro e Pequenas Empresas*), around 20% of the credits requested were denied by the banks, highlighting the difficulty to access money (SEBRAE, 2018).

It is interesting to mention the existence of the National Bank for Economic and Social Development (BNDES, for *Banco Nacional de Desenvolvimento Econômico e Social*) which is a federal public company linked to the Ministry of Economy. This bank has a main purpose: to provide long-term financing options to companies that really support the country's development. Therefore, this bank provides money with the purpose of expanding, modernizing, improving the production capacity, and increasing the competitiveness of the Brazilian companies.

The policies related to entrepreneurship executed by the Brazilian Government are efficiently coordinated through the Ministry of Economy, at institutional and operational levels. There is a specific organization, called the Permanent Forum on Micro and Small Business (FPMPE), which is responsible for monitoring the implementation of the policies and the execution of programs related to entrepreneurship (OECD, 2020b).

2.6 Social Enterprise

It has been reported that one of the most typical barrier to grow economically is the lack of understanding in relation to the purpose and natural of the sectors related to the social enterprise in Brazil (Möller et al., 2020). It is interesting to remark that social enterprises are far more inclusive than Brazilian traditional companies, having a majority of women in leadership positions.

Most of the concepts developed in Brazil related to social entrepreneurship have been influenced by countries such as the United States, the United Kingdom, or Canada.

In the literature, there are several studies that highlight the potential actions to improve the government support to perform social entrepreneurial activities. Some of those activities can be summarized as promoting the creation of an Agency for Social Entrepreneurship, supporting the creation of a database with information about the organizations and the potential support agencies, or increasing the visibility of the companies using different resources, including communication and social support (Ladeira & Machado, 2013).

2.7 Investors

Now, there is a great boom in relation to the investment in startups in Brazil. According to information published by the Brazil-American chamber of commerce, there is an attraction from investors to support startups in a country that has been long dominated by big corporations.

The support of venture capital investments for entrepreneurship in 2021 reached 33.5 billion Brazilian reals, tripling the investment volume of the previous year. It is interesting to highlight that private equity is focusing on companies that are already consolidated, meanwhile, the venture capital supports emerging companies with a very specific characteristic: a high growth potential.

3 Challenges

In previous sections, it has been possible to understand the Brazilian entrepreneurial activities, so now, it is necessary to consider and debate the challenges that the Brazilian ecosystem is suffering and also to understand the barriers that the entrepreneurs are overcoming when starting a company in this country.

- *Investment flow*: One of the most relevant challenges faced by Brazilian entrepreneurs is the flow of investment, so it is necessary to improve the deal flow and its future potential.
- *Institutional support*: In other countries, the support of public initiatives, local investors, and the implementation of programs to make startups grow are widely developed. However, in Brazil, the tradition of having local investors supporting startups is not very common.
- *Reduction of entry and exit barriers*: The entry barriers and exit barriers are the first and last challenges when funding a company, respectively.

4 Implications for ASEAN Countries

Previous sections have been focused on evaluating the main characteristics of entrepreneurship in Brazil. Now, it is time to identify the main implications that can be identified for the ASEAN countries.

As it has been detailed before, Brazil is a great entrepreneurship pole and it had a great development during the last 40 years. It can be a good example for other countries to learn about the main actions to transform a country into an entrepreneurial region.

One of the most important considerations is the support from the government to foster entrepreneurship in the Brazilian main cities. The ASEAN countries that desire to become a reference in the entrepreneurial sphere, need a strong help and support from the different levels of public institutions, including the national government, the regional government, and the local government.

It is key to highlight that the social attitudes toward entrepreneurship in the ASEAN region is generally positive, as more than half of the population consider that the entrepreneurship choice is a great option to development a career. This point helped the Brazilian population to develop a career in the entrepreneurship area.

Another relevant factor is the participation of females in entrepreneurial activities. The ASEAN region is the one with the best rate when considering gender equity for becoming an entrepreneur. In Brazil, the support for women to become entrepreneurs was one of the most relevant points to foster innovation and the creation of businesses in the area.

5 Conclusions

The main purpose of this study was to determine the main characteristics of Brazil as an entrepreneurial ecosystem.

This study contributed to the literature in two ways. The first contribution is related to the review of the status of the Brazilian entrepreneurship ecosystem. There is a growing entrepreneurship environment blowing and the government is supporting its development. There are different cities focused on entrepreneurial activities, such as São Paulo, Rio de Janeiro, Belo Horizonte, or Porto Alegre. Those cities are growing their communities related to entrepreneurship and getting international attention. The second contribution is associated with the challenges. There are several challenges Brazil has to overcome to increase the opportunities of the companies that are born in its territory and their growing possibilities.

This analysis is subject to the limitations that occurred as a consequence of the information found during the search of the literature.

A potential line of research to extend this study could be evaluating in a quantitative analysis the factors that affect entrepreneurship in Brazil. Another potential line of research could be focusing the analysis on the characteristics of female entrepreneurship or social entrepreneurship in Brazil.

References

Booker, L. C. (2013). Encouraging Entrepreneurship: Brazil's Bid in Latin America. *Urbanization in International Affairs, 74*(1).

Camargo, R., Lourenço, M., & Ferreira, J. (2018). Entrepreneurial women in Brazil: What are their fears? *Review of Business Management, 20*, 178–193. https://doi.org/10.7819/rbgn.v20i2.3578

Distrito. (2021). *Female Founders Report 2021.* Available at: https://materiais.distrito.me/dataminer-female-founders-report

Ferreira, V., Andreassi, T., Silva, G., Borges, C., & Bezerra, E. (2018). Entrepreneurship policy in Brazil: Its focus and gaps. *International Journal of Entrepreneurship and Small Business, 34*, 183. https://doi.org/10.1504/IJESB.2018.10013257

GEM. (2014). *Global Entrepreneurship Monitor Report 2014.* Available at https://www.gemconsortium.org/report/gem-2014-global-report

Ladeira, F., & Machado, H. (2013). Social entrepreneurship: A reflection for adopting public policies that support the third sector in Brazil. *Journal of Technology Management & Innovation, 8*(17). https://doi.org/10.4067/S0718-27242013000300017

Möller, G., Perfeito da Silva, P., & Valiati, L. (2020). *Creative and social enterprise in Brazil.* British Council.

OECD. (2020a). *Financing SMEs and entrepreneurs 2020: An OECD scoreboard.*

OECD. (2020b). *SME and Entrepreneurship Policy in Brazil 2020.* Available at: https://www.oecd-ilibrary.org/sites/cc5feb81-en/1/2/4/index.html?itemId=/content/publication/cc5feb81-en&_csp_=a785eb8de77c906eb32397f9c2e77129&itemIGO=oecd&itemContentType=book

Pioneer. (2020). *Female black power: The Rio de Janeiro entrepreneurship group finding solidarity amid crisis.* Available at: https://www.pioneerspost.com/news-views/20200807/female-black-power-the-rio-de-janeiro-entrepreneurship-group-finding-solidarity

SEBRAE. (2017). *Serviço Brasileiro de Apoio às Micro e Pequenas Empresas* (2017). Edital de Credenciamento SEBRAE/PR N° 01/2017.

SEBRAE. (2018). *Anuário do Trabalho nos Pequenos Negócios, Brazilian Micro and Small Business Suport Service (SEBRAE).*

Stinchcombe, A. L. (1965). Social structure and organizations. In J. March (Ed.), *Handbook of organizations* (pp. 142–193). Rand McNally.

World Bank. (2020). *Doing Business 2020.* Available at: https://documents1.worldbank.org/curated/en/688761571934946384/pdf/Doing-Business-2020-Comparing-Business-Regulation-in-190-Economies.pdf

World Bank, World Development Indicators. (2019). *Cost of business start-up procedures.* Retrieved from https://data.worldbank.org/indicator/IC.REG.COST.PC.ZS

Learning Intention in Brazilian University Students: Self-Legitimation of Independence and the Search for Entrepreneurial Culture

Jocilene Gadioli de Oliveira, Serena Cubico, Romina Fucà, Piermatteo Ardolino, and João Leitão

Abstract This research chapter uses a self-anchored scale that aims to enhance the importance attributed to the promotion of an "entrepreneurial culture" among university students in Brazil. This last is seen as a crucial reference point to ensure the new Brazilian generations will deal with higher awareness of their future educational and professional development. In partnership with the CIG—Center for Entrepreneurial Youth of the University of Verona, Italy, the authors have conducted in 2015 an empirical survey merged into a PhD thesis' sample of 553 Brazilian university students. The outcome of about 417 final respondents has provided findings for identifying how the educational institutions in Brazil may respond also to the demands for a stronger entrepreneurial culture able to consolidate sustainability in the country. The chapter is divided into four sections, each of which is a stepping stone for the construction of a kind of FIFO (First-In, First Out) measurement of peoples' entrepreneurial leanness and performance ability (ELPA).

Keywords Entrepreneurial culture · Learning intention · University bonds with the entrepreneurial world · Entrepreneurial leanness and performance ability (ELPA)

J. G. de Oliveira
SEDU - State Department of Education, State of Espírito Santo, Vila Velha, Brazil
e-mail: jocilene.oliveira@educator.edu.es.gov.br

S. Cubico · R. Fucà · P. Ardolino
Department of Business Economy, School in Public Management, University of Verona, Verona, Italy
e-mail: serena.cubico@univr.it; romina.fuca@univr.it

J. Leitão (✉)
Department of Management and Economics, NECE - Research Center in Business Sciences, University of Beira Interior, Covilhã, Portugal
e-mail: jleitao@ubi.pt

J. Leitão et al. (eds.), *Brazilian Entrepreneurship*, Studies on Entrepreneurship, Structural Change and Industrial Dynamics,
https://doi.org/10.1007/978-3-031-09392-0_11

1 Introduction: Entrepreneurial Culture and Learning Intention

Defined as the commitment that an individual has to start his own business, entrepreneurial culture is the culture that intentionally corroborates, especially in Higher Education Institutions (HEIs), integration efforts between the entrepreneurial world in a country and the pool of university students (Jardim et al., 2021; Kreiser et al., 2010; Wong, 2014). It is also "an environment where people are motivated to innovate, create and take risks" (Ioannidou, 2020). Within this standpoint, students then should have to look for awareness of uniting forces with the entrepreneurial sections of society, trying to profit from accessible and integrated programs aimed at establishing partnerships also with the labor force at large. More than on traditional research apprenticeships and dependent work perspectives, entrepreneurial culture coupled with a learning intention means to synthesize (1) the ability to cope with risk and uncertainties; (2) the ability to take advantage of close family a/o friends' economical support; (3) the acknowledgment of country-specific institutional characteristics; and (4) the awareness that public financial backing for the innovation of products and services will be hard to achieve when not discouraged by bureaucratization of the process (Newman et al., 2019). An immense country with a very agriculturally based economy, and a flourishing start-up acceleration aimed at transforming solutions and approaches with foreign investors Brazil is the special gateway of the decision-making processes that may allow the development of business best practices (Cubico et al., 2010). The current economic-financial crisis which, to a large extent, has also affected the Brazilian labor market, involving, besides an increase in youth unemployment rates a deep rethinking of the concept of employment, has pushed increasingly the market orientation toward the so-called "self-employment." In turn, a leaning toward humanistic values in the educational settings is arising, or rather the awareness HEIs should not only be boosting competitive expectations by students but also prone to fostering awareness toward both a favorable and an unfavorable admission to the job world.

Though, political, economic, and socio-cultural environment factors that influence entrepreneurship may be somehow deferred by the acquaintance students may acquire during their studies with working conditions tend to rethink both models and scenarios of economy. Developing entrepreneurial skills in the context of the Brazilian university setting respond then to the actual demands of the labor market. In Brazil, it is in fact currently fashionable to promote sustainable growth and entrepreneurial co-shared opportunities. Last but not least to be considered, small local businesses owe an intrinsic utilitarian importance given to education, i.e., "education aimed at economic growth" (Nussbaum, 2011, p. 37).

2 The Empirical Survey on Brazilian University Students

The present study makes a number of references to systematic literature on the integration between schools, universities, team networks, and the labor market. Identification of established relationships among actors and resources is paramount not only for the development of a country's economy, but above all from the perspective of a social consciousness of an entrepreneurial culture. We intended to develop a model of students who is more active, more aware of their own skills, more independent, and with the ability to cope with transformation, research, and a high likelihood of lifelong learning paths.

2.1 The Sample

In the study carried out by J. Oliveira (2015) and the Centre for Entrepreneurial Youth of the University of Verona, Italy, in two Brazilian universities, 553 college students took part in the research, with 417 valid results through the implementation of a ESeOQ—Entrepreneurship and Self-Employment Orientation Questionnaire. Of the total of 417 university students in Brazil, 57.1% were students of the Universidade Federal do Espírito Santo, 42.2% of the Universidade de Vila Velha, and 0.7% of other Brazilian universities who had access to the survey by chance. More than focusing on personality traits and self-efficacy (Danish et al., 2019; Fitzsimmons & Douglas, 2011; Manolova et al., 2007) or other descriptive features such as gender and age, this survey levered on socio-economic factors and pre-existing entrepreneurial background among respondents.

While personality traits and gender features are often used as an explanation of organizational success enhances also gender differences about innovative creativity (Na & Shin, 2019), our perspective has chosen the angle of the trust Brazilian students could nurture through university entrepreneurial courses to prepare them to face risks and solve unexpected challenges. "Starting a business is a complex process which involves a variety of motivations and stimuli," (Birley and Westhead, 1994 in: van der Zwan et al., 2016, p. 278) though earlier evidence of some experience in firms as well as the opportunity to enter entrepreneurship through the back door thanks to some relationship in the entrepreneurial family/friends circle is an asset considered in our research as a turning point. This ensures students' learning will drive the intention for running a business after finishing university studies. Brazilian students are asking for specific entrepreneurship courses that may enable themselves to overcome financial barriers as well as increase in value of their entrepreneurial traits. By our sample, the more prevalent in Brazilian students are: *Determinação para alcançar objetivos* or determination in achieving goals (49.4%), *Espírito de iniciativa* or spirit of initiative (45.3%), and *Independência* or independence (42%). In Fig. 1 some of the sample's key descriptive features.

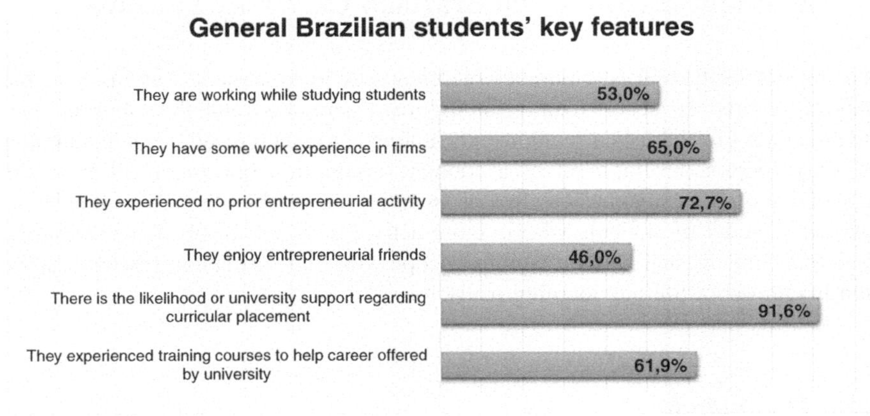

Fig. 1 General Brazilian students' key features. *Note: The shown percentages in the graph are the more prevalent in the 2015 sample by Oliveira and the Centre for Entrepreneurial Youth (University of Verona, Italy)

As a matter of fact, 53% of the Brazilian sample is made up of student workers, and 45.8% of people have no job while studying. In addition, 19.9% did not know or answer which investment may be required to become an entrepreneur; while 20.4% have never worked or already had some work experience in firms (65%).

2.2 *Entrepreneurial Network, Prior Work Experience, and Awareness of Skills*

We have therefore focused on "Entrepreneurial leanness and performance ability" (ELPA) of Brazilian students. They could have from findings a certain ground from where to take logical, reasoned decisions to deal with specific behaviors (Fishbein & Ajzen, 1975; Ajzen & Fishbein, 1980) like the starting of a new business—of those who were not already entrepreneurs, 6.7% said they had tried in the past to start a business considering also a high percentage (55.9%) of them have entrepreneurs in their family/social circles. However, both the Theory of Planned Behavior (TPB) and the Theory of Reasoned Action (TRA) have been translated in our chapter into the Perceived Behavioral Control (PBC) regarding the intention to become an entrepreneur (Vamvaka et al., 2020; Heuer & Kolvereid, 2014).

Assumptions about their entrepreneurial family/friends circles (46% have entrepreneur friends, 20.9% have entrepreneur father, 23.7% have entrepreneur grandparents and uncles, 11.5% have entrepreneur mother, 20.9% have entrepreneur

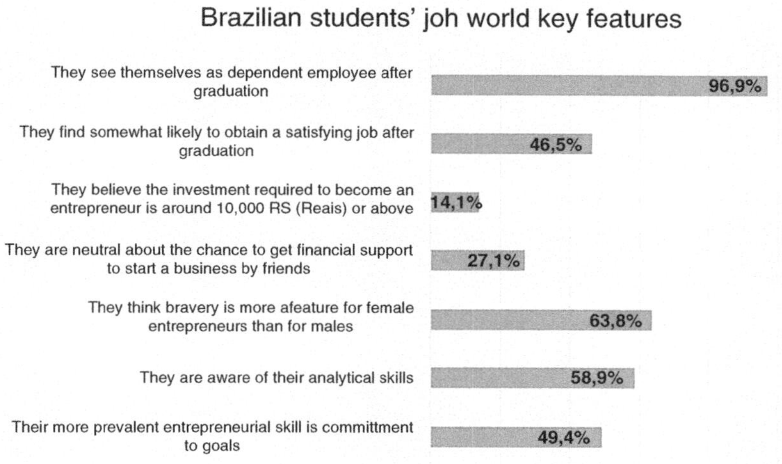

Fig. 2 Brazilian students' job world key features. *Note: The showed percentages in the graph are the more prevalent in the 2015 sample by Oliveira and the Centre for Entrepreneurial Youth (University of Verona, Italy)

brothers, 2.6% have a spouse or 0.2% siblings who are entrepreneurs)[1] as well as about the skills that Brazilian students feel to owe (*Capacidade de reconhecer pontos de melhoria* or ability to identify your strengths in the 50.6%; *Capacidade de análise* or analytical skills in the 58.9% and *Capacidade de planejamento* or Planning capacity in the 48.4%) has allowed us to construct a measure of ELPA, consists mainly of their self-trust in the likelihood of university support regarding curricula placement. From there it comes the consequent search and demand for tools, expertise, ties, and specific competences to become an entrepreneur in Brazil (Darling-Hammond et al., 2020). Their awareness of personal skills essential to become an entrepreneur (58.9% of respondents answered to owe analytical skills), and the more pertinent prevalent skills among them (49.4% are committed to goals) have both been considered not as effects but instead as assumptions motivating the consequent search and demand for entrepreneurial culture and learning intention in Brazilian educational settings (Ferreira et al., 2017). In Fig. 2, some of the sample's key descriptive features related to respondents' background in the job world.

[1] Multiple answers were possible.

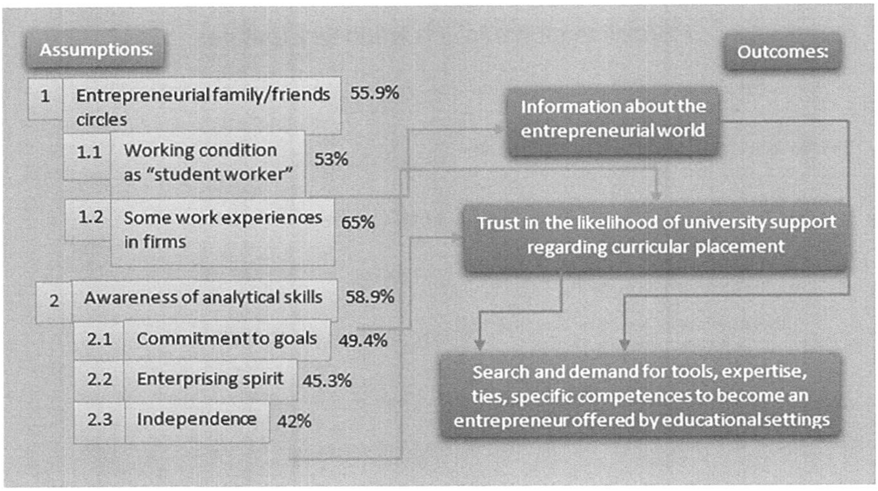

Fig. 3 Assumptions and outcomes for ELPA. *Note: The shown percentages in the graph are those in the 2015 sample by Oliveira and the Centre for Entrepreneurial Youth (University of Verona, Italy)

2.3 *Education and Entrepreneurial Training*

About the likelihood to find a satisfying and fitting job after graduation, the Brazilian students answered positively since higher percentages have demonstrated a trust in the likelihood of university support regarding curricular placement, as well as to have enjoyed a previous experience in training courses to help career offered by the university (46.5% and 12.5%, respectively).

It is important therefore to note that Brazilian students showed confidence in the university system, as they see the university as a driving force to understand jobs and careers. When asked whether the university can help young people to become entrepreneurs, the outcome shows that 61.9% of students believe the university can help through the training courses it offers, of which 23% through specific consultancies, while only 13.9% believe the university is not helpful. Especially students coming from the following areas: Management, Economics, Tourism and Accounting (20.2%), Electrical, Electronics and Mechanics (16.3%), and Mathematics and Computing (11.5%), showed a significant trust on career paths and opportunities offered by the university.

In Fig. 3, a graphic representation of both assumptions and outcomes for ELPA, a measure of Brazilian students' entrepreneurial leanness and performance ability obtained through the 2015 sample.

Although a strong difference can be traced between opportunity- and necessity-motivated business owners, our students have not yet the instruments to discern pros and cons about self-employment versus paid employment. They have enjoyed the chance to be more independent, optimist, and competitive, though not perceiving to the fullest which factors are key to a balanced understanding of time, money, and maximization of resources available for entrepreneurship (Cubico et al., 2018). Notwithstanding apparently, respondents seem to consider themselves future dependent employees (96.9%)—because likely tailored educational paths are expensive and inaccessible to most of the population, or the official administrative substrates somehow hamper competition and entrepreneurial capacity—in reality, Brazilian students may take advantage of their information about the entrepreneurial world and turn their personal background in a more transformative future.

3 Entrepreneurial Skills and the Brazilian Educational System

In Brazil, entrepreneurship keeps on being considered since years one of the most powerful strategies to overcome the social and economic troubles, because it is intended as a drive of social inclusion and "it refers to culture, which has the power to induce or inhibit entrepreneurial competencies." (Dolabela, 2003, p. 15). A continuously developing number of practices, initiatives, or activities that exist in the Brazilian country show that citizens believe in the likelihood of gaining competencies and preparation for a career switch is significantly tied up with the entrepreneurial world. In Brazil, over the years, especially from 2002 to 2019 was more visible an "entrepreneurship by necessity"—people who because of lack of employability took themselves the risk of starting a business. This has now decreased in view of an "entrepreneurship by opportunity," together with participating institutions are invited to contribute to the quality of "agents of transformation and wealth creation for societies" (GEM, 2019, p. 56).

The Brazilian labor market is equally featured by a mechanism of fruitful social inclusion, in which one finds micro or small entrepreneurs who, to escape from poverty, start their own business, or else young people who seek to access opportunities surfing transversally various sectors. Companies are evolving into hybrid organizations that have the "dual purpose of earning money for its stakeholders and of addressing defined social objectives" (Comini et al., 2012, p. 389). Entrepreneurship centers, business incubators, and both minors and majors in entrepreneurship education, as well as business plan competitions, are all increasing in number, as well as the events that stimulate entrepreneurship and business ethics.

Within this relevantly evolving educational frame, we have enhanced the research top 9 "transformational independence performance ability indicators" (TIPAIs) in Brazilian students are further elaborated using the data obtained through the ESeOQ—*Entrepreneurship and Self-Employment Orientation Questionnaire* entrepreneurial culture and learning intention: (1) working condition (Wcon), (2) prior experience in firms (Pef), (3) entrepreneurial direct activity (Eda), (4) ties with the entrepreneurial world (Tew), (5) the university as a driving force to understand jobs and careers (Udf), (6) career paths and opportunities offered by universities (Cpo),

(7) likelihood to find a satisfying and fitting job after graduation (Lffj), (8) investment required to become an entrepreneur (Ir), and (9) likelihood of support to start a business by friends (Lsbf).[2] In Table 1, we show the results of this merging of different data in a view of ensemble for the 417 respondents.

This means we had by one side a 3-point measurement thorough data collection of sampled respondents on some of the students' features and by another side a submitted 5-point Likert scale's results about some of the respondent's behaviors. Unifying these two typologies of data, we have created a from 1 to 5-point scale showing the estimating raw numbers of respondents for each of the 9 TIPAIs.

After a prior evaluation of feasibility, through a chi-square statistic 655.5924, with p-value at <0.00001 and a result significant at $p < 0.05$ for the first five indicators, and a chi-square statistic 576.3632, with p-value at <0.00001 and result significant at $p < 0.05$ for the second four indicators, we have then self-assigned again a random scoring from 1 to 5 to the 417 respondents for each of the 9 TIPAIs on a case by case basis related to the raw numbers of respondents showed in Table 1. This has generated the ELPA for each one of the respondents is equal to the below formula:

$$((\text{Wcon} + \text{Pef})^{*}(\text{Eda} + \text{Tew} + \text{Udf} + \text{Cpo}) - (\text{Lffj} + \text{Ir} + \text{Lsbf}) \qquad (1)$$

Figure 4 shows ELPA scores per group of respondents with average values and relative standard deviations.

Total final scores had a mean of 50,67, with median at 48,08, standard deviation of 24,63, kurtosis at 0.58, and skewness 0.78. Minimum score by respondents was 4.75 and maximum was 150.41. The ELPA final scale for all the 417 respondents shows results clustered in 5 big clusters with respective ranges (a) poor entrepreneurial leanness and performance ability (from 1 to 30 lower scores), (b) fair entrepreneurial leanness and performance ability (from 31 to 60 place of scores' range), (c) good entrepreneurial leanness and performance ability (from 61 to 90 place of scores' range), (d) very good entrepreneurial leanness and performance ability (from 91 to 120 place of scores' range), and (e) excellent entrepreneurial leanness and performance ability (from 121 to 150 place of scores' range).

4 Final Considerations

Effectiveness of a committed preparation and the consequent search for university programs may enable students to take advantage of business opportunities, develop business models, and develop marketing plans is first and foremost an essential

[2]These items have been drawn from the sample either from the submission of a 5-point Likert scales, and of a 3-point data collection we have converted into 5-point with the simple following IBM method: $(5-1)*(x - 1)/(3-1) + 1 = 4*(x - 1)/2 + 1 = (4/2)*x - (4/2) + 1 = 2*x - (-1)$.

Table 1 Data outputs

Conversion of a 3-point scale to a 5-point scale		Wcon	Pef	Eda	Tew	Udf	Cpo	Fp	Lffj	Ir	Lsbf
1 = 1.0	Not likely = 1 (or 1.0)	95	67	153	104	14	29	103	18	93	89
2 = 1.5; 2.0	Somewhat unlikely = 2 (or 1.5)	97	69	150	104	14	29	103	35	87	89
3 = 2.5; 3.0	Neutral = 3 (or 2.0)	5	9	64	1	6	5	1	84	102	154
	Somewhat likely = 4 (or 2.5)	109	135	25	103	192	177	104	221	56	52
	Very likely = 5 (or 3.0)	111	137	25	105	191	177	106	59	79	33
	Column totals	417	417	417	417	417	417	417	417	417	417

[a]Note: Some of the raw numbers of respondents obtained during data collection are split between one extreme or another of the scale. This is because we could not exactly state in relation to the 3-point measurement how many of these would have chosen "not likely" or "somewhat likely" by one side, and "somewhat likely" or "very likely" from the other, and then these raw numbers are to be considered alike estimates of the true raw numbers

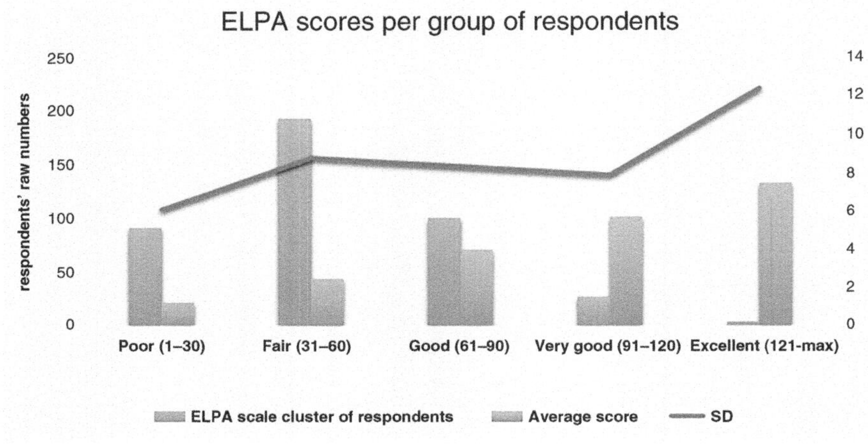

Fig. 4 ELPA scores per group of respondents. *Note: ELPA final scores per group of respondents with average values and standard deviations

element of the dissemination of the entrepreneurial culture in university settings. Individuals and societies are more and more integrated into multidisciplinary levels of education, giving priority to the awareness of risk and rapid transformation of the best-praised quality features for growth. Entrepreneurship is a challenge not only for a personal pursuit of self-interest to be effectively long-lasting must be in accordance with the demands of the society at large, but also an interconnected attractor and detractor of perception, effort, information, gain, and why not failure (Hoogendoorn et al., 2019). In this sense and further, the limitations of our study refer to the actual moving landscape for environment, health cooperation, and communication of skills. Our referenced empirical survey dates back to some years ago, and therefore Brazil could experience still new facilitators for secondary and higher education programs. Another limitation is we have not pondered our data by gender, and notwithstanding inclusion of women in entrepreneurial businesses as well as in other positions in the labor market has grown over the years in Brazil, women make up still a more modest percentage of stable over time entrepreneurs (GEM, 2019).

By another way, we are confident our findings provide evidence that also small prior experience in firms coupled with ties with the entrepreneurial world encourages the students to have trust on the university as a driving force to understand jobs and careers as well as it enables them to search for theoretical inconsistencies and gaps in the materials offered by educational settings.

References

Ajzen, I., & Fishbein, M. (1980). *Understanding attitudes and predicting social behavior*. Prentice-Hall.

Comini, G., Barki, E., & de Aguiar, L. T. (2012). A three-pronged approach to social business: A Brazilian multi-case analysis. *R. Adm., São Paulo, 47*(3), 385–397. Accessed March 30, 2022, from https://www.scielo.br/j/rausp/a/Yx53pdPkT55yvJcX6fMm3Kc/?format=pdf&lang=en

Cubico, S., Bortolani, E., Favretto, G., & Sartori, R. (2010). Describing the entrepreneurial profile: The entrepreneurial aptitude test (TAI). *International Journal of Entrepreneurship and Small Business, 11*(4), 424–435. https://doi.org/10.1504/ijesb.2010.036295

Cubico, S., Favretto, G., Leitão, J., & Cantner, U. (Eds.). (2018). *Entrepreneurship along the Industry Life Cycle: The changing role of entrepreneurial activities and knowledge competencies*. Springer.

Danish, R. Q., Asghar, J., Ahmad, Z., et al. (2019). Factors affecting "entrepreneurial culture": The mediating role of creativity. *Journal of Innovation and Entrepreneurship, 8*(14). https://doi.org/10.1186/s13731-019-0108-9

Darling-Hammond, L., Flook, L., Cook-Harvey, C., Barron, B., & Osher, D. (2020). Implications for educational practice of the science of learning and development. *Applied Developmental Science, 24*(2), 97–140. https://doi.org/10.1080/10888691.2018.1537791

Dolabela, F. (2003). *Pedagogia Empreendedora. O ensino de empreendedorismo na educação básica, voltado para o desenvolvimento social sustentável*. Editora de Cultura.

Ferreira, J. J. M., Fernandes, C. I., & Ratten, V. (2017). The influence of entrepreneurship education on entrepreneurial intentions. In *Entrepreneurial universities* (pp. 19–34). Springer.

Fishbein, M., & Ajzen, I. (1975). *Belief, attitude, intention, and behavior: An Introduction to theory and research*. Addison-Wesley.

Fitzsimmons, J., & Douglas, E. (2011). Interaction between feasibility and desirability in the formation of entrepreneurial intentions. *Journal of Business Venturing, 26*(4), 431–440. Accessed March 29, 2022, from https://www.researchgate.net/publication/227418360_Interaction_Between_Feasibility_and_Desirability_in_the_Formation_of_Entrepreneurial_Intentions

Global Entrepreneurship Monitor [GEM]. (2019). *Empreendedorismo no Brasil*. Accessed March 16, 2022, from https://ibqp.org.br/wp-content/uploads/2021/02/Empreendedorismo-no-Brasil-GEM-2019.pdf

Heuer, Annamária; Kolvereid, Lars. Source: European Journal of Training and Development, Volume 38, Number 6, 2014, pp. 506-523(18).

Hoogendoorn, B., van der Zwan, P., & Thurik, R. (2019). Sustainable entrepreneurship: The role of perceived barriers and risk. *Journal of Business Ethics, 157*, 1133–1154. https://doi.org/10.1007/s10551-017-3646-8

Ioannidou, N. (2020). *Entrepreneurial culture. Erasmus plus project result*. Slide 6. Accessed March 28, 2022, from https://ec.europa.eu/programmes/erasmus-plus/project-result-content/0566697d-2625-48a9-b3ad-574fb75085ee/B5%20-%20Entrepreneurial%20Culture.pdf

Jardim, J., Bártolo, A., & Pinho, A. (2021). Towards a global entrepreneurial culture: A systematic review of the effectiveness of entrepreneurship education programs. *Education in Science, 11*(398). https://doi.org/10.3390/educsci11080398

Kreiser, P. M., Marino, L. D., Dickson, P., & Weaver, K. M. (2010). Cultural influences on entrepreneurial orientation: The impact of national culture on risk taking and proactiveness in SMEs. *Entrepreneurship Theory and Practice, 34*(5), 959–983. https://doi.org/10.1111/j.1540-6520.2010.00396.x

Manolova, T. S., Carter, N. M., Manev, I. M., & Gyoshev, B. S. (2007). The differential effect of men and women entrepreneurs' human capital and networking on growth expectancies in Bulgaria. *Entrepreneurship Theory and Practice., 31*(3), 407–426. https://doi.org/10.1111/j.1540-6520.2007.00180.x

Na, K., & Shin, K. (2019). The gender effect on a firm's innovative activities in the emerging economies. *Sustainability., 11*(7), 1992. https://doi.org/10.3390/su11071992

Newman, A., Obschonka, M., Schwarz, S., Cohen, M., & Nielsen, I. (2019). Entrepreneurial self-efficacy: A systematic review of the literature on its theoretical foundations, measurement, antecedents, and outcomes, and an agenda for future research. *Journal of Vocational Behavior,*

110(B), 403–419. Accessed March 28, 2022, from https://www.sciencedirect.com/science/article/pii/S0001879118300587
Nussbaum, M. C. (2011). *Non per profitto. Perché le democrazie hanno bisogno della cultura umanistica*. il Mulino.
Oliveira, G. J. (2015). *Formazione e Sviluppo delle Competenze Imprenditoriali nei Giovani*. QuiEdit.
Vamvaka, V., Stoforos, C., Palaskas, T., et al. (2020). Attitude toward entrepreneurship, perceived behavioral control, and entrepreneurial intention: Dimensionality, structural relationships, and gender differences. *Journal of Innovation and Entrepreneurship, 9*(5). https://doi.org/10.1186/s13731-020-0112-0
van der Zwan, P., Thurik, R., Verheul, I., et al. (2016). Factors influencing the entrepreneurial engagement of opportunity and necessity entrepreneurs. *Eurasian Business Review, 6*, 273–295. https://doi.org/10.1007/s40821-016-0065-1
Wong, M. A. (2014). *Entrepreneurial Culture: Developing a theoretical construct and its measurement*. Electronic Thesis and Dissertation Repository. 2138. https://ir.lib.uwo.ca/etd/2138.

Brazilian Entrepreneurship: Future Research Avenues

Vanessa Ratten and Leila Afshari

Abstract Brazilian entrepreneurship is a new area of research inquiry that merits further attention. It builds on existing literature and practice regarding innovative, risk-taking and proactive business activity. Brazil as a country is amongst the world's largest in population and land size so influences the economic growth of surrounding countries. This chapter proposes that a distinct research track regarding Brazilian entrepreneurship is needed in the broader entrepreneurship literature in order to incorporate more cultural and historical meaning. This will enable new research to add to the existing research but go a step further by highlighting innovative research directions. Some fruitful and exciting research avenues that should be followed are stated in this chapter.

Keywords Brazil · Culture · Entrepreneurship · Geography · History · Social relations

1 Introduction

Interest in Brazilian entrepreneurship has grown substantially in the past decade (Fishlow & Vieria Filho, 2020). This has coincided with a global interest in entrepreneurship as a source of economic activity (Ratten, 2011a). Unlike other countries that focus more on formal forms of entrepreneurship, there is a high number of informal entrepreneurial activities in Brazil (Ratten, 2014). The aim of this chapter is to discuss in more detail Brazilian entrepreneurship in terms of future research suggestions. This will be helpful to practitioners, researchers and policymakers involved in entrepreneurship.

Before discussing entrepreneurship in a Brazilian context, it is important to highlight what entrepreneurship is and why it matters in society. Entrepreneurship is a future-oriented activity that is used to achieve desired ends (Ratten, 2022).

V. Ratten (✉) · L. Afshari
La Trobe University, Melbourne, VIC, Australia
e-mail: v.ratten@latrobe.edu.au

J. Leitão et al. (eds.), *Brazilian Entrepreneurship*, Studies on Entrepreneurship, Structural Change and Industrial Dynamics,
https://doi.org/10.1007/978-3-031-09392-0_12

Recently, entrepreneurship has been utilised to manage responses and recovery regarding the COVID-19 pandemic (Ratten, 2020). This has involved designing and delivery of products to suit new market conditions. To be entrepreneurial can be more easily said than done. This is due to it being hard to actually act in an entrepreneurial way. Entrepreneurial behaviour can range from minor to major changes depending on the context (Sarma et al., 2022). Therefore, when we discuss Brazilian entrepreneurship, it is important to take into account different types of entrepreneurship (Schwartz & Bal-El, 2015). Entrepreneurship can be used to reconfigure social relations, particularly in terms of inequality. It can be used to save regions and promote sustainable activity. It can be used to adapt and change infrastructure based on new technological developments. Thus, the way entrepreneurship occurs in Brazil varies greatly (Woodson et al., 2019).

Entrepreneurship (and its associated activities) are widespread in Brazil (Franco et al., 2011). Indeed, there has been an emphasis on entrepreneurship in Brazil in order to develop new ideas (Goedhuys & Veugelers, 2012). Much of the traditional forms of entrepreneurship involve opening up new stores or establishing additional business ventures (Maalaoui et al., 2020). However, recently there is an emphasis on entrepreneurship in education programmes in order to help build an innovative mindset. This is due to entrepreneurial thinking being associated with desirable outcomes.

In the context of emerging technology and changing market conditions, entrepreneurship brings into view new possibilities. This means that entrepreneurship can be seen as an intervention in terms of providing societal change. Entrepreneurship in Brazil requires novel forms of innovation that have a transformational effect (Andersen, 2012). Thereby the entrepreneurship is inclusive as well as sustainable.

Socialised forms of entrepreneurship are needed in Brazil (Cassiolato et al., 2003). This is due to the need to get multiple entities involved and collaborate on projects. Entrepreneurial leadership means focusing on future trends but also managing projects. Thereby committing to a broader objective in terms of how entrepreneurship creates value. Until recently, entrepreneurship literature has largely focused on general stereotypes related to entrepreneurship rather than taking into account country contexts. This has changed with more emphasis on country contexts in terms of history and culture. Entrepreneurship is not exclusively related to an individual's behaviour but can be socially based. This means entrepreneurship is community centred and focused on social objectives.

In this chapter, we summarise the opportunities for research on Brazilian entrepreneurship and the networked forms of entrepreneurship occurring in the country. We consider how Brazilian entrepreneurship can be better linked to other entrepreneurship topics including business model innovation, sustainable development and dynamic capabilities.

2 Future Research Avenues

2.1 Avenue 1: The Need for Studying Brazilian Entrepreneurship from Multiple Lenses

The literature on Brazilian entrepreneurship is fractured as it is spread across multiple subject areas (Marcon et al., 2017). This has positive effects in terms of its depth and applicability to different fields of studies but also disadvantages in terms of being hard to find. Some studies suggest there is a specific field of Brazilian entrepreneurship whilst others embed the Brazilian culture into entrepreneurial studies (McMahon & Thorsteinsdóttir, 2013). These contradictory approaches work in practice but make it hard to consistently define what is Brazilian entrepreneurship (Nagano et al., 2014). I recommend researchers advance research by integrating existing theories on Brazilian entrepreneurship to better understand its complexity.

A theoretical or conceptual framework integrating different antecedents and causes of entrepreneurship would be a good approach. This could include micro, macro and meso factors that are specific to Brazil (Oura et al., 2016). This would enable culture, religion and the environment to be better understood in an entrepreneurial setting. It would be meaningful to ask the following research questions: Does culture and environment influence an entrepreneur's decisions, and if so, how? How do different ethnic groups within Brazil become entrepreneurial? Are there some ethnicities that are more entrepreneurial than others? How do different people in Brazil become entrepreneurs? Is there a difference between urban and rural areas? What are the practical implications for people in Brazil wanting to become entrepreneurs?

More information about socio-demographic factors such as age, gender, location and family size need to be studied. I suggest future studies consider the way talent in Brazil can be better managed. This could include entrepreneurial training programmes that seek to build entrepreneurship in society. There are family factors such as parents' entrepreneurial history and use of family businesses that should be analysed in more detail.

Many believe that entrepreneurship scholarship will change in a radical way post-COVID. Whether this occurs is a matter of debate due to the still ongoing changes. What is clear is that the world has changed and with it entrepreneurship scholarship. Whilst we have learned a great deal about entrepreneurship in Brazil and how firms improvise and innovate, there is still much to learn. We need to know more about the changing nature of entrepreneurship in society.

2.2 Avenue 2: Performance Measures of Entrepreneurship

Performance is mostly measured through financial or economic indicators such as economic growth rate, profitability or change in market share (Ratten, 2011b). This means there are already well-established measures for performance existing in the literature. It is difficult to measure performance as it often can take time for actions to be evaluated. This can mean it is better to have a wait-and-see approach regarding how entrepreneurial activity affects a country. In addition, entrepreneurship as an activity can occur in a number of different ways including through the establishment of a new business venture to a change in mindset. Therefore, Brazilian entrepreneurship performance can be measured using existing scales although cultural differences always need to be considered. Entrepreneurship whether it is of a profit or non-profit form needs to involve value creation (Zaluchu et al., 2022).

2.3 Avenue 3: Comparative Studies

Within the literature on Brazilian entrepreneurship, there is much research on individual entrepreneurs or companies. Whilst this provides good data, there is a need for more comparative studies between different regions in Brazil regarding entrepreneurial behaviour. This includes contrasting urban and country areas in terms of the type of entrepreneurship that occurs in these regions.

The study of entrepreneurship cannot be limited to a single person or type of business. It needs to be inclusive in terms of taking into account new contexts. This can include focusing on how religion influences entrepreneurship and the effects of history on entrepreneurship (Ratten & Welpe, 2011). Entrepreneurship is the responsibility of many who work in partnership. This means more emphasis is needed on stakeholder engagement regarding entrepreneurial activities in Brazil (Ryan, 2010). The stakeholders can range from direct engagement in business ventures to support people that help facilitate the growth of the business. Moreover, more emphasis is needed on consumer involvement in entrepreneurial ventures. This will help to understand whether there are any cultural elements specific to Brazil that influence entrepreneurial activity. Due to the many different ethnic groups existing in Brazil, it would be interesting to characterise their attitude towards entrepreneurship to see if it is different or the same. This means more research is needed on areas such as Indigenous, ethnic and minority entrepreneurship in Brazil.

2.4 Research Avenue 4: Value Creation

There is a need to think about the value that is created from entrepreneurial activity (Ratten & Dana, 2017). This means how entrepreneurship creates benefits and for what purpose. Early studies on Brazilian entrepreneurship focused more on technological innovations, financial innovation (e.g. Crisóstomo et al., 2011; de Oliveira et al., 2018), export innovation (Cirera et al., 2015) and knowledge innovation (Dantas & Bell, 2011) neglecting the entwinement of social context and history. Entrepreneurship requires a broader view as to its impact as it is a steering activity that orientates people towards certain goals.

2.5 Research Avenue 5: Entrepreneurs' Well-Being and Culture

Whilst a growing body of research has focused on the topic of entrepreneurship in the last decade, entrepreneurs' well-being has remained under-researched worldwide and, more particularly, in Brazil (Sánchez-García et al., 2018). Entrepreneurship activities have been associated with uncertainty and involve persevering through challenges in order to transform innovative ideas into economic and social outcomes. Entrepreneurs are hardworking individuals who are willing to take risks and deal with uncertainty. Although the key entrepreneurial attributes, including proactivity, competitiveness, and risk-taking, have been inextricably linked to the issues undermining employee well-being at work, the topic of well-being, however, has received scant research attention (Williamson et al., 2021). This is despite the fact that issues compromising entrepreneurs' well-being are more prevalent in countries with high scores on Hofstede's cultural dimension of uncertainty avoidance (Hofstede, 1980). Due to strong uncertainty avoidance, individuals in Brazil feel threatened by ambiguous and uncertain situations and tend to avoid such situations. Uncertainty causes anxiety in cultures with a propensity to avoid uncertainty (Çelikkol et al., 2019). Thus, entrepreneurs in Brazil are more likely to experience stress whilst proactively seeking to take advantage of the opportunities in uncertain entrepreneurial environments. This means that entrepreneurs are prone to be exposed to situations that can potentially compromise their well-being.

In addition to the cultural dimension of uncertainty avoidance, Brazil's cultural attributes correspond to high power distance acceptance (Hofstede, 1980). Power distance refers to the unequal distribution of power in society. There is a high level of acceptance for inequality in societies with high scores on the cultural dimension of power distance. Less powerful members of such societies tend to accept that power is distributed unequally, and activities challenging the power imbalance are not tolerated (Çelikkol et al., 2019). Thus, achievement-oriented entrepreneurial behaviour can be perceived as a violation of social norms, and power holders in such cultures can challenge entrepreneurs who have aspirations to maximise their outcomes. This highlights the prevalence of issues diminishing entrepreneurs' well-being in Brazil and calls for further research on the topic.

3 Implications for Policymakers

The discussion in this chapter suggests that there is a need for policymakers to provide more supportive programmes. This will help to take into consideration the multiple challenges Brazilian entrepreneurs face in the business environment. In order for policies to properly work there needs to be a focus on how human capital can be utilised for entrepreneurial gain. This means encouraging policies regarding networking and teamwork. Thereby the policies will have a positive impact on evolving entrepreneurial practices and business relationships. In this way, different stakeholders involved in entrepreneurship can be assisted in developing their ideas.

4 Conclusion

Research on Brazilian entrepreneurship has reshaped how we think about entrepreneurship. Due to the variety of entrepreneurship occurring in Brazil, there have been numerous insights into the role of culture and context. However, further research is required and I believe the research on Brazilian entrepreneurship is just starting. I hope this chapter has highlighted other research paths needed in order to advance the scholarship on this topic.

References

Andersen, A. D. (2012). Innovation systems and natural resources–the case of sugarcane in Brazil. *Innovation and Development, 2*(1), 194–195.

Cassiolato, J. E., Lastres, H. M. M., & Maciel, M. L. (Eds.). (2003). *Systems of innovation and development: Evidence from Brazil*. Edward Elgar Publishing.

Çelikkol, M., Kitapçi, H., & Döven, G. (2019). Culture's impact on entrepreneurship & interaction effect of economic development level: An 81 country study. *Journal of Business Economics and Management, 20*(4), 777–797.

Cirera, X., Marin, A., & Markwald, R. (2015). Explaining export diversification through firm innovation decisions: The case of Brazil. *Research Policy, 44*(10), 1962–1973.

Crisóstomo, V. L., López-Iturriaga, F. J., & Vallelado, E. (2011). Financial constraints for innovation in Brazil. *Latin American Business Review, 12*(3), 165–185.

Dantas, E., & Bell, M. (2011). The co-evolution of firm-centered knowledge networks and capabilities in late industrializing countries: The case of Petrobras in the offshore oil innovation system in Brazil. *World Development, 39*(9), 1570–1591.

de Oliveira, J. A. S., Basso, L. F. C., Kimura, H., & Sobreiro, V. A. (2018). Innovation and financial performance of companies doing business in Brazil. *International Journal of Innovation Studies, 2*(4), 153–164.

Fishlow, A., & Vieira Filho, J. E. R. (2020). *Agriculture and industry in Brazil: Innovation and competitiveness*. Columbia University Press.

Franco, E., Ray, S., & Ray, P. K. (2011). Patterns of innovation practices of multinational-affiliates in emerging economies: Evidences from Brazil and India. *World Development, 39*(7), 1249–1260.

Goedhuys, M., & Veugelers, R. (2012). Innovation strategies, process and product innovations and growth: Firm-level evidence from Brazil. *Structural Change and Economic Dynamics, 23*(4), 516–529.
Hofstede, G. (1980). *Culture's consequences: International differences in work-related values*. Sage.
Maalaoui, A., Ratten, V., Heilbrunn, S., Brannback, M., & Kraus, S. (2020). Disadvantage entrepreneurship: Decoding a new area of research. *European Management Review, 17*(3), 663–668.
Marcon, A., de Medeiros, J. F., & Ribeiro, J. L. D. (2017). Innovation and environmentally sustainable economy: Identifying the best practices developed by multinationals in Brazil. *Journal of Cleaner Production, 160*, 83–97.
McMahon, D., & Thorsteinsdóttir, H. (2013). Pursuing endogenous high-tech innovation in developing countries: A look at regenerative medicine innovation in Brazil, China and India. *Research Policy, 42*(4), 965–974.
Nagano, M. S., Stefanovitz, J. P., & Vick, T. E. (2014). Innovation management processes, their internal organizational elements and contextual factors: An investigation in Brazil. *Journal of Engineering and Technology Management, 33*, 63–92.
Oura, M. M., Zilber, S. N., & Lopes, E. L. (2016). Innovation capacity, international experience and export performance of SMEs in Brazil. *International Business Review, 25*(4), 921–932.
Ratten, V. (2011a). Sport-based entrepreneurship: Towards a new theory of entrepreneurship and sport management. *International Entrepreneurship and Management Journal, 7*(1), 57–69.
Ratten, V. (2011b). Social entrepreneurship and innovation in sports. *International Journal of Social Entrepreneurship and Innovation, 1*(1), 42–54.
Ratten, V. (2014). Future research directions for collective entrepreneurship in developing countries: A small and medium-sized enterprise perspective. *International Journal of Entrepreneurship and Small Business, 22*(2), 266–274.
Ratten, V. (2020). Coronavirus (covid-19) and entrepreneurship: Changing life and work landscape. *Journal of Small Business & Entrepreneurship, 32*(5), 503–516.
Ratten, V. (2022). Stakeholder entrepreneurship: The role of partnerships. In *Stakeholder entrepreneurship* (pp. 1–5). Springer.
Ratten, V., & Dana, L. P. (2017). Gendered perspective of indigenous entrepreneurship. *Small Enterprise Research, 24*(1), 62–72.
Ratten, V., & Welpe, I. M. (2011). Community-based, social and societal entrepreneurship. *Entrepreneurship & Regional Development, 23*(5–6), 283–286.
Ryan, M. P. (2010). Patent incentives, technology markets, and public–private bio-medical innovation networks in Brazil. *World Development, 38*(8), 1082–1093.
Sánchez-García, J. C., Vargas-Morúa, G., & Hernández-Sánchez, B. R. (2018). Entrepreneurs' well-being: A bibliometric review. *Frontiers in Psychology, 9*(1696).
Sarma, M. M., Hidayati, N., Nanere, M., Trebilcock, P., & Ratten, V. (2022). Entrepreneurial marketing and its relationship on business competitiveness in footwear and agro industries of small and medium industries. In *Stakeholder entrepreneurship* (pp. 19–44). Springer.
Schwartz, D., & Bar-El, R. (2015). The role of a local industry association as a catalyst for building an innovation ecosystem: An experiment in the State of Ceara in Brazil. *Innovations, 17*(3), 383–399.
Williamson, A. J., Gish, J. J., & Stephan, U. (2021). Let's focus on solutions to entrepreneurial ill-being! Recovery interventions to enhance entrepreneurial well-being. *Entrepreneurship: Theory and Practice, 45*(6), 1307–1338.
Woodson, T., Alcantara, J. T., & do Nascimento, M. S. (2019). Is 3D printing an inclusive innovation?: An examination of 3D printing in Brazil. *Technovation, 80*, 54–62.
Zaluchu, S. E., Usmanij, P., & Ratten, V. (2022). Market Bank as alternative to MSMEs fund provider: Lesson of entrepreneurship from Indonesia. In *Entrepreneurial innovation* (pp. 43–52). Springer.